Peter Bamm, a German physician, first made his mark as a writer with one of the most impressive accounts of war experiences: *The Invisible Flag,* a vivid eye-witness story of what actually happened in the struggle between the giant armies of Russia and Germany, 1941-45, written from the viewpoint of a surgeon. *Early Sites of Christianity* was spectacularly successful in the original German edition. It sold 70,000 copies within the first six months after publication.

PETER BAMM

Early Sites of
Christianity

PANTHEON BOOKS

Title of Original Edition:
Frühe Stätten der Christenheit
Kösel Verlag, München

Translated by STANLEY GODMAN

Contents

List of Illustrations

Early Sites of Christianity

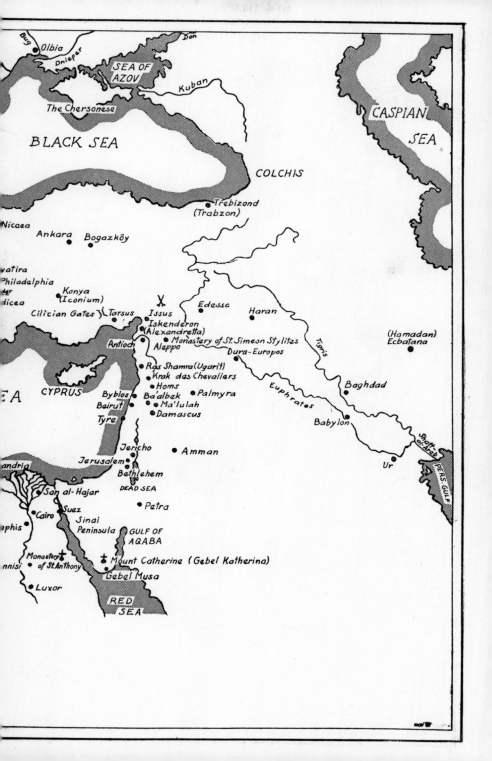

"In the beginning God created the heaven and the earth"

The first chapter of the Book of Genesis represents the beginning not only of the world but also of the history of the world. Adam was a historical figure.

For fifteen hundred years it was the aim of European scholarship to explore the truth of the Bible and to bring its truths into accord with Greek philosophy. The Bible is far and away the most widespread and the most widely read book in the world. Islam also includes large parts of the Bible in its sacred writings. According to the prophet Mohammed, one hundred and four revelations have been granted to the human race, of which four have survived—the Pentateuch of Moses, the Psalms of David, the Gospel of Jesus, and the Koran of Mohammed. Isa ben Mirjam, Jesus, the Son of Mary, is a prophet of the Mohammedan faith. For a journey into the history of the Western world the Bible is an indispensable source.

According to the religions of the ancient Orient, the cosmos arose from chaos. The cosmos, the world of order, arises from the pre-existent, from chaos and the inchoate. Chaos is part of nature. In the ancient Babylonian account of creation, chaos is symbolized in Tiamat, a female dragon, which is a symbol of archaic horror. Tiamat is slain by the god Marduk, and the universe is formed from Tiamat's corpse. This myth shows an awareness of the fact that chaos is contained within the cosmos.

This realization is in accordance with the assumption of modern physics that absolute disorder holds sway in the realm of the atoms and that all events resulting from the movements of the atoms are the product of chance. The Marduk of physics, who introduces order into chaos, is the calculation of probabilities, the branch of mathematics that formulates the laws to which accident is statistically subject. The ancient Oriental myths of creation proceed from the assumption that nature is all-embracing and that the cosmos contains nothing outside nature. The classical natural science of the nineteenth century was based on the same conception. The human race has, however, had in its possession from an early period the account of creation contained in the Old Testament, which transmits a more exalted idea than the accounts of creation recorded in other early civilizations. The God of the Old Testament is a transcendent God, a God who transcends nature, who "surpasses" it, and to whom it owes its very creation.

This is not the place to discuss the question as to how man can acquire consciousness of an idea of this kind, surpassing as it does the bounds of his own nature. We merely wish to state that the idea of a transcendent God who creates the world from nothing is of a higher order than any purely abstract conception of nature, however all-embracing.

Natural science can no longer offer a convincing theory of the origin of the human race. All that it can supply is an astrophysical hypothesis of the origin of the universe. For astrophysics the account of creation contained in the Bible is as immediately interesting as ever. The latest results of astrophysics are directly related to the first words in the Bible. "In the beginning" allows for the possibility that our earthly time was also created in the act of creation. Einstein's general theory of relativity implies that if matter did not exist before creation space cannot have existed either. Our space was created at the same time as creation. It must also be assumed that time, at any rate time as we know it on earth, first came into being with the creation of the world.

The world is finite. It had a beginning. That is the belief held by modern physics. Ultimately, the world will have an end. We do not know the age of the story of creation. A splendidly polished, sparkling diamond of archaic beauty, this account of the creation shines forth from the earliest memories of the human race through all the millennia of history right into our own time.

When the library of King Ashurbanipal was excavated in 1853 in Nineveh in the Temple of Nabu, who was a god of literature and whose symbol was the stylus, numerous parallels to the Bible stories were found in the cuneiform texts. The parallels between the Sumerian, Assyrian, and Babylonian traditions on the one hand and the traditions of the Bible on the other were used to deny the originality of the Bible. It was declared a literary composite with no possible value as a revelation—an argument that was continued until scholars inquired into the differences between the traditions. Then it became apparent that only the Hebrews had the idea that God was the creator of nature.

From the very first moment in which we find this idea in the Hebrew tradition it is free of the mythological and symbolic; it is monotheistic. Ancient Hebrew did not even contain a word for "goddess." From the very beginning the Hebrew people were in sole possession of this idea of the highest intellectual order. Furthermore, the Jews were not merely the vehicles of the idea of God, they were also the first to engage in theology.

The account of creation was probably written at the beginning of the first millennium before the birth of Christ, that is, between the time of Moses and King David and only about a hundred and fifty years before Homer. In these very early times, however, the date of the actual recording of a tradition tells us nothing about its age. There is in fact good reason to suppose that the account that has come down to us really was based on earlier written sources.

Historical scholarship, which has achieved such great successes through the systematic study of sources, is inclined to overrate the importance of written traditions. In times when most men were unable to write, oral traditions were just as safe as, if not safer than, written traditions. The written tradition that attempts to preserve the memory of events is no more trustworthy than the oral tradition that actually preserves the memory of events.

Even today there are scholars in the East who know not only the whole of the Koran but also many volumes of commentary by heart. In Bethany, where Jesus raised Lazarus from the dead, the name "Lazarus" survives in the Arab village name "el-Azariyeh." The Arabs thought that the L in "Lazarus" was an article. In the Nile delta, in the land of Goshen, where the Hebrews settled before Moses led them into the wilderness and to freedom, a place name, San al-Hajar, has survived, which is certainly of Hebrew origin. In Ma'lulah, a hamlet deep in a mountain valley in the northern Anti-Lebanon, the peasants speak Aramaic, the language that Jesus spoke, to this day.

As has been shown by the excavations in Mycenae, in Agamemnon's Palace, and in Pylos, the home of Nestor, Homer was not a poet who merely imagined things. He was clearheaded, exact, and endowed with a splendid memory. What he described in the *Iliad* must have been passed on for three hundred years by oral tradition. That Homer was a clearheaded and exact poet is one of the reasons for his position among the great poets in the literature of the world.

Abraham, who was still quite a legendary figure only a hundred years ago, has meanwhile become a clearly defined historical personality. Probably only a few people are aware, however, that the patriarch Abraham came from a port with a hundred thousand inhabitants on the Persian

Gulf, that he was heir to an ancient civilization that had lasted more than a thousand years, and that it is possible to walk along a brick pavement on which he played as a child. I have done so.

Abraham lived two thousand years before Christ, which is not really so very long ago. Research has pierced the veil of legend. It has staked out with the trigonometrical landmarks of historical research a world that was hitherto veiled in obscurity. The Sumerian kings are earlier than Abraham. The great Babylonian legislator King Hammurabi is more recent.

How remote Abraham still is from modern consciousness is evident from the fact that, compared with any of the apostles, he hardly rouses any impression of holiness in us. In very early medieval pictures Abraham is still sometimes depicted with a halo, but later on he appears without it. For the Jews and the Moslems, however, he never lost the numinosity of holiness. The legendary quality of early Old Testament figures is beginning to dissolve, and the more clearly they emerge from the mists of oblivion the more they regain the quality of sanctity.

While Western man stares into the arctic wildernesses of modern science, fascinated by every spot that is illuminated by its searchlights, the old humane sciences, archaeology and history, have regained a whole realm pulsating with the life of man in the glory of his victories and defeats. At what point in the tradition of the Bible will archaeology and history come up against the frontier that they will be unable to cross? If American archaeologists are now looking for Noah's ark on Mount Ararat, the search is by no means as far-fetched as it might seem. Admittedly, it is not very likely that traces of the ark will be found, but it is not impossible. It is quite conceivable that a fragment of the stone tablets of the Law may still be found, which Moses shattered when he came down from Mount Horeb and saw the people dancing round the golden calf. There are in existence inscriptions that are older than the tablets of Sinai.

It is impossible to forecast what knowledge the excavators' spades may dig out of the ground in years to come. Will Adam's tomb be discovered? According to a legend that is full of deep significance, Adam's tomb lies under Golgotha, and when the blood of Christ dripped down through a chink in the rock onto Adam's corpse he rose from the dead.

The discovery of Adam's tomb is, admittedly, even more unlikely than the discovery of Noah's ark. But after his banishment from Paradise the man Adam died somewhere and was buried somewhere. It is not impossible that his tomb will be found.

Whatever scholars may discover in the future, the wealth of facts that has been discovered already is stupendous and exciting. It gives us a conception of our historical past that is not lacking in elements of the sublime. However much our own age seems to be lacking in sublimity, let us, like Cyprian, the Bishop of Carthage in the middle of the third century—an age not unlike our own—stand erect among the ruins and not grovel on the ground with those who are without hope.

On the Coasts of the Aegean

"Ye men of Athens!"

The propellers swept away the dust of Rome airport as we made for the Campagna. The heavy aircraft rose from the ground. Its destination was Athens. After twenty seconds it crossed an aqueduct, one of those ancient Roman aqueducts whose broad arches, broken here and there by the destruction wrought by centuries of time, soar across the countryside from the Alban Hills. These aqueducts supplied the marble baths of Imperial Rome with fresh water. Sometimes a pagan was christened by the hand of an apostle filled with water at whose springs nymphs were worshipped.

The cloud ceiling opens up over the Greek mainland. Just before we reach Athens the sky clears. On the earth below night has fallen. Tiny white islets of cloud, wads of cotton wool in the evening calm, hover above, alongside, and below the aircraft. The stars shine above. Down below the silvery filigree of the harbor of Piraeus sparkles. Numerous ships, their masts adorned with festive lights, lie in the bay.

As the airplane prepares to land it describes a curve over Athens. Suddenly the Acropolis appears in my cabin window, the ancient citadel of Athens, a marble building supported by columns, shining in a mysterious white light. The Parthenon, which shines out of the Attic night, this jewel in the crown of Europe, hovers above the city's sea of light.

Athens today is a lively and elegant metropolis. Tradition has preserved a noble remnant of the distinguished position that the Greek woman enjoyed in antiquity, compared with the other nations of the ancient Orient. The women of Athens are presumably no less efficient than the women who live in other great cities, but they attach no importance to being valued on that account. They want to be beautiful.

Homer testifies to the beauty and intelligence of the Greek woman. Pictures on vases show their charm. The New Testament praises their spiritual receptivity. But the fact that the shoeshine boy is called Themistocles, the newspaper seller Socrates, and the money-changer Odysseus is admittedly a tradition that goes back more to Lord Byron than to antiquity. It is a delightful symptom of the renaissance of the Greek people that began with the War of Liberation after the dull and dreary centuries of Turkish dominion.

Athens lies a few miles from the coast in a broad, undulating valley hemmed in by mountains. To the east rises the Hymettus, which was renowned for its honey; to the northeast, the Pentelikon, even more famous for its marble. The Hellenes produced their statues and temples from the glorious stone of the Pentelikon. To the southwest the valley of Athens opens out into the Saronic Gulf. In the blue distance the island of Aegina floats on the water like a ship of the gods. All around, the mountains are over three thousand feet high. In ancient times they were wooded. Today their slopes are gray and bare.

From the sea of houses in Athens there rise a few hills crowned with ruins, whose walls plunge abruptly into the depths below. The highest of these hills, the Lycabettus, which is nine hundred feet high, lies in the northeast. The white houses surge against the dark rock like the white crests of waves. In the middle lies the Acropolis. West of it stands the Areopagus, the Athenians' ancient court of justice.

The plateau of the Acropolis is 295 yards long and at the center 170 yards wide. If one climbs up the road to the citadel on the southern side one passes the well-preserved Theater of Dionysus. This is the place where the first dramatists in world literature—Aeschylus, Sophocles, and Euripides—had their plays performed for the first time.

The gently rising road winds around the narrow western side of the mountain up to the Acropolis. A broad flight of high marble steps leads to the Propylaea, the entrance hall, divided into three aisles by rows of columns—a solemn climax to the mighty flight of marble steps. The outlines stand out sharply against the sky.

The Attic light is an intense, bright, penetrating light. It is the light in which the intensely bright, penetrating Logos of the Greeks achieved its creative purposes. The sun burns down from the October sky, but it has none of the scorching relentlessness that makes it man's enemy in the deserts and steppes of the South and East beyond the sea. Apollo the Lord of the Muses is the God of this Attic sun.

Proceeding through the Propylaea, one comes to the platform of the mountain citadel. The Parthenon is built close to the outer edge of the platform, its longitudinal axis diverging at a peculiar, well-calculated angle from the longitudinal axis of the plateau. The building is even more tremendous than one had imagined it from pictures; in its majesty, it has retained something of the pride of those who built it. The weathering influence of the centuries has transformed the whiteness of the Pentelic marble into a warm yellow.

Enclosed by columns, the original structure had seventeen on each side, and eight at each end. Part of the middle section of the temple has been destroyed and only the stumps of some of the columns have survived. The columns incline slightly inwards. The slight tapering of the whole building that results gives it an impression of strength. The horizontal lines appear to the eye completely straight, but in fact they run in carefully calculated curves—an architectural trick that offsets the distortion of perspective which would otherwise result from a view at such close quarters. These subtleties in construction and the exquisite proportions give the building that scintillating life which has aroused the admiration of the world for more than two thousand years.

The temple was dedicated to Athene Parthenos, the owl-eyed daughter of Zeus, maiden goddess of wisdom, tutelary goddess of Athens. The building was begun thirty years after the destruction of the Persian fleet in the naval Battle of Salamis and the land victory over the Persian army at Plataea. The age of Pericles, in which the Parthenon was built, was the most brilliant period of Hellenistic civilization. It stands between the threat to Greek freedom by the Asiatic Imperium of the Persians and its actual destruction as a result of the coincidence of external disaster with the Greeks' own political folly. While Phidias was creating his statue of Athene for the Parthenon in gold and ivory, the philosopher Protagoras was declaring that man is the measure of all things.

While the splendid processions in honor of the goddess moved up the marble steps of the Propylaea, Socrates strolled around the Agora in Athens teaching men to listen to the voice of conscience. While the government sent deputations to Delphi to question the sacred oracle, Democritus, the founder of theoretical physics, propounded the atomic theory. While Hippocrates was giving medicine a scientific foundation, a danger was approaching from the depths of Asia far more terrible than the menace of war. The age of Pericles was brought to an end by a plague that killed a quarter of the citizens of Athens. This was the age in which the Jew Nehemiah returned to Palestine with the authority of the Persian king and rebuilt the city wall of

Jerusalem in fifty-two days. The Greeks of the age of Pericles and the Jews of the exile in Babylon—each of these peoples created one of the prerequisites of Western civilization. The Greeks of the classical period created a world culture, and the Babylonian exile brought to a close a development in the life of the Jewish people in which the foundations of a world religion had been laid.

If Socrates had met Nehemiah on the Agora and involved him in one of his famous and dreaded disputes, he would not have found Nehemiah wanting for a single answer. Socrates would have been able to learn from Nehemiah wherein the mystery of the human conscience consisted. Nehemiah would have learned from the philosopher that a man can be devout without knowing anything of the teaching of the prophets. Each would have been rather amazed by the other. An argument between the two intellectual worlds of antiquity that had an all-important influence on the development of human civilization might also have taken place a hundred and fifty years before Socrates and Nehemiah, when Solon the Athenian legislator was sojourning at the Egyptian court at the same time as the prophet Jeremiah.

Opposite the Parthenon on the northern side of the Acropolis lies the Erechtheum, with its celebrated caryatids, the female figures which, instead of columns, support the beams. The name of the temple is derived from Erechtheus, legendary founder of the city of Athens.

When one looks down on the city from the Erechtheum one sees the ancient Agora. The excavation site is only a pile of broken stones, but the diligence and genius of scholars have made these stones speak. All the men who constitute the splendor of the Greek name walked on the pavement of this most famous of all market places. It is the square where the first encounter took place between Greek culture and the world religion that had taken its rise in Judaea. We have a detailed account of this event in the seventeenth chapter of the Acts of the Apostles:

"Those who were escorting Paul on his journey saw him as far as Athens, and then left him, with instructions for Silas and Timothy to rejoin him as soon as possible. And while Paul was waiting for them in Athens, his heart was moved within him to find the city so much given over to idolatry, and he reasoned, not only in the synagogue with Jews and worshippers of the true God, but in the market place, with all he met. He encountered philosophers, Stoics and Epicureans, some of whom asked, What can his drift be, this dabbler? while others said, He would appear to be proclaiming strange gods; because he had preached to them about Jesus and the Resurrection. So they took him by the sleeve and led him up to the Areopagus; May we ask, they said, what this new teaching is thou art delivering? Thou dost introduce terms which are strange to our ears; pray let us know what may be the meaning of it. (No townsman of Athens, or stranger visiting it, has time for anything else than saying something new, or hearing it said.) So Paul stood up in full view of the Areopagus, and said, Men of Athens, wherever I look I find you scrupulously religious. Why, in examining your monuments as I passed by them, I found among others an altar which bore the inscription, To the unknown God. And it is this unknown object of your devotion that I am revealing to you. The God who made the world and all that is in it, that God who is Lord of heaven and earth, does not dwell in temples that our hands have made; no human handicraft can do him service, as if he stood in need of anything, he, who gives to all of us life and breath and all we have. It is he who has made, of one single stock, all the nations that were to dwell over the whole face of the earth. And he has given to each the cycles it was to pass through and the fixed limits of its habitation, leaving them to search for God; would they somehow grope their way toward him? Would they find him? And yet,

26

after all, he is not far from any one of us; it is in him that we live, and move, and have our being; thus, some of your own poets have told us, For indeed, we are his children. Why then, if we are the children of God, we must not imagine that the divine nature can be represented in gold, or silver, or stone, carved by man's art and thought. God has shut his eyes to these passing follies of ours; now, he calls upon all men, everywhere, to repent, because he has fixed a day when he will pronounce just judgment on the whole world. And the man whom he has appointed for that end he has accredited to all of us, by raising him up from the dead. When resurrection from the dead was mentioned, some mocked, while others said, We must hear more from thee about this. So Paul went away from among them. But there were men who attached themselves to him and learned to believe, among them Dionysius the Areopagite; and so did a woman called Damaris, and others with them."

The writer was obviously an eyewitness of the incident he described. Every detail accords exactly with the prevailing situation in Athens. At one time it was questioned whether Paul's speech was inserted in the text much later. Adolf von Harnack has demonstrated with very convincing arguments, however, that the speech forms an original constituent of the Acts of the Apostles.

At that period Athens was a unique place. Politically powerless, it was nevertheless a place of pilgrimage for all the cultured people of the Greek and Roman world. It is quite wrong to imagine that the worship of the Olympian gods was still the only form of religion in Athens at that time. Four hundred years had passed since the ages of Pericles and Socrates. The mysteries, especially the mystery cult of Eleusis, the neighboring holy city on the Saronic Gulf, had become increasingly important. It is true that the worship of the gods of Olympus was still the official, State religion, but the gods were above all depositories of national memories. Public worship in Athens had decreased in importance as the importance of the mysteries had increased. Alexander the Great had conquered Asia. Greek civilization had penetrated as far as the borders of India, while numerous Asiatic cults had been introduced into Athens. Thus the city was a most vivid reflection of the religions of the great Roman Empire. The ancient piety of the Athenians had turned into a superstitious fear of the gods. On the other hand, from the earliest times there had existed the service of a supreme god worshipped without a statue, the Zeus Hypsistos, the father of gods and men. The simple festivals of this supreme god were popular holidays in Athens with a venerable tradition.

The scene recorded in the Acts of the Apostles was not a trial. The word "Areopagus" does not signify the hill of the Areopagus where the judges met on certain days of the month to pass sentence in the open air. "Areopagus" in this case is the government authority which met in the royal hall on the Agora. This authority did not sit in judgment on Paul. No sentence was passed. The accurate reporter of this scene would certainly have mentioned that. The authority simply wanted to hear Paul speak in order, if necessary, to forbid his preaching in public. That did not happen, either.

The people were present at these interrogations as listeners and witnesses. Paul brought them all into his speech, this motley crowd of locals and strangers: the dignified officials of the office of the Areopagus, elegant philosophers contemplating their well-cared-for fingernails with expectant smiles, literary loafers, distinguished strangers, joking porters, inquisitive slaves, a dandy with his whippet, and peasants with their donkeys. And confronting all these was the poorly clad Jew from Tarsus, this man of whom tradition has it that he sometimes looked "like an angel." He does not find public speaking at all easy; but he knows his message. He is alone, but he has the future of the world in his heart.

Paul concentrated his attention on the sophists who had joined the crowd to indulge in their favorite and most Greek of all vices, curiosity. With gentle irony, he begins his speech with "Men of Athens," the famous words that Socrates had used at the beginning of his defense. The northern part of the Agora was the market place where business was transacted; the southern part was a public meeting place. The incident occurred on this international stage where every new doctrine on earth had to pass the test of public interrogation.

Who in this vanity fair could have suspected that the everyday occurrence that was taking place before the eyes and ears of all of them was pregnant with meaning for the whole world? Who of them could have had an inkling that one day the emperors of the world would bend their knees before the unknown god whom the tentmaker from Tarsus was proclaiming?

Paul begins his speech with urbane courtesy. Flattered by the whole world, the Athenians were as convinced of the uniqueness and unmatched quality of their city as the French are of that of Paris today. A little flattery was therefore a diplomatic necessity.

From the Agora it is possible to see the Acropolis. Thus, as the sun sparkled on the golden helmet of Phidias's Athene, Paul declared that God is not like the golden, silver, or stone images made by human art and thought. The expression "carved by man's thought" is a translation of the Greek *enthymeseos*. Paul must have meant the thoughts that man puts into his works, the source from which works of art arise. He uses the rare and very highbrow word to show, perhaps, that he is no Anatolian peasant and, in any case, to suggest how foolish it is to pay divine honors to things that are the expression of purely human thoughts. He proceeds toward his listeners with an almost cunning awareness of their reactions. He quotes some of their poets who testify that mortals are of divine nature and origin. The wonderful phrase "it is in him that we live, and move, and have our being" is Christian in feeling but Greek in its thought. For the Greeks the father of gods and men was no abstract pantheistic being but a personal god, near to every individual and to be found by those who seek him. With this phrase Paul touches the fundamental religious awareness of the Greeks.

A man so deeply rooted in Greek thought and so dedicated was eminently fitted to spread the gospel in the Greek world.

The Greeks already owed more to the Semites than they could possibly know. Europa, the daughter of Agenor, King of Phoenicia, who was raped by Zeus, was a Syrian princess. The Phoenicians had brought to the Greeks the alphabet, copper, wine-growing, and the olive. Paul, from the race of Semitic Hebrews, brought the new world religion to Hellas in the Greek tongue. The world was ripe for this historical encounter. We know the thoughts that stirred in Paul as he walked to the Agora, by the splendid monuments of the past, by the great reminders of a history that had brought into being the civilization of his own age. His spirit grew angry within him. And the anger of this spirit changed the world.

Aspects of Eternity

A café on the banks of the Aegean between Olympus, ancient mountain of the gods, and Athos, the "Holy Mountain" of the Eastern Church, is a worthy place in which to dream a little. A slight breeze passes lightly across the Bay of Salonika. Although the year is already well advanced, the sun is still gloriously warm. The café lies on the quayside where lively business transactions are taking place. Salonika is today the export harbor for the famous Macedonian tobacco. It is the Thessalonica mentioned in the Acts of the Apostles. The name derives from the half sister of Alexander the Great, Thessalonica, the wife of King Cassander of Macedonia, who renamed the old city of Therma after her.

There is a lively throng of sailors, porters, fishermen, orange sellers, and good-for-nothing boys around the ships and boats lying by the pier. Charming little donkeys stand around, quietly and peacefully, touching to see. Some of the crowd are feverishly busy, others are gadding about doing nothing at all, just enjoying life. The existentialists! All over the Orient they are the picturesque marginal figures in the great theater of public life. One of them, wearing an old military cap, has his hands thrust deep in the pockets of his torn trousers. One cannot be certain that the pockets are still there. The one thing one can be certain of is that even if they do exist there is nothing in them. Another of these existentialists stalks along through the peaceful sunshine on crutches. A third is lighting one of the delightful Macedonian cigarettes. Shabby though their clothes all are, these old men still know how to wear their rags gracefully. They can all boast of emulating the lilies of the field in the Bible.

Surrounded by a multitude of tiny boats, an elegant snow-white passenger liner rides at anchor near the docks. In an hour's time it will depart for Istanbul. Sea gulls play around its mast. An airplane drones across the bay. Behind this scene of merry bustle and cheerful idleness ancient Olympus towers up in the southwest, rising almost ten thousand feet into the deep blue sky. Below, to the south southeast, the Gulf of Salonika is hemmed in by the green hills of Chalcidice, which extends three long peninsulas southward into the Aegean Sea. The Holy Mountain of Athos lies on the extreme tip of the most easterly of the three peninsulas, beyond the horizon.

Piety has always sought out the finest landscapes for its site. Even though the devout endeavor to turn away from the world, they cannot turn away from creation. To enter into harmony with God they do not need to forgo living in harmony with nature. Between the beauty of creation and the piety of those who praise it harmony is possible, and on Mount Athos it is at its most impressive.

And so we set out for the tenth century A.D., which has survived a hundred miles away from Salonika's great seaport. I have been on Mount Athos twice in my life. The first time I entered it with a gun, the second time with true veneration. The biographies of our time have a remarkable spread.

We decided to take the country road across the peninsula of Chalcidice. For the first part of the journey we travelled along a famous road, the Via Egnatia. Immediately following the conquest of Macedonia, the Romans, those great road builders, built the Via Egnatia right across the Balkans, from Dyrrachium, the modern Durazzo, or Durrës, to Thessalonica. Later on, the road was continued to the mouth of the river Maritsa. Parts of the ancient Roman paving are still used today. Great commanders, returning home from victories or defeats, rich merchants from every

The Parthenon, Athens

A Monastery on Mt. Athos, Greece

Courtyard of the Monastery of Vatopedi, Mt. Athos, Greece

land, high government officials with important commissions in the outlying provinces of the Roman Empire, travelled along this road on horseback. Veterans returning to their native lands, adventurers and vagabonds without a home, trudged along it barefoot in the heat and dust. All trace of them has vanished. Only the travels of one man, whose home was not of this world, are still remembered. It was on this road that the apostle Paul travelled westward, coming from Philippi in the East to establish the first Christian church on European soil in Thessalonica, in sight of Olympus, where the Greeks believed the gods to be enthroned. Paul always cherished a great love for Thessalonica. His letters to his first church are full of warm affection.

It is not easy to visit Athos. One needs a permit from the Greek Home Secretary, and unless one intends to go there as a poor tramp, or a pilgrim, one must be able to present a letter of introduction from the Archbishop of Athens to the Holy Synod in Karyai, the little capital of the monastic republic.

We had left Salonika just before sunset. Night was falling on Chalcidice. After roughly fifteen miles we came to the mountains that cross the peninsula from west to east. We drove along hundreds of narrow bends up and down the passes. At one point a big rock lay right in the middle of the road. We got out to remove it for the sake of our successors on the road, and stopped for a breather. From the depths of the forests came the uncanny howling of wolves. Finally, toward midnight we came to a lonely house by the roadside, which looked like an inn. We entered a big room. Half a dozen men were sitting around a glowing iron stove. A dismal, smoking, oil lamp hung from the ceiling. A Greek girl, pretty as a picture, was busy behind the counter. The men hardly acknowledged our greeting. Alexander—my travelling companion, who spoke excellent

Greek—looked at me. The men were foresters. Their axes and one or two guns were leaning against the wall. Doubtless they had been Partisans. The civil war had only just come to an end. In a situation like this one has to be very careful. As long as one knows the rules it is all right. But what were the rules here? We each lit a cigarette. In this country offering cigarettes right away is just not done. It is thought to be importunate. One must offer a cigarette only after a fairly long conversation, to show one likes the other man. Alexander was aware of that.

We ordered an ouzo, the pungent Greek aniseed liqueur. The beautiful girl, a Nausicaa of the backwoods, brought us two fairly large glasses. We pretended not to see the girl and tossed down the drink. Alexander shook himself vigorously, looking at his bearded neighbor with a twinkle in the corner of his eyes. The bearded man was old. He smiled. The game was won. In the lively conversation that ensued, we found there was no political topic on which these ex-Partisans were not prepared to express shrewd opinions in their passionate and vivacious manner. They offered us one or two ouzos. For ten years these men had waged war legally and illegally. For ten years they had seen nothing but misery. The Greeks are a very ancient people. They have gone through much, far too much, in their history. The bearded old man said it is a wise art to be able to forget.

We were now able to tell Nausicaa how beautiful she was. She received our admiration with a smile. The woodsmen gave us the sheepskins they use as coats, and we stretched out on them for a few hours among the axes and guns. When we set off before dawn the men gathered around the car. One of them came with us for a bit. To bid us farewell they offered us coffee and ouzo. Poverty is generous.

The first streaks of dawn were appearing in the east. We reached the chief pass of the mountains at a height of three thousand feet. The mountains are covered with forests, and we drove past gigantic old walnut trees, cypresses, holm oaks surrounded by laurel, chestnuts, broad plane trees, bizarre eucalyptus trees, figs and mulberries. Wide meadows lie between the woods, which are interspersed with a brushwood of hawthorn, myrtle, valerian, oleander, lemon, and wild rosemary. This countryside has not changed since the days of antiquity.

In the valley and far out to sea there lay a thick layer of morning mist. Down below, the cupola of a church emerged from time to time. In the distance Mount Athos towered up as on the fifth day of creation. It stands out in an incomparably proud line against the horizon. When the sun has risen, the ancient Holy Mountain hovers like a pyramid steeped in purple light above the glittering radiance that lies over the sea.

For an immeasurable period of time this sublime spectacle has taken place every morning with a lavish expenditure of beauty. Something of the freshness of creation shines through this splendor from a sphere beyond our sight but of which our minds believe they are dimly aware.

Half an hour later Alexander braked in front of the village church in the valley. There was a signpost by the roadside: Stagira. We looked at one another. The name seemed oddly familiar, but we could not place it. So we stopped in front of the little village inn, ordered a cup of coffee, and asked the landlord why his village was famous. With no little pride he explained, "Aristotle was born in this village. He was a very wise man." Only then did we remember that the great philosopher of the West is often called "the Stagirite."

How often may Aristotle have watched the sun rising over Athos when he was on the hills among the goatherds, with the other boys of the village. For Athos was already a holy mountain for the Greeks of antiquity. From its summit, where today a small chapel stands, the mighty statue of the Thracian Jupiter looked far out to sea. In Aeschylus's tragedy of Agamemnon, Clytemnestra describes with a degree of geographical precision remarkable for a woman the journey of the fire telegraph that announced the fall of Troy to Argos. The fire signal kindled by Hephaestus on Mount Ida makes its way across Mount Hermes on the island of Lemnos, the "Athoist steep rock of Zeus," the Macistus on Euboea, the Massapion mountains, the Cithaeron, and so on to Argos. The central position of the Athos massif in northern Aegea is made beautifully clear in Aeschylus's verse. The hilltops that he mentions are in fact within sight of one another, so that there can be no doubt that this splendidly organized relay actually took place. Perhaps the seed for the magnificent conception of the world's eternity that Aristotle was later to outline was sown in the boy's soul as he watched the sun rising over Athos.

We had the sunrise and the Stagirite to thank for the fact that we missed our steamer. It goes only twice a week from Ierissos—a large, prosperous fishing village on the east coast. So we left our car at the Ierissos police station and hired a caïque, a little ten-ton boat with a powerful Diesel engine. Half the village escorted us on board amidst laughter and cheerful chatter.

South of the village the remains of a canal can still be seen. This was the canal that the Persian king Xerxes had cut through the isthmus of the peninsula of Athos in the year 483 B.C. Ten years previously, the fleet of Darius, under General Mardonius, had been wrecked on the rocks of Athos. It is a dangerous corner, where storms sometimes break from a clear sky. The Persian fleet under Xerxes came unscathed through the canal to Attica, but it did not return. The Greeks destroyed it in the famous Battle of Salamis, in the year 480. This was the first time that the West was saved from conquest by a great Oriental power.

We sat on deck and drank rezina, the Greek wine that is mixed with resin. The skipper did not need much persuasion to join us. The sea was almost completely calm. Tiny waves lapped against the ship's side. Two dolphins accompanied the boat with graceful motions. Our caïque clucked bravely along the coast quite close to the shore. The sun was shining. After an hour's voyage the first monastery appeared, a fortress built on a cliff overlooking the shore. Solid and bare, the walls rise to a height of a hundred and twenty-five feet, and are crowned with a garland of windows. Tiny frail balconies supported by sloping timbers, and clinging to the wall like swallows' nests, look out to sea. Here and there a melancholy ruin rises over the blue water on a ledge of rock. Then come the Monasteries of Pantokrator and Stavronikita. After three hours' voyage we went ashore in the small harbor of the Monastery of Iviron, entering thus upon the soil of the thousand-year-old monastic republic.

Athos: The Holy Mountain

The Proigoumenos Nikardos Lavriotes, Abbot of La Grande Lavra, the oldest of the monasteries on Mount Athos, Protepistate, and President of the Holy Synod in Karyai, the seat of the government, entered the simple room where guests of the republic are received. This imposingly tall, erect old man of eighty, with his stately movements, his intense gaze from bright, wide-open eyes, his long white beard, dressed in a black cowl, adorned with a cross and a medallion inlaid with an image of the Virgin that he wears on a silver chain around his neck, his snow-white hair covered with the high black biretta of the Byzantine monks, presented an awe-inspiring picture of dignity—a dignity resting on many centuries of piety. We made a deep obeisance.

The Abbot was accompanied by an older monk who carried an ivory staff with a weighty pommel embossed in silver in his right hand to signify that the Abbot was appearing in his capacity of reigning Protepistate. With exquisite courtesy, the Abbot's companion asked us to be seated. Manners are not unimportant; they are the expression of a moral attitude. We wanted to wait until the Abbot was seated, but in the East the guest is honored so highly that we were not allowed to wait. In due course we handed over the letter of introduction from the Archbishop of Athens. The older monk rose slightly from his chair as Alexander handed him the letter. The Proigoumenos asked for the letter to be read to him, scrutinizing his guests meanwhile. It is not easy to withstand that kind of gaze. The Abbot looked at us in a way that one is not often subjected to in the world nowadays. The fact that he rarely moved his eyelids was proof in itself of his calm and superiority. His look was friendly but penetrating, reaching the very ground of the soul and making one very conscious of one's worldliness. Not everything in one's worldly soul is calculated to arouse the approval of an Abbot on Mount Athos.

The faces of these venerable monks who renounced this world and turned their lives to heaven long ago, long before one was born, bear an expression alike of wisdom and innocence and of a peculiar transparency. Just as the face of Moses shone when he came down from the cloud on Mount Sinai, so there is on these faces a gleam of the radiance to which they have been devoted in a lifetime of asceticism and prayer.

What may this wise old Abbot have thought about these

dubious globe-trotters? We explained to him that we wanted to report to Christians of the West about Mount Athos, where the tradition of Eastern Christianity has been preserved so faithfully through the centuries. The Abbot nodded benevolently. He said that our project was the more useful since the Day of Judgment was no longer very far off. He said this very quietly but with the matter-of-factness with which one mentions a date in the calendar—perhaps the day after tomorrow. The Day of Judgment is indeed no longer *sub specie aeternitatis*. The fact that a schizophrenic madman can now destroy the world gave the quiet remark a certain topicality.

A glass of refreshingly cold water with a spoonful of delightful jam was served by an evzone and followed by a cup of mocha with a little schnapps. The evzones are a small secular body, serving the Synod as police. They are rarely needed for anything more than serving guests with jam, mocha, and ouzo. The evzones still wear the picturesque Greek national costume one sees on old engravings from the period when Lord Byron was taking part in the Greeks' War of Liberation against the Turks. The Abbot raised his little glass with an expression as if to ask us to understand that he was making this slight concession to the pleasures of the world in honor of his guests.

In spite of the proximity of the Last Judgment the Abbot was curious as to how events would develop in the near future. The conversation soon led to world politics. Russia, which only a generation ago was, in the person of the Czar, the powerful protector of the little republic, is, now that the Nazi barbarians have disappeared, the most dangerous enemy of the Church and the Faith. The Abbot was anxious, also, to know the meaning of the Communist revolution in China. Though the republic of Athos stands in the margin of history, even here the repercussions of international politics can be felt. In his early years the Abbot

Nikardos was a subject of the last Turkish Sultan. In the wars of the present century the once wealthy monasteries have lost most of their possessions in Russia, Anatolia, Rumania, Bulgaria, and even Greece. The tradition that the monks on Athos preserve is, however, not a secular one. It is the tradition of the Faith entrusted to them in the final days of Constantine XI, the last ruler on the Byzantine Imperial throne. On Mount Athos the ancient piety of Greek Byzantium, which perished five hundred years ago when the city was captured by the Turks, has outlasted the Turkish Empire.

The letter from the Holy Synod to the monasteries, which recommended us to the monks' hospitality as brothers in Christ, bore a seal with the image of Panagia, the Mother of God. At the same time, however, it was an extremely democratic seal: it consisted of four parts and was valid only after all four Epistates (magistrates) had impressed their parts of the seal on it.

The Abbot took leave of us by raising his right hand slightly, in an act of blessing. It was as though he were passing on to his guests something of the grace of heaven, the grace that hovered about his white head. The older monk escorted us to the door with the utmost courtesy. Our audience with the past was over.

The autonomous monastic republic on Mount Athos is the oldest democracy in the world. It was the model for Thomas More's Utopia. The territory of the republic extends over the whole peninsula, which is about thirty miles long and has an average breadth of six miles. The peninsula is traversed by a densely wooded mountain ridge. Rising in waves from north to south, it passes over into the bare rocky marble massif of the Athos pyramid where eagles build their aeries. Across the ridge or along its slopes a mule track runs through the woods. The path is paved in the steeper places. The broad stone slabs have been worn smooth by the passage of mule hoofs throughout the centuries. From time to time the mule track is intercepted by a flight of steps, which makes it impossible for motor travel. There is not a single motor vehicle on the whole peninsula. Occasionally one comes across a monk riding peacefully along on his mule. Then the stillness of the forest is broken for a few minutes by a friendly conversation. From the crest of the ridge paths run down on either side into the valleys. Amidst spreading trees, romantic bridges span their graceful arches across streams that leap down between the meadows and hazelnut bushes. The woods are gloriously unscathed. Sometimes one gets a glimpse of the sea glistening in the sunshine. Sometimes the blue summit of Athos can be seen above the near-by green hills. In this solitude between sea and sky the monasteries rise up with their lead-covered roofs, these twenty mighty citadels of God, defiant fortresses of piety. Their moss-covered walls preserve the peace of the heart amid the peace of nature. Some of the monasteries are built on the coast, and they usually have small harbors of their own. Others are built in the lonely forests. From their battlements it is possible to see the gleaming Aegean.

The monasteries are real fortresses. In the course of the ages important treasures have accumulated there, and it was these treasures that inspired the greed of the pirates in the Mediterranean. So the monasteries were built on high rocks and protected with strong walls. Even today the gates are closed at sunset. Anyone arriving after sunset has to spend the night in the open. Since they are built as fortresses, the rooms open onto the interior. The galleries and staircases leading to the upper floors are almost entirely made of wood and are built in the open. The katholikon, the church, is situated in the middle of the grounds. Owing to their poverty, most of the monasteries are somewhat unkempt, and so the magnificence inside the churches on this remote peninsula is all the more breath-taking. Silver lamps hang from the ceiling. Golden and silver vessels adorn the altar. The iconostasis is embellished with beautiful old paintings, and the walls have frescoes. Sometimes precious marble mosaics inlaid in the floors have been preserved. All this magnificence contrasts strangely with the modesty and simplicity of the monks themselves.

Apart from the twenty monasteries there are fourteen monastic communities in villages scattered about the peninsula. They are called "sketae" from the very ancient monastic settlement of Sketis in Egypt. There are also numerous groups of monks who live in small communities unconnected with a monastic order. Hermits are dwelling on the slopes of Mount Athos—though the word "dwelling" is actually an exaggeration. Most of them live the most ascetic life in caves, impatiently awaiting the day of their deliverance from earth.

The Holy Synod that governs the republic is made up of delegates from the monasteries. Each monastery is entitled to send a representative to the Synod. Administrative business is transacted by four monks elected annually by the Holy Synod. They are the Epistates, with their head, the Protepistate, the first among equals. The Bible is their statute book.

The republic's constitution has a long history. It begins with a Magna Charta that is inscribed on goatskin. This document is called the "Tragos" (Greek for goatskin) and dates from the year 972. The Tragos is preserved to this day in Karyai. Its authenticity is beyond dispute. The Emperor's signature—"Joannis, Emperor of the Romans, a believer in Christ the God"—is the earliest surviving example of the signature of a Byzantine emperor. There are documents and signatures of Merovingian kings from the seventh century. Charlemagne signed with his own hand, but only with a monogrammatic stroke intended merely to execute the document artistically signed for him by another hand. The earliest document bearing a Western emperor's signature in full is a papal document of the year 998 signed by Otto III.

The occasion of the Magna Charta of the Tragos was the building of the first Monastery of La Grande Lavra on the southern extremity of the peninsula, at the very foot of Mount Athos. The monastery was founded at the request of the Emperor Nicephorus Phocas of Byzantium, by his friend the monk Athanasius of Trebizond (the modern Trabzon), who was later canonized. In the courtyard of the monastery there is a cypress tree planted by Athanasius. Botanists have verified that it is about a thousand years old. In the innumerable storms that break over this headland this tree has never been struck by lightning.

The remains of St. Athanasius are buried in La Grande Lavra, in a tomb famous throughout Eastern Christendom. Many miracles have been ascribed to it. It lies in a corner of the main church of the monastery underneath a dome supported by an ancient pillar; precious lamps are suspended all around it. The walls of the tomb niche are adorned with medieval frescoes. The splendor of this tomb and the living memory of a saint who died more than a thousand years ago form a striking contrast to the shabby wooden crosses below which the mortal remains of the simple monks lie forgotten in small cemeteries overgrown with brush.

One of the frescoes in the niche occupied by Athanasius's tomb depicts the saint's burial. In its composition it reminds one of "The Burial of Count Orgaz," El Greco's masterpiece in Toledo in the Chapel of S. Tomé. I presume that the young Greco had seen the fresco on Athos. He was born in Crete, where, toward the end of the fifteenth century, the Cretan school of painting produced a final blossoming of Byzantine art. Greco derives from this school.

43

The remarkable elongation of the figures in his paintings is not just his personal style but an old tradition of the Eastern Mediterranean. It was Greco, the Greek Domenico Theotokopoulos, who went to Spain and who as representative of the Byzantine tradition became one of the originators of the Baroque style, the last great creative style in European art. To the very end of his life the painter inscribed the signature on his pictures in Greek letters.

The building of the Monastery of La Grande Lavra gave rise to controversy. For many centuries monks had been living on Athos as hermits. The first of these hermits probably came to this solitude as early as the fourth century A.D. Information about them, however, is scanty. The ascetics violently resisted the building of the monastery, which was richly endowed by the Emperor Nicephorus, and sent a delegation to Byzantium to protest to the Emperor. They considered the opulence of this foundation an attack by the devil on true religion. The Tragos, the Imperial edict, settled these disputes. It gave the monks the right to democratic self-government, which was quite unusual at that time. Simultaneously, it placed the Holy Mountain under the special protection of the Emperor. Despite great difficulties, the monks have managed to preserve this constitution through the centuries. Even before the fall of Constantinople, the Turkish sultans assumed the protectorate over Athos as successors to the Byzantine emperors. In 1430 the monks submitted themselves to the Sultan Murad II. With their respect for the shrine of their Christian subjects, the Turkish sultans set a fine example of toleration. Letters of safe-conduct from the sultans are still preserved with gratitude in various monasteries. Today the monastic republic on Mount Athos is under the protection of the King of Greece.

It is true that the dispute that caused the Emperor Joannis to draw up the Tragos has never been completely

44

settled on the Holy Mountain. Even today there are two kinds of monastery on Mount Athos. In the one, the cenobian monasteries, the ancient tradition of poverty and asceticism is fully preserved. The monks elect an abbot for life, and to him they owe absolute obedience. As individuals, they have no property. Their frugal meals are taken communally in the trapezium, accompanied by readings from the Bible.

The walls of these refectories are adorned with frescoes that depict the transitoriness of earthly life. A favorite theme is the scene where a patriarch stands beside the open marble sarcophagus of Alexander the Great, pointing mockingly to the pitiful smirking mummy into which the conqueror of the world has been transformed.

In the idiorrhythmic (self-regulating) monasteries, the discipline is less strict. The monks are allowed a certain amount of personal freedom, and they have property of their own. Only the services are communal. Their little dwellings are sometimes quite comfortably furnished, often with colorful cushions embroidered by devoted aunts. Nearly all these dwellings have a balcony with a view of the sea. The devout fathers love to spend an hour or two of meditation in the warm sun on these balconies, with a tomcat or a parakeet for company.

Eastern monasticism differs from Western monasticism. When it first arose in the third century, the world-weariness of late antiquity fused with the world-estrangement of the young persecuted Christian movement. The tendency to turn away from the world is not specifically Christian. It accords with a widespread need of human nature. When St. Anthony founded the first Christian monastery in the desert by the Red Sea, he was already building on an ancient tradition. Men who had given up high positions at the Pharaoh's court to end their lives in the desert as hermits had existed in Egypt from the earliest times.

45

Even today the Eastern monk endeavors to live like the early Christians. He devotes his life to asceticism, to the mortification of the senses, to detachment from the world and absorption in the spirit within. He is entirely devoted to the things of the spirit. The Eastern Church engages in no missionary activity. Only a few monks are ordained priests. The monastic life consists in a constant surrender to the omnipresent power of the Holy Spirit. Despite all the contrasts that this attitude affords to the active, worldly, missionary attitude of Western Christianity, it contains as its premise the pursuit of Dante's *vita felice*, the blessed life, which consists in the cultivation of one's own virtues and the contemplation of God.

The method employed by Eastern monasticism to attain the goal of the union of the human soul with God is the constant contemplation of the glory of the kingdom of heaven in a life of constant prayer. The form that this life of constant prayer assumes is the liturgy of the Eastern Church. It abounds in a sublime symbolism in which, as in a kind of religious poetry, all the details of the rite are related to the events of the Gospel. To understand this liturgy requires long study. Fully to experience it requires the constant practice of a lifetime.

Eastern monasticism played an important part in the history of the Byzantine Empire. The monks' power rested on the belief of the Eastern Christian that a monk is all the more holy the more completely he has turned away from the world, and that the holier he is the more effective will be his prayers. The power of the monks was originally a spiritual power. It was the great holiness of the fathers on Mount Athos that led to this inaccessible monastic republic's becoming the spiritual center of the Eastern Church.

There are Greek, Serbian, Bulgarian, Rumanian, and Russian monasteries on the Holy Mountain. Athos is therefore still a faithful reflection of the nations and centuries in which the teaching of the Gospel has been a living force in the East.

In the Eastern Church, Oriental traditions have been preserved that would never have been able to take root in the West. That is why women have never been allowed to enter the monastic republic. One is not born on Athos. One dies there.

According to a legend that is still utterly real in the magic world of Eastern Christianity, Mara, the daughter of a Serbian ruler, who had been married to the Sultan Murad II, wanted to visit a Serbian monastery, Agiu Pavlu, to take the monks the gifts of the three kings, gold, incense, and myrrh. When she came near to the monastery she heard a voice saying, "Go no farther. Here is the kingdom of a different queen, the Queen of Heaven." The myrrh of the three kings that the Serbian princess on the Turkish throne had brought to Athos is still preserved in the Monastery of Agiu Pavlu. Though women are not allowed to enter Athos, the Panagia, the holy Mother of God, is worshipped more devoutly in this republic of ascetics than almost anywhere else in the world.

The monks of the East have never been subservient to the Church. The very fact that the Byzantine Church acknowledged the Emperor on the throne of Constantine the Great as its secular head prevented them. It would be more correct to say that the monks have tried to dominate the Eastern Church. Usually the Byzantine rulers did not wish to forgo the aid of the monks' prayers in atoning somewhat for the crimes that the mighty of this world like to call the necessities of politics. The monks always complied with the Emperor's demands. It was their Christian duty to do so. In return, the rulers gave valuables and landed properties to the monasteries during their lifetime or at their death. The Emperor Andronicus Palaeologus, who reigned from 1282 to 1328 and died in 1332, probably ended his life on Athos. On his deathbed, Andronicus bequeathed his prayer book, with an autograph dedication, to the Monastery of the Iberians on Athos. This Imperial bequest is still in the monastery's library.

In the course of the centuries, therefore, treasures have accumulated in the monasteries on Athos which it would take many volumes to describe. They include some of the oldest and most venerable relics of Christendom. The Monastery of Vatopedi preserves the girdle of the Holy Virgin that Mary dropped into the hands of Thomas the disciple when she ascended into heaven. It is a simple linen band, kept in a golden reliquary adorned with jewels and embellished with enamel miniatures. This reliquary was originally in Byzantium. It is mentioned as early as 450 in documents in the possession of St. Pulcheria, Empress of Byzantium.

The most beautiful panel pictures of Byzantine art are to be found on Athos. The picture of the famous Iberian Mother of God, the Madonna Portaïtissa, the Madonna at the Gate, is one of the precious possessions of the Monastery of Iviron. According to legend, when a soldier pierced the picture with his dagger during the image-breaking in Constantinople, the spot that had been struck began to bleed. To preserve it from further profanation the soldier entrusted the painting to the sea; he himself gave up his own sanguinary profession and became a monk. At the end of a long life he came to Athos. When, after his arrival on the Holy Mountain, he stood by the shore and looked out across the waters of the Aegean, the waves bore the picture to land.

Nikon, the Patriarch of Moscow, the reformer of the Russian Church in the middle of the seventeenth century, once ordered a copy of the Madonna Portaïtissa to be made. As the Madonna Iverskaja, this copy became one of the most famous of holy pictures in Russia. In 1648, the

48

year of the Peace of Westphalia, Czar Alexis Romanov gave the monks of Iviron a monastery in Moscow as a mark of his gratitude. Old icons are preserved on Athos, including some of the finest examples in mosaic produced from the tiniest imaginable stones. Old Bibles and liturgical books in the libraries contain a wealth of marvellous miniatures. In addition, for hundreds of years the monasteries, to the solitude of which the devout have retired to take leave of the world, have been adorned with mosaics and frescoes of great beauty. The art historians of our time forget all too easily that the medieval pictures whose beauty we so rightly admire were painted not only by great artists but also by devout painters.

The monks did not fail to exploit the influential monopoly that they enjoyed as intermediaries between a sinful Emperor and divine forgiveness. Jesus Christ alone succeeded in resisting the temptation of earthly power. In some periods there was scarcely a bishop's see that was not occupied by a monk from Mount Athos. The monks paid no taxes. They were exempt from military service. The enormous riches that had gradually accumulated in their hands began to be dangerous. They contrasted intolerably with the everlasting financial troubles of the State. It was impossible to supervise the monks politically. They were sensitive and suffered from attacks of fanaticism. Though several Byzantine emperors tried to rid themselves of monasticism by force, none succeeded. On the other hand, however, there have always been reformers inside the monastic movement who have given fresh impetus to the ideals of early Christianity. In every succeeding century the religious life on Athos has been renewed.

Their seclusion from the world is the reason for the Byzantine monks' aversion to knowledge. The European scholars who visit Athos are fond of referring, with an arrogance that is anything but Christian, to the monks' ignorance and their lack of scholarly interest in the precious things in their libraries. The monks have a simple answer: "At the Last Judgment God will not ask you what you know. He will ask you what you have done."

The monks are not actively interested in the artistic treasures in their keeping. The age-old knowledge accumulated in their libraries is covered with dust and lies forgotten. Western scholars alone endeavor to rescue it from oblivion. The only thing that has remained alive on Athos is the passion for piety. The monks' prayers are still as full of fiery zeal as on the day when St. Athanasius consecrated the katholikon of La Grande Lavra in the full splendor of the tenth century.

We spent the night in the Monastery of Kutlumusi, near Karyai. The strange name is mentioned in a document as early as 1169. It derives from the founder of the monastery, a prince of the family of the Seljuks, Prince Kutelmish. The Prince had been born in a tent on the steppe of Turkestan. After a lifetime of wild and gallant battles he became a Christian and died a peaceful death on Athos.

When we arrived at the monastery gate the mules stopped of their own accord. No devout Christian rides past or through a monastery gate, and the mules on Athos know this. The guestmaster received us with great kindness. Kutlumusi is a monastery of the strict cenobian observance. The guestmaster showed us to a room. First he prepared a mocha for us, then he boiled eggs. An egg on Athos is soft-boiled after twelve Our Fathers. The division of time is still that of the Old Testament—the day has twelve hours from sunrise to sunset. Night had fallen. It was beginning to get cold. The guestmaster brought us a lot of blankets, and we were able to present the charming man with a recent newspaper that we had brought with us from Salonika. For another hour the companions on this journey into the past sat at the comforting fireside of the brother doorkeeper, passing in review the day's personalities, from the Partisans to the Abbot Nikardos. The peace of the monastery encompassed us. At this hour the monks are asleep in their cells, and the stillness was undisturbed.

Toward midnight, the "simandre" sounded. This is a brass instrument struck with a hammer to announce the beginning of the hours of prayer. Going to the window, we looked down onto the dark monastery courtyard. We could only just discern the outlines of the buildings. From the windows of the church the light of a few candles flickered feebly. The moon had not yet risen; only the stars were shining in the sky. The brazen sound in that deep silence came as a solemn and incredibly impressive warning of the transitoriness of the world. Lights flickered across the staircases and galleries of the monasteries, making it possible to discern the black figures of monks on their way to service with lanterns in their hands. From the light of the church of Kutlumusi the solemn singing of the monks rose through the still night to the stars, praising God in the ancient and moving accents of the Byzantine liturgy, sung by a group of men who had long since burned their boats to await eternity amidst the wastes of time.

Byzantine Mosaic

Istanbul ranks with Rome in historical importance. To this city, known to us under three names—Byzantium, Constantinople, Istanbul—the world owes the preservation of Greek literature and of Roman law; a fundamental contribution to Christian theology; the rescue on several occasions of Europe from the powers of the Orient; and the beginnings of humanism.

Hellas created the literature of Greece. But after Athens had been captured by the Romans, in the course of a few centuries it sank to the level of an insignificant provincial city. It was only when it became the political capital of the new Greece in the past century that it began to play an important role again. The scholars of Byzantium have preserved the traditions of Hellas for a thousand years. In a generous gesture of farewell, Byzantium bequeathed humanism to the West at the time of its own fall.

Rome was the capital of the Roman Empire. Although from the fourth century the political center of gravity had shifted eastward, the primate of the Roman episcopate continued to be universally acknowledged. Rome became the center of Christendom. Protected by the walls of Byzantine power, the nations of the North were able to destroy the world of antiquity undisturbed, constructing from the ruins of the past those strong states from which Europe took its rise. If Byzantium had not kept watch in the East during eleven centuries of uninterrupted conflict with Oriental powers, Rome might well have sunk to the status of a Persian or Arabian village like Carthage, and the Bishop of Rome would have become a village prelate, however venerable the tradition of the See of Peter might have remained.

The Byzantine Emperor Justinian summarized Roman law in that great collective work known to scholars as the *Corpus Juris Civilis*. Byzantium thereby preserved for the world the Roman Empire's most precious achievement and restored it to the Western world in which this law had been created. Byzantium saved the Eternal City from being merely an eternal memory.

As the boat turns from the Aegean Sea into the Dardanelles it passes between the tomb of Achilles, who fell in the Trojan War, and the graves of the Turkish, British, and

German soldiers who fell in Gallipoli in the First World War. King Priam's Troy once guarded the Dardanelles, which connect the Mediterranean with the Sea of Marmara and the Black Sea. It is more than likely that the Trojan War, which took place only a generation after the exodus of Moses from Egypt, was not waged merely for the beauty of the Greek Queen Helen. Even at that period the question of Greek exports to the Black Sea may well have played a part in causing the war.

The first ship that we know to have passed through the Dardanelles was the *Argo*, which travelled to Colchis under Jason to fetch the Golden Fleece. At the heart of many of the legends that surround the voyage of the Argonauts is the memory of one of the first great voyages of discovery in Greek history. Scholars place the voyage of the Argonauts before the Trojan War. Following the course of the *Argo*, about 660 B.C., the Dorians founded the colony of Byzantion on the Bosporus, the strait that connects the Sea of Marmara with the Black Sea. This was followed by the founding of more Greek cities in the Crimea and on the coasts of the Black Sea.

When the ship has crossed the Sea of Marmara and is approaching the Bosporus, Europe on the left and Asia on the right meet on the horizon. The Bosporus runs almost exactly from north to south. At its southern entrance, on the left-hand, European side, a bay opens out into the land. This bay is the Golden Horn, the harbor of Istanbul and one of the most beautiful harbors in the world. The part of the city south of the bay is ancient Byzantium. In the northern part, on the other side of the bay, are the modern commercial quarters of Galata and Pera. The original Constantinople stands entirely on European soil.

The entry into the harbor of Istanbul affords a magnificent spectacle. As the ship approaches the city the green Princes' Isles, covered with woods and white villas, glide past on the starboard side. Then Byzantium rises up from the sea. Like Rome, the city is built on seven hills. The mighty domes of the mosques, overtopped by slender minarets, stand out against the blue sky. The sun sparkles on the golden roofs. The ship slows down. On the left-hand side, at the entrance to the harbor, the buildings of the old Seraglio glide past: the Palace of the Turkish Sultans, with its gardens and pavilions.

Above the Seraglio towers a mighty mountain of stone, the thick-set building of the Hagia Sophia, the Church of Holy Wisdom. It, too, has four minarets—one at each corner. On the other side of the Golden Horn, a mighty Genoese watchtower reaches up to the sky. Opposite, on the Asiatic side of the strait, lies Scutari, with its extensive barracks. These barracks have been a monument to neighborly love since the Crimean War, in the fifties of the nineteenth century. While the British Ambassador's wife was giving her afternoon teas in the Embassy in Pera, the citadel of diplomacy, from which the dying Osman Empire was ruled for a hundred years, on the other side of the Bosporus, in the barracks of Scutari, Florence Nightingale, the angel of the Crimean War, was waging her heroic struggle to secure reasonable care for the sick and wounded soldiers of Sebastopol amid dirt and stench and despair—a struggle which in the end she won, to the glory of the nineteenth century, and to the shame of a stupid military bureaucracy. Only a few people now recall that one of the causes of the Crimean War was the dispute between France and Russia as to which of these two great powers had first claim to protect the Holy Places in Palestine.

Somewhat south of Scutari there lies the little harbor of Haidar Pasha, with the station where the Anatolian Railway begins. It runs down to the Taurus Mountains. From Konya onwards it bears the name of the Baghdad Railway, which has become so well known in politics. Villas and palaces, gardens and ancient fortresses line both shores of the Bosporus. And over everything, the blue sky, the shining sun, and a fresh wind from the northeast.

Great ships lie at anchor or by the pier. A merry swarm of motorboats, barges, flat-bottomed boats, and snow-white passenger boats, which plow through the water at great speed, fill the harbor as far as the nearer of the two bridges that link the banks of the Golden Horn in a great arch. Cormorants squat on the bollards. Thousands of gulls add life to the scene with their white wings and loud cries. The indescribable atmosphere of one of the great harbors of the world, saturated with the thousand and one smells of foreign parts, envelops the stranger in smoke and noise.

Travellers of all nations have at all times extolled this brilliant scene. The only trouble is that the brilliance is offset by squalor and misery. History teaches us that man has to pay with streams of blood for the glory and exaltation of world dominion. This wonderful and fabulous city lies in one of the most sensitive spots in the world, politically and geographically.

The most important events in the history of the city on the Golden Horn are reflected in its seven names. And this city is unique in that all its names have survived through all the fierce events that it has seen. It is just as much Byzantium or Constantinople as Istanbul. Oddly enough, even Istanbul, its third Turkish name, comes from the Greek: *eis tan polin*—"into the city." The fourth name is Nova Roma—"New Rome." Since Constantine the Great founded the city as the New Rome, His Holiness the Ecumenical Patriarch of Constantinople bears the title of "Novae Romae Archiepiscopus" on his seal. The city's fifth name represents a centuries-old threat. All the Slav-speaking nations call the Emperor Constantine's city Zarigrad, "the Imperial City." In early times it had the pagan sacerdotal mystery name of Anthusa—"the flourishing." For its seventh name, the Arabs call it Dar el Saadat—"the place of happiness."

The peculiar historical stability of the city on the Golden Horn is reflected in its emblem, the half-moon. At the time of Philip of Macedonia, the father of Alexander the Great, the city was saved from a Macedonian attack by means of a light with which the goddess Hecate warned the inhabitants of Byzantium of the approaching enemy. In gratitude, Hecate's attribute, the half-moon, was made the city's symbol. Through all the changes and chances of history the half-moon has remained the emblem of this city—a memorable crest, and one of the oldest in the world. The last time the power of this symbol was evinced was when the Turks hurled down the Cross from the Hagia Sophia and set up the half-moon. Constantinople did not become Osman, but the Osman Empire became Byzantine.

It is thanks to Napoleon's political insight that the city has not become Zarigrad. In 1807 at the Peace of Tilsit Napoleon described Byzantium as the hub of the world and refused to cede it to a Russia destined by the course of its rivers to strive for the control of the city. Besides the Danube, the Dniester, the Bug, the Dnieper, and the Kuban flow into the Black Sea. The first Russian fleet entered the Sea of Marmara as early as A.D. 860. Napoleon's imperial vision went so far that on his expedition to Russia he carried with him in his baggage the official robes for his coronation as Emperor of Byzantium. But Napoleon was not another Alexander. Had the world been conquered by France in the nineteenth century, this would not have had the same historical significance as the spread of Hellenistic culture in the Near East in the fourth century B.C. by Macedonian Alexander.

Istanbul is a European frontier station against the East. As such, its task is so deep-rooted that even the Turks, an Asiatic nation of horsemen, had to assume a defense post against irruptions from the East after capturing the city. Anomalously, through all history it has been Byzantium's curious destiny to have to fight repeatedly against the West as well.

While Byzantium was at war with the Anatolian Seljuks, the first Turkish people to come to Asia Minor, the Doge Enrico Dandolo of Venice persuaded the Frankish knights of the Fourth Crusade to invade, capture, and plunder Constantinople. That was in the year 1204. The old man was the first to set foot on land, and by this one unconsidered step he destroyed not only the power of Byzantium but that of Venice as well. This blow from the West weakened Constantinople so greatly that in the end it fell into the hands of the Turks. With the loss of the Eastern Mediterranean and the destruction of its trade with the Orient, the power of Venice likewise declined.

The precious things that the Crusaders brought home from Constantinople as booty—forgetting Jerusalem, which had been recaptured from the Moslems—are preserved in all the treasure houses of Europe. Even in its death throes, Byzantium gave an extraordinary impulse to the awakening art of the West through the things that had been stolen from it.

From the window of my room in Pera I was able to look out over the city, this landscape of memories in which man has fashioned the idea of infinity in stone. The ruins on which the huts of the poor are built are the rubble of a great past. This city has seen all the splendor of the earth, and all its misery. Always threatened, always in danger, amid the glory of the civilizations of which it was the center, amid the squalor of the lives of untold generations, amid the vices and virtues of its rulers and peoples, Byzantium has overcome despair with hope a hundred times. This city on the frontiers of Europe is a monument to the bravery of the human heart, and may serve to remind us that in the course of the last two thousand years the West has lapsed into historical situations that were more dangerous and more desperate than that in which it finds itself today.

When the stranger strolls through the streets of Istanbul he meets a delightful mixture of East and West. The inscriptions are in Turkish, but written in Latin characters. It is possible to read them without understanding a single word. Turkish is not related to any European language. The name of the diplomatic center, Pera, where cars rush past the elegant shops and cafés and movie houses, is Istiklâl Cadessi. It takes three days to learn this name and another three to pronounce it so that a Turk will understand you. As in the time of the Sultan Suleiman the Magnificent, dignified Turks sit in the cafés smoking the narghile, the old water pipe. It is true, however, that the Turks no longer wear the fez, the red cap of the orthodox Moslem. They wear European hats, alas. The fez was certainly more becoming.

We should always recall the great Suleiman with gratitude. The world owes him a new city wall in Jerusalem, a few poems highly esteemed in Turkish literature, and a generous edict founded on tolerance that eased the lot of Christians in his Empire at the time when the Inquisition was beginning to build its pyres.

Strolling up and down hill along the old streets of Byzantium on the southern side of the Golden Horn, one is still walking on paths trodden a thousand years ago. The design of the city was determined by the lay of the land. The Seraglio, the Palace of the Sultans, stands on the foundation walls of the Byzantine Imperial Palace. The Hippodrome has never been built on at any time. The Hagia Sophia stands on the site of the Acropolis of the ancient Greek colony of Byzantion. Today's tenement houses occupy a district that was always a populous quarter. Sometimes, between two of these tall houses an age-old staircase with age-old steps goes steeply uphill. With their stones polished smooth and round, these stairs really have a venerable air. They are old enough, one feels, for the soft paws of the tens of thousands of cats, Byzantine or Turkish, alone, climbing up and down every day through so many centuries, to have polished their cobblestones to their present roundness and smoothness. Some of these unkempt cats may have in their pedigree an ancestor stroked by a Roman Empress.

Sometimes on these strolls through the city one wanders into forsaken corners where Turkish wooden houses with beautifully carved harem windows have survived. Although Kemal Ataturk abolished the Turkish women's veil, they still pull their head shawls about their faces and hold them fast with their teeth. It has always been difficult to reconcile old customs and new laws.

The city of Byzantium has subterranean cisterns, enormous vaults resting on granite or porphyry columns. One of the cisterns has been in use since the time of Constantine. Two of the ancient aqueducts, one built by the Emperor Valens, the other by Emperor Justinian, still convey fresh water into the city from the mountains.

The bazaar is a little world of its own. The entrance into this citadel of commerce is through a large stone doorway. The roofed-in lanes run on for miles in all directions. They are rather gloomy but shady and cool in the summer. It is pleasant in the bazaars. Everywhere the traders sit with their legs crossed on carpets spread on the ground. They smoke cigarettes and drink mocha brought to them by small barefoot boys on brass trays suspended on three chains. The men chatter continuously. If one stops to look at a piece of embroidery, a copper vessel, a piece of enamel work, one is immediately drawn into the chatter and offered a cup of mocha. Friendly conversation is certainly one of the most peaceful ways of making use of language.

Sometimes, however, world-shattering national rebellions have arisen from the friendly chatter of the bazaars, rebellions that erupted during the great races in the Hippodrome and had to be suppressed in rivers of blood.

The narrow, vaulted shops, caverns open to the street, are lighted by ceiling lamps. This bazaar has been burned down more than a dozen times, but it is still in the same district where the ladies of the court of the Emperor Andronicus Palaeologus bought Chinese silk, amber ornaments, Arabian perfume, furs from Russia, rugs from Bukhara. As a reminder of the flourishing crafts of the pious city that once supplied half of Christendom with objects of value for churches, palaces, and beautiful women, golden and silver bangles can be seen piled up in the jewellers' lanes as in the times when Byzantium dominated the commerce of the world.

The Emperor Constantine, who made Byzantium the capital of the Empire and Christianity the official religion of the Roman Empire, is fully entitled to the epithet "the Great" which history has conferred on him. But it is a gloomy greatness. Constantine was born in the Balkans. He was overshadowed by that dark philosophy of life that so horrified the Hellenes when they met it among the Thracians. We know, from portrait busts, what he looked like. This face with the rather low forehead, the wide-open eyes staring with the fear of demons, the gigantic nose, the powerful chin and austere mouth, with the corners slightly drawn down—a face that rarely smiled—resembles a landscape lacerated by terrible struggles for power. In spite of the beautiful stories woven around Constantine's conferment upon Christianity of the rank of a State religion, this act of the utmost historical importance had as much to do with politics as with Christian piety.

The foundation of the New Rome was a decision of outstanding political wisdom. Constantine wanted to separate the prestige of his authority from the ancient pagan tradition, to relate it to the other-worldly metaphysics of the new religion. He therefore created a new capital to form the nucleus of a new world. In the New Rome the tradition of paganism was too weak to resist the inner force of the new doctrine. It took longer for Christianity to succeed in Rome than in Constantinople. Constantine did nothing by half measures, which is true even of his crimes. After he had made Christianity the official religion he convened bishops from all parts of the Empire to the first Ecumenical Council in Nicaea. At this Council, at which he presided, the theological principles of the Christian creed were formulated "by the Fathers," as it is termed in the old accounts of it. It is therefore not surprising that Christian historians of his own time turned a blind eye to the Emperor's errors. Constantine the Great played a decisive part in the historical success of Christianity. He achieved the political intention that he had in mind when he made Nova Roma the capital on May 11, A.D. 330. Without any violent disturbances the Roman Empire passed over into the Byzantine Empire. (It should be remembered that when Columbus was born the throne of Byzantium was still occupied by a successor of the Roman Emperor Augustus.)

Constantine chose the spot for his capital with the geographical and political astuteness of a genius. In this he surpassed even Alexander the Great. When on the evening of May 29, 1543, the Turks stormed the city wall of Byzantium, the millennium in which the city of the Emperor Constantine had been the capital of the Greek-Byzantine Empire came to an end. On the morrow of its most terrible defeat Constantinople woke up to find itself the capital of the Islamic-Turkish Empire, which it was to remain until our own day. This is unique in history.

The city wall of Byzantium, built a hundred years after Constantine by the Emperor Theodosius II, is one of the most magnificent ruins I know. The wall runs a distance of four and a half miles in the shape of a crescent moon from the shore of the Sea of Marmara to the shore of the Golden Horn. It shuts the city off completely on its western side and is still the city boundary. The tremendous fortification consists of two walls standing one behind the other. From the somewhat lower, outer wall there runs a sixty-foot-wide moat with vertical scarps. Both walls are crowned with towers, ninety-six on the outer, ninety-six on the inner wall. The towers of the outer wall are overtopped by those of the inner wall, which are tremendous bastions. From the battlements the eye ranges far into the hilly land across acacia woods, fields, villas girded with walls, and peaceful villages. The wall has ten huge gates through which in the course of the centuries victorious armies have marched in triumph as often as defeated commanders have sought safety within them. The tremendous double chain of the city wall of Byzantium, which runs through the countryside, was the bulwark of civilization against barbarism for a thousand years.

Constantine XI, of the house of Palaeologus, fought his last battle against the Turkish conquerors at the gate of St. Romanos, which still stands today. The final phase of this struggle was movingly dramatic. On the eve of the conquest the Turks lighted gigantic fires all along the city wall. This fiery crescent moon, the ancient symbol of the city, lit up the last night of the brave defenders. At that time the city can hardly have had more than a hundred thousand inhabitants. Five thousand armed Greeks, two thousand foreigners, and four hundred Genoese formed the backbone of the defense. The foreigners and the Genoese were the last help from the West in the effort to save the bulwark of Christianity in the East. The following morning, a Friday, the Emperor Constantine XI received Holy Communion with his followers in the Hagia Sophia. Then the Sultan Mohammed Fehti II attacked with the whole force of his army. Two heavy attacks were repulsed by the defenders, and if they had succeeded in repulsing the third attack, Mohammed would probably have abandoned the siege and have had to renounce the proud surname of Fehti the Conqueror. But a trifling incident led to a turning point in the world's history. The Kerkoporta, a gate that had been locked hundreds of years previously by the Emperor Isaac Comnenus to circumvent the prophecy that the Emperor Frederick Barbarossa would enter the city by this gate, had been opened during the defense for tactical reasons. As it had always been known that this gate was impassable, the local commander had omitted to protect it. Fifty Turks stole through it into the city. They were killed immediately, but a rumor that the Turks were in the city ran along the defenders' line like a cry of terror. Panic broke out, and Mohammed attacked again. When the Emperor Constantine saw that his cause, the cause of an Empire, was lost, he cried in a loud voice, "Where is a Christian who will kill me?" Then he hurled himself at the enemy and fell among the swords of the Osmanlis.

The last Eastern Roman Emperor, and the last ruler of this first Imperium of the Christian faith, went down, a great man to his very last breath. The next morning his mangled corpse was found under a heap of the slain, recognizable only by the purple shoes on his feet.

The ancient city on the Bosporus provides us with a view in all four directions of the compass of meditation. Western Christianity has forgotten that the first centuries of its history were enacted in the region around the Aegean Sea, and in North Africa. From the frontiers of modern Europe one looks south and southwest to the Christian Greek world of those early centuries: to Syria with the Holy Places in Palestine; to Asia Minor, where John the Evangelist founded the first Christian communities, the

Seven Churches of the Apocalypse; to Egypt, where, in Alexandria, Christian scholarship founded one of its most famous teaching centers, the Egypt in whose deserts the first Christian monasteries were established. In Hippo, near Carthage in North Africa, St. Augustine taught and worked. The countries where the spirit and civilization of the West had their first great Golden Age, where the Age of Faith began, have been lost to the West politically. But the city on the Bosporus is still a reflection of the ancient glory of the West that has gone down splendidly and hopelessly many times in its history, only to rise splendidly and hopefully again. The history of this city reflects all the contradictions of Europe—its glories, follies, despairs, and unparalleled will to survive. As one looks out across the roofs of Istanbul, the roofs of its churches and grand hotels, of its mosques and embassies, banks and bazaars, behind this scene of the bustling present there extends the horizon of the centuries—to the east, the Crimea, Colchis, the Caucasus, the Caspian Sea, ancient Asia; to the south, Ephesus, Tarsus, Antioch, Jerusalem, Alexandria; to the southwest, Troy, Athens, Mycenae; to the west, Philippi, Mount Athos, Rome.

The carpet of history lies stretched out at the stranger's feet. How old this continent is! The power of this world, the yearning for the other world, fear and piety, lust for power and neighborly love, blood, tears, and sweat, pride and chivalry, the glory of art, the smile of the Madonna, the thunder of organs and the roar of jet planes—how will this world look in a thousand years, or in ten years? How will it look the day after tomorrow? We do not know, but we can hold fast to the courage which it teaches us.

Inside the Monastery of Vatopedi, Mt. Athos, Greece

The Sarcophagus of Alexander the Great. Museum, Istanbul

Obelisk, Istanbul

The Church of Holy Wisdom

When, in a solemn ceremony that took place on the third day of Christmas in A.D. 537, the Patriarch of Constantinople consecrated the Hagia Sophia, which had taken only five years to build, the Emperor Justinian the Great stepped up to the altar unattended, raised his hands, and cried with a glorious blend of Roman pride and Christian humility, "Glory be to God, who has deemed me worthy to accomplish such a work. O Solomon, I have surpassed thee!"

Over the south door of the narthex, the portico that extends in front of the west side of the church, twelve yards wide and seventy yards long, there is a mosaic about fifty feet high that was painted over by the Turks but has been uncovered again. In this mosaic an unknown master throws light on the background against which this first architectural monument of the Christian faith was built.

In the center of the mosaic the Madonna sits enthroned with the Child. A little lower down on both sides are the earthly majesties of the Emperor Constantine and the Emperor Justinian. Constantine is presenting to the Madonna the new capital of Nova Roma, and Justinian is presenting the new Church of the Holy Wisdom.

This mosaic is a masterpiece of consummate beauty. Byzantium brought the art of the mosaic to an unsurpassed level of attainment. It is true that a long history prepared the conditions that led to the rise of Byzantine art, but the art itself arose from the spirit of the time as much as Athens arose from the head of Zeus.

This mosaic has the simplicity and the perfection that are characteristic of all the great works of a new epoch. The colors have faded during the centuries, but the gold of the background still glows around the Madonna, who combines the tender gestures of a mother with the sublimity of a Queen of Heaven. It is this gold that gives the work a kind of archaic austerity. The changing play of light animates the great surface in a delightful way. The mosaic stones form varying surfaces that incline slightly toward one another, so that the light strikes them at different angles and is reflected accordingly. The figures in their solemn and stiffly formal robes, with the Emperors' heads reverently inclined toward the Madonna, have been composed in space with a perfection such as only the greatest masters of the West have attained. They relate in simple allegory two hundred years of world history.

Constantine the Great's raising of Byzantium to the status of capital of the Empire was a political action. To give reality to his creation, Constantine invited ten thousand of his subjects from all parts of the Empire to come and admire the splendor of his rule with their own eyes. In the following two hundred years Byzantium became the dominating metropolis of the Imperium. The founding of the city had turned a great historical possibility into a historical reality.

In the Roman Empire of Augustus there were at the time of the birth of Jesus of Nazareth four metropolises: Rome in Italy, Alexandria in Egypt, Ephesus in Asia Minor, and Antioch in Syria. Of these four cities, three were not within the frontiers of what we now call Europe. Alexandria and Antioch were only just over three hundred years old at that time. Only Ephesus was as old as Rome. And only Rome was in Europe. Byzantium became the fifth metropolis. It soon became the most important. It had become the capital of the greatest and most stable Empire in the world. It was the seat of the most brilliant royal household of the early Middle Ages. While the Byzantine emperors waged war against the Persians they adopted the gorgeous court ceremonial of the Persian emperors. The anointing of monarchs with holy oil is a final remnant of this Eastern tradition. Even in our own day, at the coronation of Queen Elizabeth II of England, this solemn rite was enacted protected from the eyes of onlookers.

Byzantium had also become the leading commercial city in the world. Here the new Milion was set up, the golden milestone from which the distances on roads throughout the Empire were calculated.

The Emperor Justinian (483-565) was born the son of Illyrian peasants near the modern city of Sofia. He may be termed the last Roman Imperator. The wars that his commanders Belisarius and Narses waged with much success throughout the globe restored the power and splendor of the Imperium. The Imperial law was valid from the Euphrates to the Pillars of Hercules, from the Nile cataract to the Danube. Justinian ruled over sixty-four provinces containing almost a thousand cities. His gold coins were valid in Arabia, Ceylon, and Ireland. This great statesman gave the world the Pax Romana for the last time. He was a forceful theologian, also. During his reign the controversies about the doctrine of the two natures of Christ reached their culmination. Justinian enforced acknowledgment of the teaching of the Council of Chalcedon that Christ is true God *and* true man. And he was a great architect. He built many churches and crowned his life by building the Hagia Sophia. He was a devout man. He wrote hymns. He built hospitals for the sick and institutions for the poor. And the number of his crimes did not reach the quota that had become usual under former Roman emperors.

This versatile and important man was also a man of heart. He married the woman he loved. His wife Theodora was the daughter of a Syrian bear-keeper and had been an actress. Since the law forbade members of the Senate to marry actresses, Justinian had the law annulled so that he could marry Theodora. He loved her with great tenderness to her life's end. Procopius, the historian of the age of Justinian, had only words of praise for Theodora in his own lifetime. After his death, however, a pamphlet from his pen was published which made scandalous revelations about the Empress's life before she married Justinian. This little book was called *Anecdota, Unpublished Memoirs*. As Procopius is considered a trustworthy historian, the anecdotes cannot all be inventions. About the beauty, charm, wisdom, and virtues of this remarkable woman there has never been any dispute, but for thirteen centuries scholars have been quarrelling about Theodora's vices.

Within the framework of political power that Justinian had restored, the encounter of late antiquity with Christian doctrine led to the rise of a new civilization in the metropolis of Byzantium. The tension between Imperial power and Christian contempt for the world dominated the whole life of Justinian and was to dominate the whole further development of the history of Byzantium. The Emperor Justinian the Great gave a soul to the city of the Emperor Constantine the Great.

The Curia of the Senate, the Forum, and the Temple of Jupiter Capitolinus had constituted the heart of Rome. The Imperial Palace, the Hippodrome, and the Church of Holy Wisdom became the heart of Byzantium. Thus, Emperor Justinian completed Constantine's creation. Byzantium became the first completely Christian city in the world.

Only in one regard did Byzantium have to leave the primacy to Rome. Even in Constantine's time, when the decline of Rome was well advanced and the center of power was beginning to shift to the East, it was never questioned at any time or by anyone that the Bishop of Rome was the first Bishop of Christendom. Even Antioch, where the apostle Peter had sojourned before going to

Rome, did not dispute this claim. Yet it was in Antioch that the followers of Christ were first called Christians.

That the honor of Pontifex primus did not devolve on the Bishop of Jerusalem was probably due to the fact that in the first Christian centuries Jerusalem was an utterly pagan city. The Emperor Hadrian had called Jerusalem "Aelia Capitolina" after his family's name and erected a Temple of Venus over the Holy Sepulcher. The Bishop of Rome, on the other hand, resided in the capital of the Roman Empire, which the world had for centuries been accustomed to regarding as the center of religion. Thus the Bishop of Rome continues to bear the title of Pontifex maximus, which the supreme priest of Jupiter bore for so long. This privilege of the Bishop of Rome's, which was not taken much notice of at the time of Constantine, was the grain of seed that gave rise to the mighty tree of the Catholic hierarchy. It was only when the patriarchs of Constantinople had attained great power under the protection of the Byzantine emperors that they began to kick against the pricks of Rome. But even then they did not dispute the spiritual primacy of the Bishop of Rome. They merely opposed his political influence.

The division of Christendom into a Western and an Eastern Church had many causes and a long history. The immediate reason for the schism of 1054, which led to the separation of the two Churches for nine centuries, was a trivial one. It was the termination of a development that had already begun in the fourth century.

One must remember that up to the year 1054, there had existed one Church embracing the whole of Christendom. The alternation between classical antiquity and Christianity, between Greek philosophy and the Christian faith, which can be deduced from the history of the ecumenical councils, took place for the most part in an area that now belongs to the Eastern Church. The Christian tradition lives just as much on the fruits of the world of the Greeks as of the Latin Church Fathers. Furthermore, many of the great apostles of Christianity in Gaul, on the Rhine, and in Britain were Syrian Greeks.

It is impossible to do justice to these facts if one bases one's attitude to the Greek Orthodox Church on what happened in the year 1054. Today, the Eastern Church differs from the Western. Up to the year 1054 there was a common Christian doctrine, a common Christian culture for East and West alike.

These are important facts. They concern the very heart of Western historical consciousness. In doctrinal matters the differences are merely on matters of detail. Nor are the differences in the forms of worship decisive. What separates the two Churches is a purely emotional factor. The Western Christian feels that the background of the Eastern Church is alien to the history of the true faith. There is no justification whatsoever for this feeling.

As I looked at the Church of Holy Wisdom I realized with astonishment how little we are aware of the significance of this creation of the Christian spirit. The Hagia Sophia is a monument and a witness to our own history. I visited it many times. South of the church there is a large open square, the former site of the Hippodrome. Some of the rows of seats have survived. For centuries this was the scene of the most violent struggles on matters of internal policy. The parties called themselves the Blues and Greens. It proves great political intelligence to distinguish between political parties by the simple means of colors. And no doubt political life acquires a freshness of outlook when it is enacted in the open air.

On the Spina, the ancient middle wall of the Hippodrome, there are two monuments as remarkable for their differences as for their age. One is a bronze column thirty-four feet high, consisting of three intertwining serpents.

It is the remains of a votive offering of the Greeks to the shrine in Delphi, in gratitude for the victory over the Persians at Plataea in 479 B.C. Constantine moved the column to Constantinople. It is still possible to decipher the names of the thirty-one Greek cities that took part in the battle for the defense of the West.

The other monument is still more remarkable. It is an obelisk of Egyptian granite the sides of which are covered with perfectly formed hieroglyphics. Julian the Apostate, the last pagan Emperor on the throne, brought the obelisk to Constantinople, Theodosius the Great had it erected, and ever since it has stood on this site. During the course of time it had sunk twelve feet into the ground, but the foot of the obelisk has now been dug out again. It is based on four copper hexahedrons. Owing to this construction, the obelisk has never collapsed in any of the many earthquakes that have occurred in this area.

The obelisk has stood in the Hippodrome of Constantine the Great for one and a half thousand years. But when Theodosius had it erected it was already two thousand years old. According to the inscription, it was erected for the first time by Thutmose III, fifteen hundred years before the birth of Christ, in Heliopolis, the City of the Sun, in Lower Egypt. That was the period when the people of Israel were living in the land of Goshen, in the Nile delta, remembering the remote past when Joseph had come to Egypt. There are other similar obelisks in Paris, in front of St. Peter's in Rome, in London and Potsdam, and one— "Cleopatra's Needle"—in New York City's Central Park.

From the obelisk of Theodosius it is possible to see the mosque built by the Sultan Achmed I between 1608 and 1614. Overtopped by elegant minarets and adorned inside with delightful gleaming blue faïence, it has a rococo spirit of delicacy and gaiety. On the other side of the obelisk, the Hagia Sophia rises.

At first sight, from the distance, the building appears to weigh heavily on the ground; it seems repulsive, foreign, and austere. The soaring delicacy of the four minarets fails to offset its severity. To begin with, the dome and the minarets give one the impression of looking at a mosque rather than a Christian church. The Hagia Sophia so impressed the Turkish conquerors that for two hundred years they tried to surpass the glory and grandeur of its construction. This Christian church therefore had a decisive influence on the development of the Turkish mosque.

"Hagia Sophia" means "Holy Wisdom," a term derived from Hebrew philosophy. In the eighth chapter of Proverbs, wisdom appears as a personified character of God. It is the creative Logos to which the Church is dedicated.

Whereas the names of the builders of our great medieval cathedrals are wrapped in mystery, the names of the builders of the Hagia Sophia are known. They are Anthemius of Tralles and Isidorus of Miletus. They were quite a modern team: architect and engineer. Anthemius, the artist of the team, was the most famous architect of his time. We do not know much about Isidorus, but it is certain that he was a great mathematician. What has survived of the mathematical works of Archimedes we know only from an edition published by Isidorus.

The structural problem that Anthemius and Isidorus had to solve was the combination of two types of building, the cupola type and the basilica. Both had a long history. The square building surmounted by a cupola has been native to the Orient since the beginnings of architecture. The basilica, an elongated rectangular building with one or three naves, was the church of early Christendom. The permeating of the old Oriental cupola structure with the new Christian nave was the task that confronted the architects.

Hardly ever has a more exacting task been set an architect. For centuries antiquity and the Orient had permeated one another and become increasingly blended. To have transmuted the final phase of the Roman Empire into Christianity and to have blended the two in a higher unity is what constitutes the essential achievements of Byzantine culture. The Emperor Justinian set the architects the task of representing the historical process of the interpenetration of late antiquity and Christianity in a great building that was to combine the Oriental cupola with the Christian basilica. It was a clear-cut problem. In the Hagia Sophia it was solved in crystalline beauty.

When the visitor walks around the church the close-up impression is somewhat embarrassing at first. Certainly the building makes an even more tremendous impact at close quarters, but it gives the impression of a gigantic, unformed mountain of stone. The cupola seems flat and squat above the broad substructure, with its great masses of stone. The reason for this impression is that the building had to be supported by a number of enormous brick buttresses between eight and twelve yards across. The base of each of these is many feet deep, and they end two thirds of the way up the outside wall of the church. Hiding the contours of the original structure, they give it a feeling of squat solidity. They were added at a later period to save the building from caving in. This proved necessary not because of a fault in the original construction but because of the frequent earthquakes from which the building had to be protected.

I walked many times around the mountain of stone. Gradually I succeeded in grasping the original form of the building, and in the end I was able to discern the boldness of the design. The entrance to the interior leads through the narthex. The outer portal is closed by a bronze door of the sixth century: a costly, ornamental piece of work with inlaid silver, the last example of this Byzantine craft from this early period that is preserved in Istanbul. Above the inner portal there is the radiant mosaic representing the Madonna with Constantine and Justinian.

From this high, spacious, and generously proportioned hall, the walls of which are lined with marble, nine doors lead into the interior of the church. The center door was the Emperor's portal. It was here that the Patriarch received royal personages on high festivals. In the old days the wings of this portal were inlaid with silver.

Through the Emperor's portal we get our first sight of the main interior. There is a surprising contrast between the colossal and gloomy exterior and the brightness, breadth, and spirituality of the interior. Four tremendous arches rest on four tremendous columns that stand in the corners of the central square. The columns are made of limestone blocks, the joints of which are filled up with lead on clay. The cupola rises above the four arches to a height of 180 feet. This central square with the cupola is the Oriental element in the building. The walls in the north and south are built right up to the apex of the arches. They are broken by rows of pillars that make it possible to look through to the side aisles.

The two other arches are free of supports. They demarcate tremendous demicupolas that rise from smaller apses. The Christian element in the building, the basilica, permeates the Oriental structure from west to east. The two elements have been blended perfectly in a structure that flows and rises on every side with consummate ease up to the light-footed cupola from which the Christus Pantokrator looks down. In the harmony and audacity of its proportions the spirituality of the building verges on the heavenly. In a single glance the eye takes in the spirituality of this interior where Christians have prayed for a thousand years in human misery and glory, in victory and defeat, in hope and despair. The Hagia Sophia existed a thousand years before St. Peter's in Rome. The people of the sixth century believed that God himself had held his protecting hand over this building and that angels had helped in its construction. Today the church is empty. Its treasures have been scattered to all parts of the world. It is no longer used as a mosque or as a church. Kemal Ataturk turned it into a museum.

From traditional records and the reports of famous travellers we are able to imagine something of its original splendor. Its fame spread over the whole world. The building cost 320,000 pounds in gold—in other words, about 130 million dollars. To posterity Justinian bequeathed his fame, but to his heirs he left an empty public purse.

Forty silver chandeliers hung from the edge of the cupola. The whole interior of the church was adorned with precious things from all corners of the world. Green marble columns from the Temple of Artemis in Ephesus, red porphyry columns from the Temple of the Sun in Baalbek were brought to Constantinople. The veins in the marble floor were intended to imitate the waves of the sea. An early writer said that the variegation of the marble gave the impression of a meadow of flowers.

The ceiling and vaults were adorned with mosaics of unprecedented magnificence and grandeur. Gold, silver, ivory, and precious stones were lavished in inconceivable quantities. The canopied chair of the Patriarch was of massive silver, the altar of gold, embellished with precious stones. The whole of Arabia a generation before the birth of Mohammed would not have been rich enough even to furnish the altar of the Hagia Sophia. No other building on earth combines so much magnificence with so much good taste, and both qualities with so much piety.

Let me recall one of the most beautiful of the many legends that have been woven around the building of the church. During a midday break an angel in a radiantly white robe appeared to a boy whom the masons had given instructions to look after the tools. The angel asked the boy why there was a pause in the work on the holy building, and ordered him to fetch the masons. The boy explained that he could not go away because he had to look after the tools. The angel promised to stay until he came back, and the boy ran off to call the workmen. Then there was great excitement. The boy was taken to Anthemius to tell him what had happened. The appearance of an angel seemed so important an event that the Emperor was informed. Justinian proved himself a master of heavenly diplomacy. The angel had promised to stay in the church until the boy came back. Justinian therefore forbade the boy to return. He kept him in the palace and later sent him with a big reward to an island in the Aegean. And so, ever since, the angel has guarded the Church of Holy Wisdom.

When the Turks occupied the city the priest who was celebrating Mass vanished in a pillar. He will not finish the Mass until the Cross adorns the cupola of the Hagia Sophia once again. In Greek folksong the lament for the ancient glory of the shrine can still be heard today.

Within the splendid framework of the Church of Holy Wisdom the earthly power of the Byzantine Empire celebrated the glory of heaven for nine hundred years. After capturing the city, the first place that Mohammed II visited was the Hagia Sophia, where part of the terrified population had taken refuge. Tradition marks a spot on one of the pillars where the Sultan's Arab mare kicked out a piece of marble with its hoof. The infidels respected the sanctity of the place, however, and the Christians in the Hagia Sophia were saved. After thirty-three days the Sultan put a stop to the murdering, plundering, and destruction in the city. The Christians were guaranteed their life and faith. A new Patriarch was installed. His successor still resides in Istanbul.

When the Turks hauled down the Cross and set up the half-moon in its place, it was a day of mourning for the whole of Christendom. On the third day after the conquest, prayers were said to Allah in the Hagia Sophia. For a further five hundred years, though a mosque, the shrine continued to maintain the venerable name that it had borne for almost a thousand years as a Christian church. As an orthodox Moslem, Mohammed II, the Turkish Sultan, respected the wisdom of Solomon no less than did the Emperor Justinian.

Anatolian Impressions

Foreign warships are no unfamiliar sight in the old harbor on the Golden Horn. In the fifth century B.C. the first Persian fleet anchored off Byzantion. In A.D. 750 the first Arabian fleet cruised up the Bosporus. In 860 the first Russian, in 1204 the first Venetian, in 1420 the first Turkish, in 1807 the first British, and in 1953 the first American fleet appeared outside Istanbul.

Warships in the Sea of Marmara have always been a highly political affair. This was also true of the visit to Istanbul of the American fleet with aircraft carriers and cruisers. It was intended to demonstrate to all whom it concerned that the President of the United States is a friend of the Turkish people.

This ancient city has seen so much—Greek civilization, the dominion of the Persian kings, the world empire of Alexander the Great, the Roman Empire, the brilliance of the Byzantine court, the government of the sultans, and the rule of Britain in the Mediterranean. Power and decay, splendor and misery, victories and defeats have all had their day in Byzantium. Now, American sailors, young, fresh, healthy boys, immaculately clean-shaven, in clean uniforms, and protected by a regiment of military police in white leggings and white belts—the might of the United States of America—poured into this ancient city.

To study this sight I sat in a bar by the harbor. The dollars were piling up on the counter. The bartender, a white-haired man with one of those primeval, leathery, Oriental faces that tell of centuries of suffering, took the bills calmly in his slender, delicate hands. In the course of the evening I ascertained that he had no difficulty in translating Turkish currency into American dollars. Over a hundred-dollar bill that had just crossed the ocean and was now crossing the counter the bartender exchanged a glance with me. And so we fell into conversation. He spoke French.

In the Orient it is the polite thing to ask where a man comes from and where he is making for. So I asked him what country he came from.

"I am an Armenian."

"An Armenian in Istanbul?" I thought of all the unhappiness his unhappy people had gone through in the course of their history.

"Well, yes," he said. "A few always stay over." I asked him his name.

"Saroyan."

"Saroyan?" I asked him if he had ever heard of the American writer William Saroyan. He raised his left hand slightly with the kind of easy, superior gesture of which only an old Oriental is capable.

"You know, Armenians in America—none of them can speak Armenian any longer and, after all, Armenian is the most beautiful language in the world." Later I came across a remark by William Saroyan that his father had been a great writer; sometimes he would browse in his father's manuscripts, but he could not read them because they were written in Armenian.

Even though the fame of his own name in America was unknown to my Armenian friend, he knew that the kingdom of Armenia was the first State in history to make Christianity its official religion, even before Constantine the Great. How many of the fresh, fair-haired boys at Mr. Saroyan's counter knew that the genius of one of their great writers originated in the sterile mountains of eastern Anatolia? How many of them will have known that one of the precious early manuscripts of the Bible in the Armenian language is preserved in the Library of Congress?

I asked this Armenian gentleman about Ephesus and how I could get there. He recommended that I take the sleeper to Smyrna. When I asked about the time of departure of this sleeper next morning I was told it went every Wednesday.

It was a delightful journey. The Anatolian Railway not only links Istanbul with Smyrna, it also connects Nicaea with Ephesus. It was at the Council of Nicaea that the question was decided whether Christ was similar or equal to God. At the Council of Ephesus it was decided whether Mary was the mother of Christ's merely human nature or the mother of his divine nature as well. What questions!

That such difficult theological problems were preoccupying the whole world at that time shows how alive the Faith was in those days. "This city," wrote Gregory of Nyssa, about 380, of Byzantium, "is full of artisans and slaves, each of whom is a profound philosopher, and they all preach in the workshops and the streets. If you ask a man to change a silver piece he explains to you the difference between the Father and the Son; if you ask the price of a loaf you hear that the Son is less than the Father; and if you ask whether your bath is ready you get the reply that the Son was begotten from nothing. . . ."

Nicaea lies about sixty miles southeast of Istanbul on the mainland of Asia Minor, and fifteen miles from the next station on the Anatolian Railway. It is now called Isnik. Near Isnik is the beginning of a great lake that stretches from east to west, which formerly had a navigable link with the sea. In antiquity Nicaea was a great port and the junction of important roads. The Roman and later the Byzantine emperors had a summer residence there. For a time Nicaea was in the hands of the Seljuks. In 1097 it was regained by Duke Godfrey of Bouillon in the First Crusade. During the fifty years of the Latin Empire that the Frankish Crusaders established on the Golden Horn after the capture of Istanbul in the year 1204, Nicaea was the seat of the Byzantine court and of the Patriarch of Constantinople. A generation after the end of the Crusades the city fell into the hands of the Turks, under whose government it still stands today.

I visited Nicaea in an absurdly perverse way. It is quite easy to get to from the railway station that lies to the east, but I tried to get there from the west. The fact that I had relied on the map and on a Turkish waiter instead of on Thomas Cook resulted in a splendid journey that took me the best part of a day, round the lake of Isnik, through woods and mountains, villages, orchards, and olive groves, greeted by friendly peasants and shepherds, along incredible roads with bends that even a Turkish chauffeur is unable to master with the sole aid of clutch and brakes. There are stretches on these mountain roads, amid rocks and abysses, where a vehicle simply must not come from the opposite direction. Such stretches can only be surmounted with the aid of Allah.

In the late afternoon we reached the top of the mountains south of Isnik. At one of the bends in the road one looks down on the lake in the valley, to the mountains opposite and the ancient site of Nicaea. From the summit all one can see is the irregular double ring of the tremendous city wall at the extremity of the lake, with a hundred and eight enormous towers on the inner wall and a hundred and thirty smaller round towers on the outer wall. The ground inside the wall is a cultivated field. In the middle lies a small village picturesquely set among acacia and mulberry bushes.

A dozen emperors contributed to the building of this wall over a period of a thousand years. In later ages numerous ancient reliefs have been broken out of the ruined buildings and been built into the wall. Here and there the remains of Imperial inscriptions have survived. The gates through which the bishops of Christendom entered into Nicaea are now half sunk in the earth. As I deciphered the name "Flavius" on the stone arch a flock of sheep crowded through the gate. The liturgy in the Turkish language is still occasionally heard on high festivals in the decaying church of "Koimesis tes Panagias," the Church of the Passing of the Mother of God, which dates from the eleventh century.

It was in this village that the heresy of Arius, a presbyter from Alexandria, was defeated by Athanasius, later Patriarch of Alexandria, in A.D. 325, and that the dogma that the Son is identical in nature with the Father was formulated in the Nicene Creed. The Arian controversy was concerned with a single letter, an iota. The Greek word for "of the same nature" is *homousios,* and for "of a similar nature" *homoiusios.* Arianism long survived its condemnation by the Council of Nicaea—longest of all in Russia, where the last Arian divine service was held in 1870. But the unity of the Faith and the Church was saved at the Council of Nicaea.

The splendor of the city has vanished; the plow now

passes over it. The melancholy gleam of the past lies over the walls of this peaceful, sunny countryside, but the creed that the Fathers promulgated within these walls is still being proclaimed at all times and in all places.

The peasants of the Anatolian highlands are poor. The land yields little. Woodland is rare. The rocky mountains stretch in a vista of hard and strong beauty. It is only in the valleys, with their unassuming rivers, that a little green grows. The gray stone houses in the villages are grouped around simple minarets. Sheep represent wealth, for sheep are exacting. They require pasture land. The goat is the domestic animal of the poor. The goat maintains the poor, but also poverty. The peasant lives on the goat, but the goat eats up everything that tries to grow. The peasant would have to live for five years without goats to be able to live without goats. The Turkish government is making great efforts to improve the peasants' lot and has achieved considerable success in the last decades.

Turkish peasants are a tough race, unassuming, hard-working, hospitable, and full of humor. They love the stories and pranks of Nasr-eddin Hodsha, the Turkish Tyll Eulenspiegel. Hodsha was madly envied by a wicked neighbor who coveted his house. One day he went over to his neighbor to offer him the house at a low price. The only condition he made was that one nail in the living room should remain his property. The neighbor gladly accepted the offer and moved into the house. Next morning Hodsha knocked at the door. The neighbor opened it with a friendly "Good morning, Allah be praised! And what can I do for you?" Hodsha explained that he merely wanted to hang up his trousers to dry on the nail that was his property. The neighbor made no objection. The following day, Hodsha knocked at the door again. Once again the neighbor opened it, though with not quite such a friendly "Good morning. Allah be praised! And what can I do for you?" this time. Hodsha explained that he wanted to hang a bunch of garlic on the nail that was his property. And so the droll story goes on until, naturally, one day, in despair, the neighbor returns the house without recovering a penny of what he gave for it.

I continued the journey to Ephesus by train, which even has a sleeper. For very little money one can buy at the station a roast chicken, a splendid piece of embroidery, marvellous apples, excellent tea, and, if one wishes, a live sheep.

When the train has stopped for a quarter of an hour a bell is rung at short intervals three times in succession. After the third time the travellers finish their business with the peasants and proceed with measured steps back to the train. After a while it starts off again.

The books that I had with me were in harmony with the purposes of my journey. They were the Bible, Baedeker, and Tertullian's *Apologeticus*. The Bible is continually quoted in the Baedekers devoted to the Near East: the Acts of the Apostles in the section on Anatolia, the Old Testament on Syria, and the Gospels on Palestine. Tertullian's treatise, written at the end of the second century, is a spirited defense of Christianity against the attacks of the philosophers of antiquity—the most thorough in existence. The *Apologeticus* is also one of the invaluable sources from which it is possible to deduce the contents of the writings of the enemies of Christianity which have been carefully destroyed. As a Latin writer of the age of the early Fathers, Tertullian is surpassed only by Augustine. His *Apologeticus* provides an outline of the intellectual landscape as it was in the first two centuries after Christ.

The initial period of Christianity was filled with the controversy with Judaism, a dispute that was settled by St. Paul, who sees the gospel as a message to all peoples. It was therefore the obvious task of the first two centuries to awaken a response to this message in the intellectual world of the Roman Empire. This world had been conditioned by Greek philosophy. After the destruction of Jerusalem in A.D. 70 the traces of Jewish Christianity very soon vanished; but the seed that it had sown was not entirely lost. Judaeo-Christian communities continued for centuries in the land east of the Jordan and, oddly enough, in Arabia as well. There is evidence that the prophet Mohammed adopted much of the Judaeo-Christian tradition in his teaching.

Christianity would hardly have attained its world-wide historical position if it had not come to terms with the results of centuries of Greek philosophical thought. As a result of this encounter, however, Christian ideas also penetrated Greek philosophy. Islam did not evade the encounter. Ibn-Sina, the great Arab philosopher known to the West as Avicenna, attempted to reconcile the faith of Islam with the findings of Greek philosophy. It is a weakness of Islamic theology that it never went any further than this first attempt. To make up for this deficiency, however, Islam concerned itself far more thoroughly than did Christianity with the great art and the distinguished culture and ideas of ancient Persia. As a result of this preoccupation, much of Persian tradition has survived that would have been lost but for the work of Arab scholars.

While Christianity was contending with Greek philosophy, the beginnings of the hierarchy of the Church were taking shape. In the early period all that existed were congregations, though they were to be found from a very early date in all parts of the Roman Empire. Christianity not only had to come to terms with Greek philosophy: Greek philosophy itself could not avoid studying Christian teaching.

What is the nature befitting the incarnate Son of God? The Greek mind, trained by centuries of hard thinking, asked question upon question. Christian thinkers had to seek for an answer in the scriptures. These questions could not be settled by mere opinion; they had to be answered by the truth. The truth was laid down by the Church in dogmas and creeds, at the great councils, the first of which was convened by Constantine the Great at Nicaea. Christians thought that an assembly of the oldest and wisest bishops of the Church would be partaking of the enlightenment of the Holy Spirit.

Many Christian dogmas owe their philosophical precision to Greek training. It would be wrong, therefore, to think of the relationship between Christianity and Greek philosophy as one of fundamental enmity. The men who were baptized in the first centuries A.D. were members of the Greco-Roman civilization, the best minds of which had been trained in Greek philosophy. The dowry they brought to their conversion to Christianity was the wisdom of Hellas.

Our train, after traversing the passes of the Anatolian mountains, turned westwards down to the Mediterranean coast, where the climate is warmer and the land more fertile. Rice fields appear, and one is offered fresh oranges at the stations. The train passes through a picturesque river valley in the radiance of a late autumn evening. The sun sinks over the Mediterranean. We have arrived in Smyrna. Smyrna is a modern port lying in a bay on the west coast of Asia Minor. Ephesus lies in a bay thirty-five miles south of Smyrna. What kind of city is Ephesus today?

"Great is Diana of the Ephesians"

It is an extraordinary fact that a great city can vanish so completely from the face of the earth that memories of it survive only in tales and legends. Great cities arise from the coincidence of a particular historical situation and political, geographical, and economic conditions. But man has rarely been able to withstand the temptation of attributing the foundation of a city to a single individual who was either a genius of farsightedness or acted on behalf of the gods.

When one or two of the above-mentioned conditions cease to operate, great cities may dwindle into small provincial towns. When all four conditions cease to obtain, cities with millions of inhabitants can sink into the ground. The historical precondition for the rise of Ephesus was the dominance of the Greeks in the Mediterranean. Ephesus was a polis, one of those independent city-states whose power was based on the freedom and the rights of its citizens. That was the political precondition. Economically, Ephesus was the starting point of the royal Persian road to the lands of the East.

The dominance of the Greeks in the Mediterranean came to an end with the Roman conquest of Greece. The freedom of the city-state had already been threatened by the Persian kings, but it had been possible to maintain, by treaties, the basic conditions for its survival. With the Roman conquest, however, the freedom of the city-state came to an end. Then the harbor became choked with sand in the course of the centuries. We do not usually realize that the earth's solid foundations can change remarkably in the space of historical periods which, compared to the millions of years of the earth, are mere seconds. As a result of the increasing silting up of the harbor and the fact that the States founded by the Turkish peoples cut the West off from the countries of the East, the royal Persian road also lost its commercial importance.

Ephesus therefore lost its population in the course of the centuries. Finally, it was abandoned by its last inhabitants. It vanished, blown away by the wind. Its ruins have only been brought to light by the archaeologists of our own day.

Ephesus was one of the great cities of antiquity. In its heyday, at the time of the apostles, it had a quarter of a million inhabitants. Probably it was already a Greek city in the tenth century B.C., at the time when King David's army conquered the Philistines and the city of Peking was founded in China. Even at that period a shrine of Astarte stood on this site. She was the great nature goddess of the Asiatics, whom the Greeks subsequently raised to the same level as their goddess Artemis. The Romans gave Artemis the name Diana.

Later on, Ephesus became one of the twelve cities of the Ionian league of cities. It contained the greatest and most magnificent, if not the most beautiful, temple of antiquity, the Artemision, which was dedicated to the goddess Artemis and considered one of the Seven Wonders of the World. It was erected around 700 B.C.—the time when King Ashur-dan of Assyria conquered Egypt and raised his kingdom to its highest power. King Manasseh of Judah incorporated his kingdom into the Assyrian Empire, and thus the service of Baal, with human sacrifices, was reintroduced in Judah. This happened during the last years of the prophet Isaiah. At the same time Zarathustra founded in Persia the first religion to attain world-wide importance. For the first time in the history of art, winged spirits in human form, heathen angels, appeared on Assyrian reliefs. Greeks and Chinese were minting the first coins in the history of the world. In Babylon the cultivation of cotton was introduced.

The Artemision endured for nearly a thousand years. It was one of the great places of worship in the Greek world, until the Goths destroyed it in A.D. 262.

Our conception of the expansion and the main centers of the Greek world in the first half of the thousand years before Christ is influenced by modern geographical designations. Today only the land west of the Aegean is called Greece, while the land east of the Aegean is now called Asia Minor. In fact, the cities of Ephesus and Miletus in Asia Minor had been flourishing Greek cities, centers of political power and of art and learning for centuries when Athens was still only an insignificant provincial city. In the first half of the thousand years before Christ the Aegean was a sea landlocked on all sides by Greece.

Heraclitus, usually called "the Dark Philosopher," was born in Ephesus. Far from being what his nickname implies, he was in fact the first great master of the Greek philosophy of whom we know more than his mere name, the first of whose personality and work we have some idea.

Homer, the father of poetry, lived in Ephesus. A meadow on the Caÿster, the river on which Ephesus stands, is mentioned by the name of Asia in Homer. This meadow gave its name to the greatest continent in the world.

When Herostratus set fire to the Temple of Artemis, to make a name for himself, it was the very night in which Alexander the Great was born. What poetic force radiates five hundred years after Homer, from a legend according to which the flames of a burning temple lit up the night in which the conqueror of this part of the world was born!

A thousand years after the time of King David Ephesus was an important early center of Christianity. This Ephesus, which was the capital of the Roman province of Asia, was one of the Seven Churches of the Apocalypse. Two of our

Lord's disciples, the evangelists Luke and John, were buried here. There is a good deal to suggest that Ephesus was the city in the vicinity of which the Mother of Christ spent the last years of her life.

Onesimus lived in Ephesus. He was born a slave, but he became Bishop of Ephesus. He was the first to publish the letters of St. Paul, in the year 110. When one considers the influence the apostle Paul has exerted through his letters it is only right to remember the part played by Onesimus, the unassuming publisher and servant of the great work. The Council that rejected the teaching of Nestorius, the Patriarch of Constantinople, took place in Ephesus in the year 431. Nestorius had taught that Mary was only the mother of the human nature of Jesus; she could not also have been the mother of the divine nature of Jesus since God could not be born of a human being. It would be more correct to call her *Christotókos*, the Mother of Christ, than the Mother of God.

Nestorius's great opponent was Cyril, the Patriarch of Alexandria. It was in Cyril's time, and probably at his instigation, that the female philosopher Hypatia, the last important heathen in Greek civilization, was murdered in Alexandria. Cyril rejected Nestorius's doctrine as heretical. Mary was, he admitted, not the true mother of the divine nature of Jesus in itself, but mother of the incarnate Logos, the Word which contains both the divine and also the human nature of Christ. Mary was in fact *theotókos*, god-bearing, the Mother of God.

For a long time early Christianity came very near to abandoning belief in the divinity of the person of Jesus Christ. At the Council of Nicaea, the equality of the Son with the Father was made a dogma, which came to be generally accepted in the course of the following century. Its importance explains the bitterness of the controversy that it aroused.

After the equality of the two natures had been accepted, the question as to the nature of the Mother of Jesus arose automatically. It was settled at the Council of Ephesus. Cyril's thesis was accepted as the truth. Twenty years later, the Council of Chalcedon confirmed the teaching of Ephesus. In our own day the doctrine of the Assumption has been made a dogma of the Church and the dispute that began in Nicaea and Ephesus finally settled.

Nestorius's teaching survived its condemnation by the Councils of Ephesus and Chalcedon for hundreds of years. In fact, even today there are Nestorians in Kurdistan, and the theology of Nestorius survives in the Syrian Church.

The Nestorian Church spread far into Asia. In the middle of the seventh century the Nestorian monk Olopoen undertook a missionary journey to China. The Emperor T'ai-Tsung of the T'ang dynasty, one of the most important figures in Chinese history, received the Syrian monk with high honors. He imposed no restrictions on his missionary activities; on the contrary, he promoted them. As a result, Nestorian Christianity flourished in China from the middle of the seventh to the middle of the ninth century. At this period there were Christian churches in nearly all the great cities of the Chinese Empire. A remarkable memorial to the mission conducted by Olopoen has survived. In the year 1625 a great stone tablet was found when a house in the city of Singanfu (Sian) in northwest China was being excavated. The tablet contains detailed information about Christianity in the China of the T'ang period, in Chinese and Syrian script, and is surmounted by a relief consisting of griffins and dragons. It dates from the year 781, and its importance was immediately recognized by the Jesuit Father Trigault. The news that Christianity had been so widespread in China in the early Middle Ages was so sensational that the Jesuits were accused of forgery. Even

Voltaire succumbed to this error. The tablet is in fact quite genuine. Of the T'ang Emperor it says:

"When T'ai-Tsung, the glorious Emperor, began his happy reign in fame and splendor, ruling his people with wisdom and enlightenment, there lived in the kingdom of Syria a man of great virtue named Olopoen who, prophesying from the radiant clouds, brought the Holy Scriptures. He withstood the perils and difficulties of the journey by noting the harmony of the winds. In the ninth year of Cheng-kuan he came to Chang-nyan. The Emperor sent his Minister of State Count Fang Hüan-ling at the head of an escort to the western suburb to receive and escort the visitor. The writings of Olopoen were translated in the Imperial library. When his teaching was examined in the Emperor's private room the Emperor acknowledged its accuracy and truth and gave orders for it to be preached and spread abroad."

The best authority on this matter is a Japanese scholar, Professor Saeki, who believes that the China of the T'ang period was, though not *de jure*, at any rate *de facto*, under Christian influence.

Christianity disappeared again in Confucius's empire, but little is known about this process. It is true to say, however, that Chinese civilization absorbed the Christian ideas that were akin to Buddhism. One may say that all the four great world religions are spiritually interrelated, which amounts to saying that humanism is based on a world-wide foundation.

If one wants to explore Ephesus one must spend the night in an Anatolian town near the excavations. This little town, which is really just a large village, is named Selcuk or Aya Soluk. Many of these places have two or even three names —a Turkish, a Greek and sometimes an Armenian or even a Hittite one—the cause of much confusion. The name "Selcuk" derives from the Seljuks, a Turkish people who came to Asia Minor at an early period and in the eleventh century founded the great and flourishing kingdom of Rum in southern Anatolia, with Konya, the ancient Iconium, as its capital. The name Aya Soluk derives, in spite of its beautifully Turkish sound, from the Greek Hagios Theologos —that is, John the Evangelist. Every peasant boy here preserves in the name of his village a tradition that we Western Christians have forgotten.

It always gives a tingling sensation to leave the beaten track and the security and comfort of the grand hotels and to find oneself a complete stranger in a country whose language one does not speak. I stood, alone with my suitcase, on the platform of Hagios Theologos. The twenty arches of a Byzantine aqueduct, made partly from ancient materials, span the station square. The train departed. A crowd of Turks stood around eying me with restrained curiosity. Here too there is only one train a day, an event for which the whole community assembles.

For an orthodox Moslem a stranger is a gift from Allah. Obviously the man has money, but instead of proving himself worthy of the goodness of Allah by sitting in the sunshine in front of his house or taking a second wife, this man travels around the world. From this the orthodox Moslem draws the reasonable conclusion that Allah has upset the man's mind and sent him to his children so that they may enrich themselves at his expense. If the stranger is miserly, the children of Allah will get angry—not because they are covetous, however, but because they are devout. If, on the other hand, the stranger is generous, the wisdom of Allah is fulfilled and the stranger will travel through the land on a flowery carpet of Oriental kindness.

In a situation like that in which I found myself at this station, one has to find a protector. I chose a worthy man with a white beard. I spoke to him directly. Any language does in such circumstances. The old man felt honored by my addressing him, and the honor I had done him made him feel responsible for me.

It is incredible what can be said by mere gestures. I pointed to my suitcase and put my flat hand on my cheek, leaning my head to one side in the gesture of sleep. Some of those standing around me imitated the gesture to show they had understood me, and one even began to snore. At this they all laughed. The old man took me gently by the arm. Someone seized my suitcase, and off we all went to a lodginghouse of which the ground floor was occupied by a small café. There we drank some thirty to forty cups of mocha. Among my guests was a disabled man who had lost both his legs in the fighting around the Dardanelles. He insisted on treating me to a mocha.

The comfort of friendliness is better than the comfort of all the grand hotels in the world. Here it was the finest flower of innate courtesy, the friendliness of the poor. For these people are poor. The peasants subsist on cotton growing, and prices are bad. Resat Pars, my Turkish friend, said, "The peasants weep blood."

The Turkish government's press officer had kindly given me a letter that stated in Turkish who I was and the purpose of my journey. I handed this letter to the landlord. He passed it round. The government stamp evoked respectful cries from the peasants, much as a *firman* from the Sultan would have done in an earlier age. Thus, in the course of an evening filled with clouds of tobacco smoke and cozy chatter, I became "their" foreigner. This was later to save me from disaster.

The following morning I set out for the past. First of all I climbed up a hill near the village, which is crowned with the ruins of a Turkish fort. Halfway up, one looks out from this hill westward to the flat estuary of the Caÿster as it opens out to the sea, enclosed by mountains on either side.

In the distance, about five miles away, one glimpses a narrow strip of land on the horizon: the coast. The mountains on the right are low. On the left-hand side, about three miles away, the Bulbul Dag, the Nightingale Mountain, rises to between six and seven hundred feet. The Ala Dag, an extensive, roughly two-thousand-foot-high ridge, cut by deep valleys, rises up behind the Bulbul Dag. At the foot of the Bulbul Dag, a good half mile away from where I was standing, between the hill and the sea, lie the ruins of Ephesus. From this distance, the remains of the ancient metropolis are no more than a few bright specks in the landscape. The Bulbul Dag is bare, but, as its name suggests, it must have been wooded at one time. The Ala Dag, towering up behind it, is wooded in its upper regions. The woods extend, as in ancient times, far into the valleys behind the mountain. At one spot one can see a new road that ascends the steep slope of the Ala Dag in a sharp zigzag. This road leads to the Panaja Kapoulü. Panaja is from the Greek Panagia, "The Most Holy of All," in other words, the Holy Virgin. Kapoulü is the Turkish for "place." The house of the Holy Virgin lies behind the ridge of the Ala Dag, in the middle of the woods. Before us, the land as far as the sea is flat, a reedy marsh, only broken here and there by fields.

In a radius of a few hundred yards from where I was standing are the sites of four important buildings dating from four different periods of history. The first is the Artemision. The second is the church that the Emperor Justinian, builder of the Hagia Sophia in Constantinople, had built in the sixth century, over the tomb of St. John. The third is the Isa Bey-Djami, one of the earliest and most beautiful ancient Turkish buildings on the soil of Anatolia. The Isa Bey-Djami is a mosque built by the Seljuk Sultan Isa Bey at the end of the fourteenth century. The fourth building is a Turkish castle of the seventeenth century.

At the period of the Artemision, the sea still surged right up to the foot of the hill where I now stood. The marble wall of the plateau on which the Artemision was built was the wall of the quay. At the time of the Emperor Justinian, the sea was already one mile distant. At the time of the Seljuk ruler Isa Bey it was three miles away, and now it is five miles from the castle hill to the shore. The river Caÿster winds its tortuous way through the marshy flats, which it has flooded for two thousand years.

To describe how the Greeks, in the battle for Troy, hurled themselves from their ships and tents into the plain between the coast and the city of Troy, through which the Scamander flowed, Homer chose an image that had impressed itself on his mind when he was a youth in Ephesus:

> "And as the many tribes of feathered birds,
>   wild geese or cranes or long-necked swans,
>   on the Asian mead by Kaystrios' stream,
>   fly hither and thither joying in their plumage,
>   and with loud cries settle ever onwards, and
>   the mead resounds; even so poured forth
>   the many tribes of warriors from ships and
>   huts into the Skamandrian plain. And
>   the earth echoed terribly beneath the tread
>   of men and horses. So stood they in the
>   flowery Skamandrian plain." *

The gift of the Father of Poetry for observing and describing nature can still be confirmed by the evidence of the descendants of those swans and cranes that Homer saw on the Asian meadow in his youth and immortalized in the

* Translation by Lang, Leaf and Myers: *The Iliad of Homer.* Macmillan, 1927.

second book of the *Iliad*. Probably no other swans in the world can boast an older pedigree.

The excavation site of the Artemision lies about 300 yards from the castle hill. It looks like a foundation trench, a rectangle measuring about 330 by 110 yards, and deep. The pit is half filled with ground water, and a few remains of columns lie in the morass.

The Acts of the Apostles contains a description of the rising in Ephesus which the goldsmith unleashed during the sojourn there of the apostle Paul. At that time the goldsmiths of the city were doing a roaring trade with small silver temples of Artemis which were sold to pilgrims as souvenirs. They have been found in excavations as far away as Upper Egypt, Spain, and India.

Demetrius, who appears to have run a kind of holding company in this business, convened a trade-union meeting of the goldsmiths at the great Theater of Ephesus and instigated his fellow craftsmen against Paul. Luke describes this in great detail. It is amusing to note how little the world changes. He writes:

"It was just at this time that the way of the Lord was the cause of a notable disturbance. There was a silversmith called Demetrius, who used to make silver models of Diana's temple, and so gave plentiful employment to the craftsmen. And now he called a meeting of these, and of the workmen who were in the same trade, and spoke thus, 'Friends, you all know that our prosperity depends upon this business of ours. And you can see and hear for yourselves that this Paul has persuaded a whole multitude to change their allegiance, not only at Ephesus but over most of Asia, by telling them that gods made by men's hands are no gods at all. It is not only that we are in danger of finding this work of ours discredited. The temple of the great goddess Diana will count for nothing, she will be shorn of her greatness, the goddess whom Asia and all the world reveres.' At these words, they were all

Old Castle, Ephesus, Turkey

Mary's House near Ephesus, after Restoration in 1951

View of the Ancient City of Palmyra, Syria

The Citadel of Aleppo, Syria

overcome with rage, and began to shout 'Great is **Diana of Ephesus.**' Their uproar filled the whole city."

In fairness it must be admitted that Demetrius, who was no doubt a prominent member of the Ephesus Chamber of Commerce, was not unjustified in fearing that the new doctrine proclaimed by Paul would prejudice the sale of souvenirs of Artemis. Demetrius was a farsighted businessman. Cashing in on religious cults is no invention of our own time. But something else emerges from Luke's account of the revolt of the goldsmiths of Ephesus. Even in the time of the first apostles the preaching of the gospel did not take place exclusively in secret but to a very large degree in the full glare of publicity. In Thessalonica, too, the Jews organized a mass revolt against Paul. They made noisy protests before the rulers of the city: "These men are stirring up the whole world." The admirable writer of the Acts of the Apostles, whom journalists might well take as the patron saint of their profession, is so accurate in a hundred details that can be checked that there can be not the slightest doubt about the accuracy of his reports. These things took place just as he reported them.

There are many reasons why the gospel caused such a sensation in the world at that time. Some of the finest scholars of the nineteenth century wrote excellent studies of the ways in which the ancient world had been prepared for the new teaching. Vergil, the Father of the West, as he was called in the Middle Ages, has been adjudged an *anima naturaliter christiana.* His famous Fourth Eclogue is indeed extremely moving:

"We have reached the last era in Sibylline song. Time has conceived and the great Sequence of the Ages starts afresh. Justice, the Virgin, comes back to dwell with us, and the rule of Saturn is restored. The Firstborn of the New Age is already on his way from high heaven down to earth.

97

With him, the Iron Race shall end and Golden Man inherit all the world. Smile on the Baby's birth, immaculate Lucina; your own Apollo is enthroned at last.

And it is in your consulship, yours, Pollio, that this glorious Age will dawn and the Procession of the great Months begin. Under your leadership all traces that remain of our iniquity will be effaced and, as they vanish, free the world from its long night of horror." *

That was not a prophecy. It was the poetic finale to a period that had attained fulfillment. Culture, learning, political organization, and art had exhausted all the possibilities that were open to them in this world. It was impossible for them to go any further. An absolute end had been reached. Heathen antiquity could never again equal the heights of the past. There was no one to match a Praxiteles in sculpture, a Sophocles, a Cicero, a Caesar.

But all these considerations, elaborated by the learned humanists of the nineteenth century, were concerned only with the preconditions of the situation, not with the situation itself. A pile of hay under dry spars in the burning sun does not produce a fire. To produce a conflagration, a spark is needed. The spark that set the ancient world aflame was the scandal of the gospel. And the men who preached the new doctrine must have made a strange impression in the brilliant metropolises of the ancient world: Jewish fishermen from the Lake of Gennesaret, modest artisans from small Syrian towns, travelling as poor as church mice through the prosperous Empire, refusing to share the amenities of civilization. They proclaimed a new aeon.

Prophets of new doctrines from Asia, the inexhaustible source of metaphysics, were nothing unusual in the ancient world. What distinguished the men from Syria was their fearlessness. In a world of fear, not to be afraid of death is

* Translation by E. V. Rieu. The Penguin Classics, 1949.

a great source of power. Fearlessness is the reward of truth. Its price is death.

These are some of the thoughts that come to a pilgrim of the twentieth century as he sits on the marble ruins of the Church of John the Apostle in Ephesus and looks down on the pit where once the Artemision stood. The shrine of the ancient world has vanished so completely that J. T. Wood, an English architect of the middle of the last century, took seven years to discover the site of the temple. In the end he found it with the help of a Roman inscription of the period of the Emperor Trajan, about fifty years after Paul was in Ephesus. The inscription gives instructions concerning the route by which the statue of the goddess was to be taken to the theater at the annual festival. By following these instructions Wood found the site of the temple.

The excavations merely exposed the debris of debris. For centuries the temple had been used as a stone quarry. Fortunately, in late antiquity the debris of the Artemision was considered so valuable that some of the ruins were used for the building of Christian churches. Thus, eight marble pillars from the Artemision were used in the Hagia Sophia in Constantinople. Three splendid marble slabs from the temple at Ephesus line the walls of the sanctuary in the Church of St. Catherine at the foot of Mount Sinai.

The temple must have been a magnificent sight. Sailors entering the Bay of Ephesus could see it shining in the sunlight. The ruins that survive and the extant descriptions of this wonder of the world are so numerous that it has been possible to make a complete reconstruction of the Artemision.

The temple stood on a broad marble platform, and was 110 yards long and 55 yards wide, with more than a hundred columns of porphyry or marble, about 60 feet high. In very early times the idol had been a statue of wood only. The goddess worshipped in this temple in St. Paul's time was of gold and ivory. Portrayed complete with wings, between two animals whom she was leading, she was the so-called Persian Artemis, a fusion of the Greek and the Asiatic goddess.

The second building lies halfway up the castle hill. It consists of the remains of the church that the Emperor Justinian had built over the tomb of St. John. St. John was the missionary of Asia Minor. He was probably the founder of the Seven Christian Churches mentioned in the Apocalypse, the first to be established on the soil of Asia Minor. Apart from Ephesus, these places were Smyrna, Pergamum, Thyatira (Akhisar), Sardis, Philadelphia (Alasehir), and Laodicea, all of them within a radius of a few hundred miles around Ephesus.

There is solid historical evidence to suggest that John the Evangelist sojourned in Ephesus, and that the empty tomb on which Justinian built his church is historical. This church was a tremendous building, of which only the foundation walls stand today. These foundation walls suggest that the ground plan was clearly cruciform. The church was 150 yards long and was surmounted by six great domes. The building material used was marble, probably derived in part from the ruins of the Temple of Artemis. According to the information available, this church was hardly less magnificent than Hagia Sophia in Constantinople. At the time of the Crusades and right into the late Middle Ages it was the goal of devout pilgrims from all over Europe. Today the ruins stand forsaken. A few black-eyed Turkish children play among the walls. Goats graze in the sanctuary.

The third building, the Isa Bey-Djami, which dates from the year 1375 and lies at the foot of the castle hill, is still in a tolerably good state of preservation. It is a domed mosque of pleasantly simple design with a courtyard adorned with antique columns. Alongside the entrance there is a decrepit minaret. The façade is a large surface completely faced with marble slabs. The portico, which is enclosed by a broad marble framework, is unfortunately kept locked. On the right and left two flights of steps sweep upward to meet on a platform. The color of the marble slabs as they shine in the sun, a dark, warm yellow, is very striking. Only centuries of long exposure to sun and rain can produce this particular shade.

Within quite a small space, therefore, we find the remains of a Greek temple, a ruined Christian church, and a Seljuk mosque, which is slowly decaying—all on the edge of a marsh that was once alive with ships. Only Homer's swans remain unchanged.

I walked thoughtfully across the fields to the ruins of the city of Ephesus and climbed over the low walls that the peasants have put up to divide off their fields. They are made of the rubble of ancient marble. Sometimes one comes across a piece of carving in the walls.

Climbing up a wide sunken road, I arrived at the Coressian Gate. Behind it, on the left, built into the slope of a hill, lies the ancient theater, which is in an astonishingly good state of preservation. The theater has sixty-six rows of seats rising one above another. I sat down in the top row, from where I could look out over the whole city. At the foot of the hill there is a marble-paved road to the left that leads to the Agora. Straight on, toward the sea, runs the Arcadiana, a splendid road more than a mile long built around 400 by the Emperor Arcadius of Byzantium, on both sides of which the remains of numerous marble structures can still be seen. The Arcadiana terminates at the harbor, near the citadel, that is, the jail where the apostle Paul was imprisoned. From my bird's-eye view it was possible to make out quite clearly the boundaries of the ancient harbor basin, which is now completely bogged up and covered with reeds. On the right, alongside the Arcadiana, are the remains of the Church of Mary, standing half its original height, in which the Council of Ephesus was held in the year 431. I was able to see the ruins of the church in which the tomb of Luke the Evangelist was venerated, but only from a distance. Three Anatolian sheep dogs, a breed not far removed from the wolf, frustrated all my attempts to approach the ruin.

From my seat in the theater not a soul could be seen on this vast site of ruined splendor. Only two eagles flew in circles high up in the blue sky. If it had not been for the inquisitiveness of scholars, this landscape of the past would be a mere rubbish heap, overgrown with bushes and scanty grass, just enough to feed a herd of goats. The most important excavations in Ephesus were carried out between 1896 and 1908 by the Imperial-Royal Austrian Archaeological Institute in Vienna. The many valuable pieces of sculpture that were brought to light are now in the Belvedere in Vienna.

The impression the ancient Agora makes is almost one of intimacy. The Celsus Library on its south side, which a respectful son built in memory of his father, is still quite well preserved. Ten steps lead to the reading room, with the sky immediately above. There is a niche in the back wall of the reading room, reserved for the throne of Pallas Athene, the goddess of wisdom. To protect the walls with the book niches from moisture, there was a wide circular passage behind them. Under the library, in a small room, there is still the magnificent tomb of Tiberius Julius Aquila, in whose honor the library was built. The son of Tiberius Julius Aquila at any rate attained the object of his magnanimous foundation, which does as much honor to himself as to his father.

By an irony of chance the Greek word "*Sophia*," meaning wisdom, and the head of Medusa are carved next to each other in the balustrade. Wisdom and the head of Medusa, united in the Agora of transitoriness, form a two-thousand-year-old symbol of the fact that all knowledge and all wisdom can provide man with no more than a view of the demonic countenance of the serpent-haired goddess with the empty eye sockets, a view of the horror of nothingness.

On the road from the theater to the Agora I stepped on the same paving stones on which the apostles John and Paul walked amid the international throng of the great port, past shops full of the treasures of the world, among Greeks and Jews, Egyptians and Phoenicians, Persians and Romans.

In a recess in the Agora, a messenger of the present amid the sublime surroundings of the past, a Turk had sat down and was brewing some mocha. This cup of the delightfully hot, acrid drink of Arabia in the ancient market place of Ephesus, on the marble steps of the Library of Celsus, in the shade of a sycamore, under the Anatolian sky with eagles circling around, was the most thought-provoking mocha I have ever drunk in my long and varied life. The kingdoms of this age have disintegrated. The solidly based marble buildings of that time are in ruins. The goddess Artemis, who was worshipped by the whole of Asia and the world, is a far-off legend.

Panaja Kapoulü

It is the small things that make a foreign country seem so strange. Foreign peoples have different ways of inclining their heads, different ways of smiling, different ways of counting money, different ways of cooking rice. They have different wine and different bread. The animals are different too. Camels seem enchantingly exotic. Even on asphalt, they carry the atmosphere of the oasis with them. When vultures, instead of crows, sit by the roadside the metaphysical quality of the country is different. A donkey in Corsica is different from a donkey in Syria. The philosopher Seneca rode on a Corsican donkey when the Emperor Claudius banished him to that beautiful island. The Syrian donkey carried the Virgin Mary when she was forced to emigrate to Egypt. Corsica's stoic donkey has never been portrayed in art. The Christian donkey of Syria has been depicted over and over again in the art of Western Europe.

On one occasion I was travelling along a country road with a Syrian chauffeur, a first-rate driver. The excellently asphalted road ran smoothly and cleanly along a broad valley between trees, with a range of mountains clearly visible in the distance. There was nothing coming toward us. Yet all the same, the Syrian driver blew his horn every few hundred yards. In the end I asked him why. "Oh, you know," he said, "I've been a donkey driver for thirty years, and a donkey won't budge unless you shout at him at regular intervals."

Among the thousand and one tiny details in a foreign land that enchant the eye and heart like the round pebbles in a mountain stream, a sparkling diamond of a surprise may suddenly flash on the eye. One comes across something unexpected, and it is as though no human eye had ever seen it before. One of the great surprises of my journey to the early sites of Christianity was a house of which I had never heard anything before. It was the Panaja Kapoulü. It was while I was reading Baedeker in the Anatolian Express that I learned for the first time of the existence near Ephesus of a house of the Virgin Mary, a house where, according to tradition, the Mother of God once lived. Baedeker makes but a brief comment, which runs as follows: "In 2½ hours it is possible to make an excursion on horseback from Aya Soluk southwards to the probably early medieval church of Panaja Kapoulü on the Ala Dag. Since 1891 it has been held to be a house of the Virgin Mary. It has extensive views."

This house is the subject of a controversy that goes back to the fifth century. What are we to make of it? Isn't it, very likely, one of the many pious legends in which the poetry of Christendom is so rich? When I discussed the question on my return with a learned Benedictine, he warned me, with the kindest intentions, not to refer to the question at all. It was, he said, far too complicated. But in view of the exciting fact that there still exists a house in which the Mother of God is claimed to have lived, I do not dare to pass the matter over.

I had spent the morning in the ruins of Ephesus. Toward noon the warm autumn sun disappeared and the sky became rather overcast. I asked my friend Resat Pars to order a car for me. I intended to drive up the Ala Dag to see the Panaja Kapoulü. Resat Pars returned to the café half an hour later to report that none of the chauffeurs would consent to take me. It had been raining for some days; the road was still being built, and if it began to rain again they were afraid a car would not come down again. So I decided to ride up there on a mule. Resat Pars soon got me a driver with a mule. Anatolian mules are rather extraordinary creatures. Their very structure seems to be a caricature of a real animal. They are a mixture of horse and ass, but the mixture fails to produce a really new or a really credible creature. It is a purely artificial mixture. Furthermore, these mules look completely moth-eaten. They are an offense against nature. They wear neither a snaffle nor even a bit. You lead them merely by the halter strap. When I tried to greet my mule with a friendly tap on its neck it immediately snapped at my hand. What a charming creature! Yet even this animal has a classical forerunner, the celebrated mule that did service by hauling marble blocks during the building of the Parthenon. When this creature grew old and was unable to work any longer the Athenians decreed that merchants were forbidden to drive the mule of the Parthenon away from their corn racks.

The Anatolian mules are very steady on their feet. What the mule lacks in friendliness it makes up for in usefulness.

The driver, by contrast, had all the necessary friendliness. He was an Anatolian peasant of about forty, thick-set and of an unusually strong build. His thick black forelock was magnificent. When he laughed his white teeth sparkled in his sun-tanned face. He loved laughing and we got on very well together. Some of the peasants were looking with a doubtful eye at the sky in which the clouds were gathering speed, but their crazy visitor did not allow their doubts to prevent him from riding away on his mule.

And so we set off, the three of us, through the countryside of Ephesus. It was about an hour's journey to the foot of the Ala Dag. This gave me time to think things over a little. Few seats on earth are so conducive to meditation as the saddle on an Anatolian mule riding on the plain of Ephesus. It was in Ephesus in the year 431 in the reign of the Emperor Theodosius II that there took place the great Council that dealt with the Nestorian heresy. On my right I saw the Magnesian Gate, through which patriarchs, archbishops, and bishops from all corners of the world came in great splendor to determine the true nature of the Mother of Jesus.

Two hundred years before this, Tertullian had written the first great polemical treatise against the philosophy of paganism. A hundred years previously, Christianity had become the official religion of the Roman Empire. In the century since Constantine the Great, many churches had been built in Jerusalem, in Rome, Antioch, and Ephesus. It was an age of great saints and great theologians. A year before the Council of Ephesus, Augustine had died amid the radiance of sanctity and learning, in Hippo, his see near Carthage. From this unimportant little town he had moved the world. It was he who had decided once and for all the intellectual battle between Christianity and paganism in favor of Christianity.

The bishops of the great cities became princes of the Church with the political power that began to accrue to them. Leo the Great was the first to call himself the "Father of Christendom." Augustine had set the *Civitas Dei*, the City of God, against the secular State. Ireland had been converted to Christianity by St. Patrick. Ethiopia had become Christian.

The pilgrimage to the Holy Sepulcher, rediscovered by the Empress Helena, mother of Constantine the Great, had become one of the popular customs of the period. From all corners of the world pilgrims travelled to the Holy Land. Christianity, aware since the age of the apostles of its world mission, had attained world-wide significance. The century from the foundation of Constantinople to the Council of Ephesus was a period of splendid faith. Politically, however, the world was encompassed by terrible dangers. Twenty years before the Council of Ephesus the Goths had conquered and plundered Rome under Alaric, the Rome that had not seen an enemy within its gates for eight hundred years and had only once seen Hannibal outside its gates. Augustine had died while the Vandals were besieging Hippo, his episcopal city, and they captured it shortly after his death. Under the Sassanid dynasty the Persian Empire had attained great power for the second time in history. For the second time it was threatening the Greek civilization of the Mediterranean, which had meanwhile become Christian. Attila, King of the Huns, was ruling in Hungary. Even Byzantium was forced to pay tribute to him—to the tune of seven hundred pounds of gold yearly. And as yet no one had an inkling of the danger that lurked in the empty deserts of Arabia, where only a few wild Bedouin tribes were moving with their camels through the endless sand and fighting for oases.

In this politically riven world men were disputing the sublime theological problem of the nature of the Virgin Mary. Its critics have often scoffed at Christianity because theological disputes among Christians cost far more human lives than all the persecutions of Christians by the Roman emperors. That is perfectly true, but the truth is indivisible; only the heads it fails to enter can be split.

When the Ecumenical Council in Ephesus resolved to confirm the doctrine of Cyril, Nestorius was dismissed from his office of Patriarch and also excommunicated. Many of the bishops disagreed with this decision. Personally, Nestorius was a man of blameless reputation, but Cyril was relentless in his opposition. The people of Ephesus broke out in great demonstrations of joy, and the result of the Council was celebrated with a popular festival. This was not without its dangers, since the destruction of the Temple of Artemis had taken place only 170 years previously. The people have a long memory—this festival must have stirred memories of the great Ephesian festivals of Artemis. But the Church has always understood how to guide pagan streams into the channel of Christian piety. It was in Ephesus that one of the first churches in honor of the Mother of God was built. It was in this church that the Council met. Even at that time there must have been a Marian tradition in Ephesus.

As the sky grew darker and the clouds raced over the land with ever increasing speed, we came to the foot of the Ala Dag. We went up the slope of the mountain zigzag fashion on the new road. All of a sudden three of the dangerously aggressive Anatolian sheep dogs that had already kept me away from St. Luke appeared on the road. Seeing us, they began barking ferociously. The worthy driver proceeded quite calmly. When we were only three yards from the dogs he shouted a few stern words to them in a rough voice. To my amazement, the dogs turned tail and went off snarling. No doubt about it: I was in good hands.

Can the Mother of Jesus have lived in Ephesus? The Bible tells us nothing about her life after Christ's Ascension. The first three centuries maintain an absolute silence on her fate and her death. A learned theologian has remarked with some acuteness that this silence may have been God's own will: the world was not in a position to appreciate the uniqueness of Mary's personality. There was always a danger that she might become a goddess worshipped by the people, particularly in Asia, with its deep-rooted matriarchal traditions.

There are two traditions concerning the final years of Mary's life. According to the first, she never left Jerusalem. She lived in the house where Jesus celebrated the Last Supper with his disciples. She died twelve years after the Lord's Ascension, in the presence of all the apostles, and was buried by them in a tomb cut out of the rock near the Garden of Gethsemane. It was only after her death that the apostles went out into the world. According to the other tradition, Mary went to Ephesus with John and died and was buried there. According to both traditions she was taken into heaven shortly after her death, *anima et corpore*, with soul and body.

It is true that the Jerusalem theory is of venerable antiquity, but it is not found before the middle of the fifth century. It may have arisen earlier than that, but there is no evidence for an earlier date. In fact, there is much to suggest that it did not come into being until the fifth century. The visit of the Empress Helena to Jerusalem, for instance, took place in the year 326. She embellished all the well-known Holy Places with churches. Although we have detailed information about her sojourn in Jerusalem and all the details regarding the rediscovery of the Holy Sepulcher are known, there is no mention anywhere of a site dedicated to the Mother of God. Hieronymus, the Church Father who described the Holy Places, said nothing about a tomb of Mary in Jerusalem. The written evidence for the Jerusalem thesis dates from a later period. We know that Christ on the Cross entrusted his mother to his favorite disciple, John. "Woman, behold, this is thy son," and to the disciple he said, "Behold, this is thy mother." And from that hour the disciple took her unto himself. We know also that not long after the Crucifixion the Jews in Jerusalem began to persecute Christ's disciples. John's brother suffered a martyr's death. Peter was thrown into prison. It is therefore quite likely that John left the dangerous city with Mary. It is unlikely that he ever forsook her after the dying Christ had entrusted her to him. It is quite certain and beyond all dispute that John was in Ephesus in the year 66. But for deciding whether Mary was in Ephesus this date is valueless, since Mary can scarcely have still been living in the year 66. When Jesus was born she was probably 15 years old. In the year 66, therefore, she would have been about 80. According to tradition, she died at the age of 63. Admittedly, Jesus was not in fact born in the year 1. But the discrepancy between the year 1 and the actual date of his birth is certainly not large enough to bridge the gap between 63 and 80. There is a period in the life of John, between 37 and 48, on which we have no information about his whereabouts. The question is whether he can have been in Ephesus during these years. I cannot quote all the arguments that have been used in this three-hundred-year-old controversy. Many scholars think it possible that he was there, and none regards it as impossible. One of the arguments that scholars who support the Ephesus thesis consider particularly important is very curious.

When the Council of Ephesus had decided against Nestorius, the Patriarch of Constantinople, the prelates wrote a letter to the clergy and people of Constantinople. This letter has been preserved with the documents of the Council. In it there occurs a sentence that would, but for a grammatical disaster, have confirmed that in the year 431 it was generally assumed that John and Mary had lived in Ephesus. The prelates were so worked up by reason of the excommunication of the Patriarch that they forgot the verb in this important sentence. The famous passage runs as follows: "Nestorius has been condemned as a heretic by the verdict of the bishops in the city in which the theologian John and the Mother of God, the Holy Virgin . . ." At this point there is no verb. Common sense suggests that the missing words must be "have lived." But many other possibilities have also been suggested. It is diverting to study all the subtleties that have been displayed in the attempts to supplement the missing words. The question remains unsettled. The scholarly Pope Benedict XIV, whose pontificate lasted from 1740 to 1758, inclined to the Ephesus theory but did not commit himself definitely.

Even though the assumption that Mary lived with John in Ephesus and also died there is no less probable than the other traditional view that she died in Jerusalem, it is a fact that in the first four centuries it was only the tomb of John that was known and revered in Ephesus. There is no known site there connected with the Mother of God.

In the year 1891 two Lazarist priests from Smyrna made a study of the visions of Anna Katharina Emmerich, an Augustinian nun who described the house of Mary and her tomb in Ephesus in her visions in great detail. Following up the details that the nun gave in her visions, the two priests discovered in the forests of Ala Dag the well-preserved ruin of a small church that corresponded with amazing exactness to the description given by the nun. It is still possible to verify this correspondence between the vision and the reality. Furthermore, the priests learned that the church had long been called Panaja Kapoulü by the Greek Orthodox peasants of the district and was considered to be the house of the Virgin Mary. Archaeological investigation has shown that the small church discovered by the Lazarists dates from the beginning of the fourth century and was built over the remains of a house that undoubtedly derived from the first half of the first century. This dating may be trusted since it is possible to compare the style of the building with that of buildings in Ephesus of which the dates are known for certain. Archaeologically, it is quite admissible that the Panaja Kapoulü may be the place where the Mother of God spent her last years on earth.

Meanwhile, the weather had taken a definite turn for the worse. The wind had become a gale. A storm had come up over the ridge of the Ala Dag. The rain was lashing my face. At the next bend in the road it started beating into me from behind, and in ten minutes I was wet through. Lightning was flashing all around us. It was impossible to see more than twenty yards ahead. The climb had already taken us a good two hours. Daylight was failing. Only my driver went on as calmly as ever, dragging the mule up the mountain rather than leading it. Suddenly, he turned off from the road and went up a steep slope through the dense underwood. He seemed to know a path in that direction. To come down from the mountain at night would be rather risky. There was no moon, and it would be pitch-dark under the low-lying clouds. I was miserably cold on my mule. The mountain seemed to be never-ending. I got off and tried to warm up by climbing on foot, but an icy-cold wind was howling down the mountain. The mule track turned into a rivulet, and after another ten minutes it became an ankle-deep torrent. I was constantly slipping on the smooth stones. The thunder crashed, but the catastrophic conditions seemed to be making no impression at all on the driver and his mule. In the end, by going straight ahead one always arrives somewhere sooner or later. We came back to the road again. The wind subsided. The lightning became less continuous. I turned around a sharp bend and saw a sight that astonished me. In the middle of the road, which comes to an end up here in the mountains, there was an army jeep and beside it a young man who was eagerly beckoning to me. It seemed that I was to be saved from spending the night in the woods. I was almost prepared to believe in a small miracle. The driver, a young fellow with an open face, seized hold of me and pushed me into his jeep. I could not make myself understood, but everything seemed to be in order. The mule driver, who had reached us meanwhile, put his head through the tarpaulin, laughed, shook my hand, and vanished. As I had not paid him I felt sure I should be seeing him again. The young fellow drove away. I know it is possible to perform all kinds of tricks with these vehicles, which are made for the open country, but I had never come across this sort of driving before. We almost galloped along the road that was still only half built, tearing past gaping abysses at breath-taking speed. The young driver performed these feats with sovereign assurance and, indeed, indifference. And so I finally reached my destination. We stopped by a new church that was still being built. I got out. It had stopped raining. The sky was clearing. I walked two hundred steps around a small salient and came to the old house. From the platform in front of Mary's house the land falls gently down into the valley. A few steps bring one to a fountain whose gentle murmuring breaks the silence of this place. One's eye roams far across the wooded mountains that rise one behind the other. It was through one of these valleys that the Royal

Persian road from Ephesus to the East used to run. Ephesus and the world of men lie far away behind the mountain. Nothing disturbs the peace of the place, to which mighty oaks, entwined with ivy, give a natural solemnity. The house, with its dilapidated walls of gray stone and red brick, is built on a slope. Through the arch of the entrance door one glimpses a low altar with a statue of the Mother of God on the rear wall. Above the house the leaves rustle in the trees. A late bird scurries past to find its nest. The fountain sings its song. The atmosphere and simplicity of the place make it seem credible that the Mother of Christ did once live here.

On the day and at the hour when the dogma of the Assumption was proclaimed in the Basilica of St. Peter in Rome, some Christians held a service before the tiny altar in this house, after a difficult journey to reach it—crusaders of our time.

It had grown dark now. I returned to my kind driver. Beside the church in construction there was a shed where the workmen lived. They had lit a fire, and they gave me hot tea and helped me to dry myself in front of the fire. Then we drove frantically down to the valley again. The peasants in the café welcomed me back with beaming faces. It appeared that, worried lest I might have to spend the night on the mountain, they had enlisted the help of the mayor and he had sent up the jeep to bring me down safely. It was therefore really as though the Panaja had worked a small miracle of kindness in the hearts of these friendly Anatolian peasants.

From Tarsus to Aleppo

The Jew Saul, who afterwards became Paul the apostle, was a tentmaker from Tarsus. He possessed Roman citizenship as a birthright. That was a valuable privilege. At that time there were not many cities outside Italy that shared this honor.

The Romans never bothered very much about the religion of the peoples they ruled. Their main interest was in obtaining respect for the law in the occupied territories. When Paul was imprisoned on remand in Caesarea, he was asked by Festus, the Roman Governor, if he was prepared to go to Jerusalem and stand his trial in the court of the High Priest, the High Priest's court being the appropriate tribunal for religious offenses. Since Paul considered that the Jews' complaints were unjustified, he refused and declared that he would appeal to the Emperor, for every Roman citizen had the right to appeal to the Emperor as a last resort. Paul thereby created an embarrassing situation for the Roman Governor. It is questionable whether it was wise of Paul to take advantage of his right of appeal.

The appeal to the Emperor was an act of law. It meant the initiation of legal proceedings. So long as the *appellatio ad imperatorem* was not granted, the proceedings were pending. The Governor could not even do King Agrippa, who got Paul to explain the situation to him and was impressed by the apostle's personality, the small favor of releasing Paul. Neither the Governor nor the King could intervene while proceedings were pending. Paul therefore had to go to Rome.

What kind of city was the Tarsus where Paul was born?

It was in Tarsus that Antony and Cleopatra celebrated their honeymoon. The ship that bore the freight of royal beauty under a purple sail from Alexandria to Tarsus was a sensation for all the dandies of the time. What was true of the ship was also true of the Queen. An English proverb says that "a beautiful woman is like a ship with too much sail."

Cicero was Governor in Tarsus, and thanks to the talents of his brother, an excellent staff officer, he even earned military laurels.

The Stoic Athenodorus, a friend of the geographer Strabo and teacher of the Emperor Augustus, came from Tarsus. The city had an outstanding university. In Paul's time it was one of the great cities of the ancient world.

Where does it lie? On the map it will be found somewhere in the south of Asia Minor. One has to visit the city, which now has a population of thirty thousand, to realize that on its site there was once a great city of antiquity. Even today a few hundred of its inhabitants carry on the difficult trade of tentmaking, and even today the tentmakers are proud of their great fellow craftsman—despite the fact that they are Moslems.

Tarsus lies south of the Taurus Mountains, which extend, with the adjacent Anti-Taurus, from the southwest corner of Asia Minor almost six hundred miles eastward as far as Kurdistan. The highest elevations reach more than eleven thousand feet. This tremendous pathless mountain wall has always been for Syria and Mesopotamia a strong, though not always an effective, defense against military incursions from the north.

Apart from a few mule tracks, the Taurus Mountains have no passes. They are more hostile to man than the Alps. Only in one place, thirty miles north of Tarsus, is there a geological break formed by the Pylae Ciliciae, the famous Cilician Gates, where the Baghdad Railway, the continuation of the Anatolian Railway, crosses the mountains, by means of numerous tunnels and viaducts. Originally, the

Cilician Gates were impassable. But there are few mountains that man cannot overcome. The first Alpine road over the Gotthard was built in the time of St. Francis of Assisi.

Tarsus lay at the southern exit of this pass, by which the road from Byzantium and Ephesus came over the mountains. Thirty miles east of Tarsus the road divides. One continuation runs by Aleppo to the Upper Euphrates and Baghdad, the other to Antioch, Damascus, Jerusalem, and Alexandria.

Tarsus lies fifteen miles from the sea. In antiquity it was linked to the sea by a lagoon at the end of which there was an excellent harbor. Situated, with a good harbor, at the junction of the most important trade routes of the East, Tarsus was destined to become a prosperous city with a great history. It was in Tarsus that Alexander the Great quartered before setting out for the Battle of Issus.

At their narrowest point the Cilician Gates form a passage sixty feet wide, with walls that rise steeply and somberly hundreds of feet. This narrow gorge hardly has room for the river Cakit which pours through it. Human engineering has managed to build a road through this gate of rock. In antiquity the path ran along the eastern wall of the rock, partly hewn into the rock and partly projecting on timbers. The modern road has been hollowed out of the western wall by blasting.

It was through this gorge that Queen Semiramis of Assyria came, around 800 B.C., to found Tuana, north of Tarsus in the salt steppe of Lycaonia. Of this city a single marble column has survived on a hill in the middle of the salt steppe. It is still called the Column of Semiramis. Such is the trustworthiness of legends.

Sometimes legends have a kindly quality. The gardens of Semiramis, more than her military deeds, have preserved the fame of this great woman, who played an important part in her own time. Even such a great advance in military technique as the invention of the stirrup, which was made at that period in Assyria and which was no doubt greatly admired by her contemporaries, made less impression than the gardens in which the Queen delighted.

At the same period another outstanding woman founded a city that was destined to have a great future and a terrible end. Queen Dido, sister of the Phoenician King Pygmalion of Tyre, had to flee from the anger of her royal brother because of a love affair. On the coast of North Africa she founded the city of Carthage. Queen Dido came from the same city as the Princess Europa, who was once raped by Jupiter and abducted to Crete. It was to Queen Dido that Aeneas told the story of the fall of Troy: *"Infandum, regina, jubes renovare dolorem*—You bid me, Queen, to renew unspeakable grief." The fall of Troy began with the love affair of a Queen. The beauty of women made history on the shores of the Aegean.

Three hundred years later, Darius the Great, of Persia, passed through the Cilician Gates on his campaign against the Scythians. That was the century in which Solon was teaching in Athens, Confucius in China, and the Buddha in India. Solon was teaching Europe how to guarantee the social order by law. Confucius was teaching China how to place human society under the rule of custom. The Buddha was teaching India to love even the meanest creature. None of these teachings has ceased to exert an influence in the modern world.

Two hundred years after King Darius, Alexander the Great passed through the Cilician Gates. At that time Euclid, who created the mathematical foundations of geometry, was still living. Aristotle, the teacher of Alexander the Great, deduced from the phenomenon of the lunar eclipse the fact that the earth is round. And for the first time, Chinese silk reached Europe via India and Persia.

Many armies of the Byzantine emperors passed through

the Cilician Gates on expeditions against the Arabs. About A.D. 800 Harun al-Rashid, Aaron the Upright, marched through them to Asia Minor to force the Emperor Nicephorus of Byzantium to pay him tribute. Harun al-Rashid's Baghdad was the scene of the stories of the Arabian Nights. Three hundred years later, the first Crusaders under Godfrey of Bouillon passed through the Cilician Gates to capture Jerusalem.

The last army to pass through the Gates was that of the allied Turks and Germans at the end of the First World War, on their retreat from the Suez Canal. All these kings and commanders who have marched through the Gates were in Tarsus.

The ancient Tarsus now lies buried under some twenty feet of alluvial land. Only two things have survived from those early times: the magnificent view from the city looking across to the Taurus Mountains, on which the snow lies right into the month of May; and second, the excellence of the wool given by the goats that graze on the Taurus Mountains. It is from this material that the tents are made. If ever Tarsus is excavated, the finds may well be sensational.

Xenophon, the Greek commander and historian, mentions Tarsus as a great and prosperous city as early as about 400 B.C. Under the successor of Alexander the Great the city became Greek and developed into a center of learning. In the year 64 B.C. Pompey made Tarsus the capital of the Roman province of Cilicia.

In this wealthy city, in which sailors from all the ports of the Mediterranean, merchants from Gaul, Spain, Persia, and Egypt, famous scholars, and the high officials of the Roman administration came together, Paul spent his youth. Paul's father was contemporary with Gaius Tullius Cicero, the most famous lawyer in Rome, the last republican, and the most elegant stylist in the Latin tongue. He might have n Antony and Cleopatra. Paul's father also knew the ty's most famous son, Athenodorus, the philosopher who :ft Tarsus to become the teacher of Octavianus Augustus, the first Roman Emperor. How could Paul's father have had the remotest idea that it would be his own lively and unruly son who would enter the name of Tarsus in the book of history for all time?

To understand the personality of Paul it is useful to remember that he grew up in a metropolis. The horizons of an international port, the splendor of the civilization of the Roman Empire in its heyday, the culture of this enlightened Roman-Hellenistic world—all these left their mark on Paul. He was conscious of the fact that he was a member of the Chosen People. He was a devout Jew. The Jews were older than the Romans and older than the Greeks. Yet Paul spoke exceptionally good Greek and was proud of his Roman citizenship.

Antony made Tarsus a free city. Augustus confirmed the city's rights. If Antony's generosity toward Tarsus was merely an expression of gratitude for his honeymoon with a queen, in the case of Augustus it was gratitude for the wisdom of his teacher Athenodorus. Paul, a man of penetrating intelligence, a brilliant student of human nature, widely travelled, was an urbane man of the world. In an apocryphal story of the apostles he is described as of small stature with thin hair, of strong build, with eyebrows that met, and a sharply bent nose. He is said to have been a man full of charm. Sometimes he seemed a human being, sometimes he had the expression of an angel.

Antioch, the modern Turkish city of Antakiya, on the lower course of the Orontes, lies thirty miles south of Alexandretta. Seleucus Nicator I, Alexander the Great's commander-in-chief and heir to part of his gigantic empire, founded the city in the year 301 B.C. on the site of an altar that Alexander had dedicated to Zeus. At the time of the apostles Antioch was the capital of the Roman province of Syria. It was one of the four largest cities in the Roman Empire, and played an important part in the history of Christianity.

I could not help wondering why the city was established in such a curious spot, surrounded by mountains and about twelve miles from the coast. When one looks at it carefully, however, the reasons are not difficult to understand. It was easy to supply the city from the fertile plain of the Orontes. The mountains formed a defensive wall against attacks from the Syrian Desert or the coast. And at the same time, thanks to the Orontes, Antioch had good communications with its harbor at the mouth of the river on the Mediterranean. It was possible to supply water to the city from the mountain springs. The great caravan route from the Euphrates via Aleppo ended at this well-protected and easily defended place.

Antioch must have been a peculiar city. It was neither a Greek nor a Roman foundation. It was a Macedonian city. Its first inhabitants were the war-hardened veterans of Alexander the Great, men who had conquered the world.

The King had married a marvellously beautiful princess whose birthplace was at the foot of the Hindu Kush. She was Roxana, daughter of King Oxyartes of Bactria, one of the hundred kings conquered by Alexander. Alexander, an aristocrat, who paid no attention to racial theories, ordered his soldiers to round off the conquest of the beautiful land by conquering its beautiful girls. He organized the mass marriage of Susa. His veterans were not so broad-minded as their great king, however, and the marriage of Susa was followed by the mutiny of Opis, in which the soldiers protested against Alexander's policy of racial amalgamation. The mutiny was fruitless, but the results of the marriage of Susa were ineradicable. It initiated the long process in which the Asiatics were Hellenized and, since the Asiatics had an ancient culture themselves, the Greeks Orientalized.

At the time of the apostles Antioch was a magnificent city adorned with splendid temples, luxurious baths, and mile-long colonnades. The Circus of Antioch, built in the century before the birth of Christ, was the greatest in the Roman Empire. At night the paved streets of Antioch were brightly illuminated with lamps. No other ancient city is known to have been lighted in this way.

In Antioch, Greek, Syrian, Phoenician, Persian, Aramaic, and Latin were all spoken. There was a large and prosperous Jewish community. Artists, scholars, naval captains, merchants, harlots, camel drivers, sailors, soldiers, and slaves filled its lively streets.

The Roman writer Juvenal, who lived from about 60 to 140, describes the Antioch people as restless, covetous, proud, turbulent, and inclined to satire. The adventurous blood of the soldiery never entirely came to rest in this city.

In Antioch all the religions of West and East were practiced. This no doubt contributed to religious toleration but hardly to the strengthening of morals, since vices and virtues differ in the various religions. Juvenal complained that a stream of superstition and immorality flowed from the Orontes into the Tiber.

The history of the city was as turbulent as the nature of its people. Antioch was frequently troubled by earthquakes. In the year 83 B.C. the city was captured by King Tigranes of Armenia, and, twenty years later, by the Romans. Caesar, to whom the city passed with flying colors after the Battle of Pharsalus, rewarded its disloyalty to Pompey by giving it an elegant new theater and a magnificent bath. Furthermore, he added a new boulevard to the already famous ones of Antioch.

My Turkish chauffeur first drove me through Antakiya, up a steep and narrow road, about five miles into the mountains. I gave in to him, though I had no idea where he was making for. In fact we came to Daphne, of which I knew nothing. Daphne was the summer residence of the Roman officials and the rich Syrian merchants, whose villas and baths were grouped around a unique natural phenomenon. On a steep mountain slope, a hundred or so yards up, under laurel trees, cypresses, oaks, and eucalyptus trees, twenty springs, each the breadth of a human arm, gush out from the rock. The springs combine in a delicate silver filigree, divide again, form waterfalls of varying size, and finally collect in a whirlpool from which a tremendous waterfall plunges down to the Orontes. The sun shines through the foliage of the old trees and sheds a quivering light on the scene. Now and again tiny rainbows form under the roof of the foliage. It was here that the nymph Daphne was changed into a laurel tree when she was pursued by the lustful Apollo. This enchanting—though, for Apollo, somewhat disappointing—incident actually took place in Thessaly. The Macedonians took the legend with them, and it is an indication of their cultural energy that they were able to give new life to the legendary laurel tree on the conquered soil of Syria.

To console the cheated god, a great Temple of Apollo was built in Daphne. This shrine afforded asylum to fugitives from justice, and the right of asylum offered by the lascivious god probably contributed a good deal to the low moral repute of Antioch at this time.

It was in Daphne that the Roman commander Germanicus, exiled by his uncle, Tiberius, recovered from the exertions of his campaigns against the Germans. It was in these surroundings of seductive pagan beauty that Julian the

Apostate, the last Roman Emperor who resumed the struggle against Christianity, wrote his famous polemical treatise against the new doctrine in a winter in which he was preparing an expedition against the Persians.

From Daphne I drove back to Antioch. Midway of the slope one gets an expansive view of the plain, surrounded by mountains, as far as the Lake of Antakiya. Here and there the Orontes sparkles in the sun, as it meanders through the fertile landscape. The size of the ancient city can still be gauged from this bird's-eye view.

It was here in Antioch that the first Christian church to be independent of the synagogue was founded. It was here that the disciples of Christ were first called Christians. Peter was here. The Christians of Antioch venerate him as their first Bishop. This tradition was the foundation of the claim that the city later made to occupy a place second only to Rome in the hierarchy of the centers of Christianity. It was in Antioch that Paul the apostle began his work. It was here that the Holy Spirit had said: "Separate me Barnabas and Saul for the work to which I have called them."

Between the middle of the third and the beginning of the sixth century thirty great ecclesiastical assemblies were held in Antioch. As early as A.D. 325, at the Council of Nicaea, Antioch was called the center and eye of Christianity. It was a place of Christian learning, taking the lead in historical and grammatical criticism and exegesis of the Bible, whereas the school of Alexandria was more inclined to the mythological and allegorical.

The Emperor Constantine built a magnificent church in Antioch, as he had done in Byzantium and Ephesus. The luster of the name of Antioch is so great that the title "Patriarch of Antioch" is still bestowed by four churches. There is a Roman, a Greek, a Maronite, and a Syrian

Patriarch of Antioch. None of them resides in the city any longer.

The city began to decline in the fifth century. In the year 526, in the reign of the Emperor Justinian, there was an earthquake that cost a quarter of a million lives. A hundred years later the city was taken by the Arabs. In 1098, during the First Crusade, the Norman Bohemund, Prince of Tarentum, son of Robert Guiscard, founded the first Latin duchy in Syria. He called himself "Prince of Antioch." This duchy was to last for a hundred and fifty years. About this time most of the Christian churches were still in existence. Until the time of the Crusades the Arabs maintained a tolerant regime. Today, only fragments of all the precious and glorious things of the past remain. The excavation of Antioch might also cause a sensation.

When we had returned to the city, my driver stopped outside a modern and strikingly beautiful building, with two classical statues outside, and beckoned me to go in. To my amazement, I found myself in the most remarkable museum I have ever seen. The museum contains fifty large Roman mosaics in excellent condition, from the first century A.D., which were excavated in the Roman villas in Daphne. They give one some idea of the luxury and splendor of that ancient city, which was able to boast that three Roman Emperors—Caligula, Trajan, and Hadrian—had built aqueducts to supply its baths with water. The mosaics depict scenes from Greek mythology: the Judgment of Paris, the drinking contest between Hercules and Dionysus, and contemporary hunting and drinking scenes. Some of the faces are terrifyingly alive.

The museum also contains a number of Hittite sculptures, which are still very rare, and a collection of coins, some of them of great beauty. The coins cover a period ranging from the Achaemenidae to the last Turkish Sultan. In the room where the coins tell the well-known history of the

last three thousand years there is one case that tells the unknown story of the previous three thousand years. The
collection that it contains is incomparable. It consists of
a number of small cylindrical seals, each of them no bigger
than a thumb. With each seal is shown its impression in
wax or clay. All these seals come from the Açana Höyügü,
a small hill about twelve miles north of Antioch in a valley
of the Orontes. One day a peasant turned up in the museum
with a fragment of a clay vase. The peasants know that
there are queer people who are prepared to pay for pot-
sherds. The fragment had come to light during the plowing
of a field on the slopes of the Açana Höyügü. The archaeologists of the Oriental Institute in Chicago, aided by the
Turkish government, proceeded to cut a trench through
the hill. They found fourteen archaeological strata. The
oldest dates from 4500 B.C., which is earlier than the earliest
known dynasty of Egypt, and older than the civilization
of the Sumerians, which has been excavated in Ur of the
Chaldees. Cylindrical seals were found in each of the
fourteen strata. Those from the oldest stratum have geometrical patterns. Their artistic quality is enchanting; their
design and composition have the delicacy of antique gems.
Some of the seals have not been assigned to a particular
culture. Further excavations and investigations will no
doubt throw more light on their origin.

After leaving the valley of the Orontes on the journey
from Antioch to Aleppo, the desert begins. It is a steppe
desert in which only an occasional thistle, bramble, or blade
of grass grows. Every twenty or thirty miles we came to a
small village of mud huts. From time to time we met a
group of gypsies. Even the gypsies do not ride through
this world of sand on carts. Their tents are carried by
camels.

The Turkish-Syrian frontier post lies at the center of a
mountain chain that rises in the middle of the desert. When

I emerged from the passport office, my suitcase had vanished. Now, it is impossible to be robbed in the desert; you can only have your pockets rifled. If a thief tried to walk off with a suitcase he could be seen plodding through the desert for five hours. Hence it is not simply owing to virtue that the Bedouins do not steal. Only an armed robber can afford to steal. In the end it turned out that a kind Italian, who came up to me and invited me to accompany him to Aleppo, had simply loaded my bag in his car. The second guest on whose behalf the Italian had come to the frontier came from Baden. His task in life was to sell sewing machines to the Bedouins.

In 1460 my Italian's family had come to Aleppo from Venice, and ever since it has traded in this desert city and obviously done well. When, later on, I was invited to this charming man's house I discovered a Carpaccio on the dining-room wall, which one of his ancestors had bought in the master's studio in Venice and brought with him into the desert. The picture shows a few Moslems, in turbans and Oriental robes, standing before the lovingly painted façade of St. Mark's. They may well have come from Aleppo. Thanks to the dry air, the colors have retained to the full the freshness that the master gave them. This surprise was supplemented in the most agreeable way by my host's generous hospitality. I now have a real friend in Aleppo.

As on all frontiers, the road was bad to begin with. Then it became excellent. The Near East has skipped the Age of Railways. To compensate for this omission it has good motor roads. We drove across the monotonous sand hills of the Syrian Desert, up and down, up and down. From the crest of one of these waves of sand, one can see into infinity, but all one sees is nothingness. The landscape is quite bare, the horizon empty. Then, suddenly, as we emerged from one of the depressions, Aleppo stood before us. It lies, sharply defined against the desert, a sand-colored sea of houses in the radiant sunshine. Numerous cupolas and minarets are to be seen, but not a single tree. From among the houses the citadel rises up on a steep hill. Enormous masses of stone are piled up on this cone as though prehistoric giants had built here.

This is Aleppo, which the Arabs call Haleb. Three hundred thousand people live in this city in the desert. Haleb is very old. Abraham watered his cow at a well in the citadel, where the Moslems have built a mosque in his memory. Here I had the feeling of really being in a foreign land. The Moslems wear the fez or turban. The women wear black veils. Admittedly, only the veils worn by the peasant women are opaque. The smart Arab women wear veils made of soft woven materials, which enable them to practice a strictly moral form of coquetry. In the evening hardly any women are to be seen in the streets, and the coquetry of those who are can hardly be described as strictly moral. The innumerable cafés are occupied entirely by men.

When G. K. Chesterton was first shown Broadway by night by his friends he stood still, looked at the illuminated advertisements, and said, "How nice it would be if only one were illiterate!" He could have had that experience in Aleppo in the Syrian Desert. All the inscriptions, including the illuminated advertisements, are in Arabic script. It looks enchanting. Arabic characters might have been especially made for neon tubes.

The history of Aleppo-Haleb goes back to the third millennium B.C. The conquerors of these ancient cities have always been the same—Amorites, Hittites, Assyrians, Egyptians, Babylonians, Greeks, Arabs, Mongols, and Turks. Haleb was mentioned on Egyptian monuments as long as four thousand years ago.

Near Aleppo, in the middle of the desert, is the Monastery of St. Simeon Stylites. Simeon spent thirty or forty

A Cedar of Lebanon, Syria

Krak-des-Chevaliers, Syria

*The Courtyard of the Omay-yad Mosque, Damascus, Syria.
Eighth century*

*A Village of Mud Houses on
the Desert near Ur, Iraq*

years of his life on a pillar, preaching from that elevated position. In his love for the meanest creatures he may even have surpassed the Buddha. Once when a worm dropped from one of his wounds he picked it up and put it back in the wound, saying, "Eat what God has given thee." In the fifth century a church was built around the place where the pillar stood. It was one of the first churches designed in the form of a cross, and its ruins can still be seen.

The Djami Cakariya, the Great Mosque of Aleppo, was built by the Omayyads, the first Arab dynasty in Damascus, on the site of a basilica of the Empress Helena. It contains the tomb of Zachariah, the father of John the Baptist. The mosque is surmounted by a four-cornered minaret. It is very old, beautifully simple, and embellished with precious ornaments. A remarkable manuscript, the Codex of Ben Asher, is preserved in the synagogue of the Sopherim in Aleppo. It is a Hebrew manuscript of the Old Testament dating from the tenth century. The Biblia Hebraica, which has been produced with the aid of many collaborators in our own time, and which is now considered authoritative, gives the text of a Petersburg manuscript that is based on the Codex of Ben Asher, now preserved by the Rabbi of Aleppo.

The citadel is a Cyclopean fortification. The steep slopes of the hill on which it is built are paved. Arab writers maintain that the hill is artificial and that the citadel rests on eight thousand pillars. I crossed the deep moat by a bridge that leads to a high gate adorned with two magnificent lions, reminiscent of the lions on the Gate of Mycenae. One of the lions is laughing, the other is sad. Innumerable stories are told of the contrary moods of the king of the desert who was the symbol of so many of the kings of history and therefore has equally good reason to laugh or to cry. Tremendous walls, never-failing wells, and great subterranean storerooms make this fortress almost impregnable. Only the

Hittites took it once by force of arms. The Crusaders tried in vain to subjugate Aleppo from Antioch. It is true that the inhabitants were forced to pay tribute to the Franks, but the knights failed to take the citadel.

From the battlements of the citadel one looks far out across the desert into a very remote past. Here are the beginnings of Syria, the land of those civilizations that form the colorful tapestry into which the history of the people of Israel was woven. Even today the chalk figures that the children of Aleppo draw on the pavements for their games are men with Assyrian beards. In the town museum there is a statue of the Good Shepherd carrying the Lamb, a favorite motif in Western art; but the statue in Aleppo is of Sumero-Babylonian origin, from the second millennium B.C., and was found in Tel Hariri on the Euphrates.

The view across the town from the citadel of Aleppo into the sun-scorched desert has not changed since Abraham came from Mesopotamia on his way to Canaan in Syria, the land where our tradition has its origin and our civilization its roots.

Between the Euphrates
and the Nile

Syrian Horizons

The history of the world seems to consist of nothing but wars, bloody cruelties, treason, the lust for fame, and the creation of empires doomed to destruction. What is the result of history but mourning for the slain, the despair of the refugee, and the destruction of ancient splendors? The history of the world, which began with Paradise Lost, now confronts, with the splitting of the atom, the possibility of its end. But ancient, splendid, and precious things have existed from the earliest times. Amid despair and destruction, again and again new works have been created that have become ancient, splendid, and precious things after centuries have passed.

The history of Syria is a tremendous drama in the world's theater. Traces of man's existence in this corner of the earth go back to the Old Stone Age. They are therefore 150,000 years old. At that period the climate in this area was still tropically humid and hot. The oldest discoveries of human remains in Syria are 100,000 years old. They were found near Lake Gennesaret. The earliest settlements of which the remains make it possible to distinguish between different civilizations go back to the beginning of the fifth millennium B.C. Of the three world religions that proclaim only one god, the Jewish and the Christian originated in Syria. Islam attained its supreme flowering in Syria. From all parts of the world the faithful of the three religions look to the shrines that are scattered about Syria. It was in Syria that a kingdom of the spirit was established for the first time in history, in Syria that for the first time an idea established its rule over all the power and glory of the earth: the idea that the world was created by God and that man was made in the image of God.

Here in Syria it was proclaimed for the first time that man is the brother of man. Syria has been the moral teacher of the whole human race. Philip K. Hitti, the historian of Syria, rightly says that every educated man has two native lands: his own and Syria. This Syria that occupies such a high position in the history of the human spirit has also been the most terrible battlefield in human history. There is scarcely an inch of soil in this land that is not the grave of some hero or some poor devil. In peacetime Syria has always been a land of world trade, whose exports and imports have ranged from China to Spain, from the Nile to the Baltic, even in the earliest times. In Palmyra, Mycenaean pottery from the second millennium, together with a piece of Chinese silk, was excavated from a tomb of the age of Augustus.

The Syrians invented the alphabet. They put copper to use. Probably, Syria is the land where man planted corn for the first time and burned clay into pottery. The plow, the wheel, and the wagon came from neighboring Mesopotamia.

When I refer to Syria I do not mean the modern State whose frontiers are a result of the First World War. I mean what was understood by Syria in antiquity. This Syria was bounded by the Euphrates on the east, by the Taurus Mountains on the north, by the Mediterranean coast on the west, and by the Sinai Peninsula on the south. The fact that the country was situated between the Sumero-Babylonian civilization in the Land of the Two Rivers to the east and the Egyptian civilization to the south had a decisive effect on its spiritual development.

For geographical reasons, Syria has always been the scene of great events. The land is so split up that it has never been possible to unite it in a tightly organized State. It has never been possible to defend its extended frontiers. Again and again it has become the spoil of every conqueror who coveted it. Its strategic position between the continents of Asia, Africa, and Europe exposed Syria to innumerable invasions. Babylonians, Assyrians, Amorites, Phoenicians, Egyptians, Hittites, Aramaeans, Hebrews, Greeks, Persians, Macedonians, Parthians, Romans, Armenians, Arabs, Mongols, all invaded this land, and it was in Syria that the drama of the Crusades took place. Finally, the land was conquered by the Turks.

At the beginning of the nineteenth century Napoleon marched to Syria. Later on, the land was again invaded by European powers. In both world wars fighting took place there, and even today it is a troubled country. This incredible country has repeatedly played a part in political history, but nearly always under the heel of conquerors.

In the eleventh century B.C. the Aramaeans ruled in northern Syria. They were a people closely related to the Hebrews who had come to Syria from the deserts of northern Arabia across Mesopotamia. The Aramaic language was destined to play an important part in history. Not only did Jesus and his disciples speak Aramaic, but probably the Jewish patriarchs did too, before they adopted the language of the Promised Land. Hebrew is a Phoenician dialect. Rebecca as well as Leah and Rachel, Jacob's wives, were presumably Aramaeans.

In the tenth century King Solomon created his mighty empire. In the year 301 B.C. Seleucus Nicator I had established the city of Antioch on the Orontes and made it the capital of Syria. The rule of the Seleucid dynasty lasted until 64 B.C.

In the second half of the third century A.D. a female ruler of Syrian blood gained for the country the position of a great power. This was Queen Zenobia. The capital of her kingdom, Palmyra, lay in the middle of the desert.

The last brilliant period of world-wide importance in Syria was, after its conquest by the Arabs, the caliphate of the Omayyads, with Damascus as the center. The rule of the Omayyads lasted from A.D. 661 to 750.

Today there are four independent States on the soil of ancient Syria: the Republic of Syria with Damascus as its capital, the Republic of Lebanon with Beirut as its capital, the Hashemite Kingdom of Jordan with Amman as its capital, and the State of Israel. The Sinai Peninsula belongs to Egypt. The only thing shared by all four States is the Syrian Desert.

Man loves recalling the splendors and forgetting the miseries. What sufferings these peoples have been through in the seventy centuries through which we can trace their history! A wise Jew said imploringly, after the persecutions of our own time, "May God's goodness preserve man from having to suffer all that he can endure."

The Old Testament tells us the story of the sufferings of one of the peoples of Syria. It is a trustworthy source, but it mentions world-political events only when they affect the people of Israel. When the Jews left Egypt the Mycenaean Empire was in a flourishing state. Numerous Mycenaean vessels have been found in Egypt, where they were regarded as objects of great value. It is impossible to believe that Moses, that cultured man who was educated at the Pharaoh's court as an Egyptian prince, knew nothing of this civilization, to the high standards of which Homer bears witness. But the Old Testament makes no reference to any such knowledge.

Homer lived only 150 years after Solomon, whose empire was a great power. It is inconceivable that Homer knew nothing of the fame of King Solomon and the splendor of his capital, of which even the Queen of Sheba in southern Arabia had heard. Yet Homer tells us nothing about King Solomon, just as the prophets tell us nothing about Homer. Only the history of Syria from the end of the thirteenth century B.C. gives us an idea of the kind of world amid which the Jewish people lived.

Surrounded by ruthless enemies, conquered again and again, deprived of their political independence, deported, always tempted to doubt in Yahweh and to serve the mighty gods of the victors, the Jews achieved the historical feat of surviving, of holding fast to the Law of Moses, despite all the temptations, and of believing in the prophets until their prophecies were fulfilled.

An hour before sundown, at the end of November, I drove from Homs eastward into the desert. Homs is a small rural town on the eastern border of northern Lebanon. It is the ancient Emesa, which was a center of Syrian Baal worship in late antiquity.

My destination was Tadmor, an oasis in the Syrian Desert, a hundred and ten miles east of Homs. Tadmor is mentioned in inscriptions from as far back as the eighteenth century B.C. Under the name of Palmyra, the palm city, it became the prosperous capital of the kingdom of Queen Zenobia. Even today the Arabs call Palmyra the Bride of the Desert. It was destroyed by the Emperor Aurelian in A.D. 273. Blasted by sand and wind, what remains are the largest surviving ruins of a late Hellenistic city—unaltered ruins, for no further building was carried out on the site after the destruction of the city. No one was in a position to use the ruins as a quarry. Palmyra was surrounded by the silent desert. Only a few Bedouins lived in the oasis.

In the year 1173, at the time of the Crusades, the medieval traveller Rabbi Benjamin of Tudela visited the site. We owe to this learned Spanish Jew much valuable historical information. Rabbi Benjamin found a small Jewish colony in Palmyra. Then the place sank into complete oblivion.

At the close of the seventeenth century it was rediscovered by an English doctor in Aleppo, Dr. William Halifax.

One hundred and ten miles is no great distance for a car in the desert. With luck, this distance can easily be covered in two hours. There was a sort of road here, but as a result of the constant wind its surface was like corrugated iron. The strips ran athwart the direction we were travelling. It is true that it is possible to whisk across a corrugated iron surface at roughly fifty to sixty miles per hour, but at that speed it is easy to break a spring. My driver did not want to risk doing that. We could have driven alongside the road, since in the meantime the full moon had risen, like a big red orange, above the horizon. But we might easily have lost our way and I did not want to do that. So we drove hour after hour at the discouraging speed of twelve miles per hour, and even so the driver complained about the damage this was doing to his car. I promised him an additional fee. But money is not worth much in the desert. After travelling for two hours we met a truck in a tremendous cloud of dust. Both drivers sounded their horns —almost a human sound. It began to be painfully cold. As the moon rose the light became white. Right and left of the road, at a distance of five or six miles, chains of hills undulated on the horizon in silvery solitude.

For thousands of years man has travelled the desert with his caravans from one shore of fertility to another, through the sandy desert of solitude, loneliness, and danger. The desert is the authentic metaphysical landscape. Mountains create Olympuses. Forests are populated by trolls, fairies, and dwarfs. In the sea dwell demons of the deep. Nothing of that kind is possible in the desert. Neither gods nor spirits nor demons can exist in its emptiness. The desert is the true landscape of God. The revelation that the world was created by God could have come to man only in the desert. Abraham travelled through the desert from Haran in Mesopotamia to Canaan. It is in the desert that the mount of the Law rises up, and the desert through which the Holy Family fled into Egypt from the fury of King Herod.

The caravans brought the precious things of India and China to the West and the artistic treasures of the Mediterranean to the East. More important than the precious things that world trade took from one distant people to another was the nonmaterial freight, the freight of ideas. The monk Olopoen travelled across the Syrian Desert to spread the gospel in China. About the same time, knowledge of the Prince Gautama Buddha penetrated from the East to a solitary monastery on the Dead Sea. In the Monastery of St. Sabas, southeast of Jerusalem, a monk called John wrote the life story of the Indian Prince Josaphat. This Prince was canonized by the Church. The monk must have obtained his knowledge of the Prince's life from India. It has been established by scholars that the story the monk told corresponds in every detail with the story of the life of the Buddha. The monk on the Dead Sea took it for granted that a prince who taught love for all creatures and lived a life of grace could only be a Christian. Thus—an enchanting historical arabesque—as a result of the devotion of a scholarly monk, at least the spirit of the Buddha's teaching has been canonized.

Meanwhile, according to my calculations of the mileage, we should have reached Palmyra by now. But as we had left the road with the corrugated iron surface we might have taken a slightly wrong turning. It was now 10 P.M. A light appeared. A light in the desert! A tiny, friendly, reddish light! It came from a tent. Someone came running up. It was a sergeant of the Syrian army, a big strong man of thirty with thick, rather dishevelled black hair and the open face of a simple soldier. He was beaming with pleasure at the sight of human beings and invited us to enter his tent. He told us he had served in the French army, and he spoke good French. When an Arab invites a stranger in the desert into his tent the stranger at once acquires the privileges of an age-old tradition, the tradition of the hospitality of the desert. In the desert man is either man's enemy or his brother. The greeting with which the sergeant invited me to take a seat is an example of the magic of the Arabic language: "My hut is poor and dirty. Be seated in the radiance of my eyes."

The Arabs have a proverb that Allah has made three perfect things among men—the hand of the Chinese, the brain of the Frenchman, and the tongue of the Arab. For the European the hospitable sergeant brought up a packing case, which he carefully covered with his lambskin coat. If only we had been taught to sit on the ground when we were young, instead of having been made to bend our knees! As we settled down there was the delightful feeling of casting anchor in the ancient harbor of brotherliness.

With a Syrian it is impossible to decide whether the brotherliness goes back to the Patriarch of the Jews, the Indian Prince, or the Arab Prophet. Under this tent Abraham, the Buddha, and Mohammed live peacefully together. The excellent man immediately set about preparing mocha. After so many hours' dusty travelling it tasted wonderful. We exchanged friendly words. We enjoyed a moment of happiness between the past and future. It was as if Cain had never lived. I was able to delight my host with a gift that is valuable in the desert—the gift of Prometheus—a box of matches. After a cheerful palaver we said good-by under the silvery desert moon. The sergeant showed us the way. Ten minutes later we were driving past the mighty Temple of the Sun, along the colonnade of the Grand Boulevard of Palmyra. The marble shone a ghostly white. Finally, we landed safe and sound in the small desert hotel "Queen Zenobia."

Desert and arable land, Bedouin and peasant—this antithesis has dominated the history of the country from the earliest times. The never-ending battle between the wandering nomads and the sedentary peasants has been waged here for seven thousand years. Under good government arable land has been wrested from the desert. In times of anarchy the wind has buried the peasant's labor under the sand. Foreign conquerors have not always ruled the land badly. Under the pharaohs, the Roman emperors, and the caliphs, the land has known long periods of peace and prosperity.

Syria, which has been governed by so many foreign rulers, has repaid the debt. Around A.D. 200 there was a Syrian dynasty on the Roman Imperial throne, founded by the Empress Julia Domna. She came from Homs, which I had left in the afternoon. She married Septimius Severus, a general commanding a Syrian legion. In the year 193 Septimius Severus ascended the throne, the only Roman Emperor to be born in Africa. He never learned Latin properly all his life.

Julia Domna was one of the beautiful women in the history of the world, as is proved by her coins and portrait busts. She was also one of the unhappiest. Caracalla, her son, had his brother Geta murdered in his mother's arms in order to start his own cruel regime. During the assault Julia's hand was pierced as she tried to protect her son.

Heliogabalus, who had inherited the office of High Priest of Baal at the age of thirteen and became Roman Emperor at the age of fourteen, was a member of this dynasty. After a dissolute reign of three years, the Oriental excesses of which had become too much even for the Romans, he was murdered. Twenty years later, another Syrian, Philip the Arab, sat on the throne of the Roman Emperors. The Roman Emperor who had to celebrate the festival of the thousandth anniversary of the City of Rome was an Arab who had been awarded the title of Germanicus Maximus for his victories on the Danube. The world of late antiquity was a world without prejudices.

From the fourth century to the beginning of the seventh, Syria was a Christian country. So this amazing people sent a great ruler to the Byzantine throne as well, the Emperor Heraclius of Byzantium. He came from Edessa. Just as Antioch was an intellectual center of Greek Christianity, so Edessa was the intellectual center of Syrian Christianity. Heraclius restored the Church of the Holy Sepulcher in Jerusalem, which had been destroyed by the Persian King Khosrau. When Heraclius set up the True Cross of Christ in Jerusalem again on September 14, 629, Christendom rejoiced, and the fourteenth of September is still observed by the Church as a feast day. The Syrian Heraclius made a further attempt to settle the dispute concerning the nature of Christ which was devastating Christendom. He introduced the doctrine of Monotheletism, according to which Christ has only one will.

But the Battle of Yarmuk was imminent. Syria was to become Arabian.

With each new conquest Syria's political viewpoint changed. It thereby acquired a many-sided outlook on the world.

Three times this land has changed its language. Until the time of Alexander the Great, Aramaic was spoken in Syria. From then until its conquest by Islam the main language was Greek. Then Arabic became the official language, and so it has remained until the present day. Old Syrian, a derivative of Aramaic, has survived in the liturgy of the Syrian Church. Syrian translations of the Bible have existed from very early times.

At sunrise I entered the vast field of the ruins of Palmyra. The colonnade of the main street has survived. It leads through the ruins, past the amphitheater, which is just being excavated from the sand. Through the triumphal arch at the entrance to the Grand Boulevard you see to the north the bare hills of the desert which protect Palmyra. On one of their summits the pinnacles of a medieval Turkish fortress sparkle in the sun. Steep and menacing, the citadel towers up into the sky. On the other side, toward the plain, lies the mighty Temple of the Sun, of which parts of the roof have been preserved. A great portico leads to a courtyard—a tremendous site of ruins. The color of the stone is a glowing, reddish yellow. The contours of the temple stand out against the sky with extreme grace and elegance. A few Bedouin women in black, with pitchers on their heads, walk along as of old. Date palm groves extend behind the Temple of the Sun. Then the desert makes a clean start again.

For many hours I strolled among the ruins, down to the remarkable stone towers in the side valleys, the Towers of Silence, where the dead were buried in tiers one above the other.

The city once had more than 100,000 inhabitants. How was it possible for such a great city, with its luxury, its splendor and riches, to arise in the middle of the desert? The answer is "water and trade." There is plenty of water here. Water in the desert means a source of fertility. That was one form of the city's wealth. The other was trade. In the course of the centuries the caravan route from East to West has changed its direction several times. For many hundreds of years it passed through Petra, the rock city to the south of Jerusalem. Then the whole of the trade between East and West passed, for an equally long period, through Palmyra.

The city was rather in the nature of a port in the desert, its wealth the wealth of a seaport. Politically, Palmyra lived on the jealousy of its great neighbors, on the tension between the Roman Empire and the kingdom of the Parthians on the other side of the Euphrates, which was never conquered by the Romans. Under its last ruler, Queen Zenobia, the Palmyrene kingdom had extended throughout Syria and Mesopotamia. Zenobia was a remarkable woman. She spoke Arabic, Greek, and Aramaic. She wrote a history of the East. Greek philosophers received honors at her court. To judge by the coins that have been preserved, she must also have been a beautiful woman.

In the end, Queen Zenobia was defeated by the Emperor Aurelian. She fled through the desert to the East on a camel but was captured in the middle of the night while attempting to cross the Euphrates. In the splendor of her jewels and pearls she adorned the victor's triumphal procession in Rome. But the Emperor was thoroughly chivalrous to his beautiful captive. He gave her a villa near Tivoli. In the luxuriant park attached to this villa Queen Zenobia of Palmyra dreamt for many long years of the sterile but sublime beauty of the desert.

Like a meteor moving across the sky, the splendor of Palmyra shone in the desert for a few short centuries. There were many such places in this incredible landscape of Syria, most of which have vanished from the earth. The archaeologists are only gradually bringing them to light again.

The numerous frescoes that have survived in Palmyra constitute the bridge between the ancient Semitic art of Syria and the beginnings of Christian art. In the fortress of Dura-Europos, on the Euphrates, the border citadel of the Palmyrene kingdom, a very early church has been excavated, which dates from the year 232. A few frescoes have survived in this church, including a picture of Adam and Eve. Only a few hundred yards from this Christian church there is a synagogue from about the same period. It contained frescoes which are the earliest known pictorial representations of subjects from Biblical history. They are now in the Damascus Museum.

Thanks to favorable circumstances, Palmyra, the Bride

of the Desert, has left a last reflection of the glory of its golden days. The beauty of the ancient buildings in the brilliant sunshine is a monument to the genius and bravery of man beneath the sublime horizon of the desert, which praises the beauty of creation.

Krak-des-Chevaliers

Twenty-eight miles northwest of Homs, the Emesa of the Empress Julia Domna and Heliogabalus, there stands on a northern spur of the Lebanon one of the most remarkable monuments ever built by Europe in the Orient. It is Krak-des-Chevaliers, the greatest medieval fortress I have ever come across.

"Krak" is Turkish for citadel. "Les chevaliers" were the Knights of the Cross. The Arabic name for it is Husn-el-Akrâd, meaning Castle of the Kurds.

As we left Homs a strong west wind was blowing against us which developed into a gale. It drove the clouds from the sea into the Syrian Desert. On the summits of the Lebanon the clouds were being torn into shreds. As it began to rain, my small friendly driver looked doubtfully at the sky. He thought it madness to go up a mountain in such weather.

For a bit we had to drive through Lebanese territory. Because of the frontier, the road immediately worsened. The mountains, with elevations of from two thousand to twenty-six hundred feet, had begun. Remains of forest have survived on the lower slopes; on the summits the rains have washed the soil away and left the rocks naked.

At a bend in the road Krak-des-Chevaliers appears about four miles distant as the crow flies. It stands on a salient.

From the round ridge of the mountain it stands out in a sharp geometrical outline against the gloomy gray clouds. We took three hours to cover those four miles. First we had to stop at the customs office in a drafty shed where a few freezing officials were sitting. A charcoal fire was burning in a brazier. Dry camel dung was mixed in with the charcoal, producing a pungent but not unpleasant smell. It is one of the smells which even over the distance of many years conjure up whole worlds when they are met again. We were given a mocha, and warmed our fingers on the cups. The Syrians are delightful people; their kindness, their natural hospitality, their sociability and fondness for a chat, ranging from the weather to politics, quickly win over any stranger with a heart.

In this tiny customs shed we recruited a guide who knew the way. The road winding up to the Krak of the Knights round practically the whole mountain still consists of thick slabs of basalt, which the rain has made as smooth as glass. Fortunately, the driver was not a nervous man, and he steered the skidding car up the winding road with graceful ease. From time to time a blast of the gale drove the car slightly off its course. The higher we climbed the more glorious the view became. No doubt about it, this track is really only intended for mules. If another car had come from the opposite direction it would have created an insoluble problem. The Prophet was with the driver. The Angels were with me. There was no other car.

Suddenly, behind a bend in the road, the fortress towered up in front of us, only a hundred yards away, a gigantic citadel rising high into the sky. The hilltop on which it is built plunges steeply, on the south, east, and north sides, into the depths below. On the west it branches out into a small ridge, in the hollow of which lies a village. Among the black-eyed children who immediately crowded around our car as it stopped was one with hair as fair as wheat, with bright blue eyes.

We crossed a bridge that took us over a deep moat with almost vertical sides, and then we passed through the gloomy entrance. From here a paved road covered with semicircular arches runs for some three hundred yards in a plain curve and at a slight incline. About every thirty yards there is a break in the wall with a view below and out into the distance. The desire to outdo the citadel of Aleppo probably had something to do with the incredible dimensions of this fortress. Finally, one comes to wide, open courtyards. The hall where the knights dined has been preserved. At its entrance two crests have been carved in the stone, the only surviving ornament in the whole castle. Opposite the hall is the castle chapel, its walls still standing. Between the hall of the knights and the chapel is a square where carousing occasionally took place at stone tables in the open air. We may imagine the arrival one day of a knight from France who recounted the latest literary sensation—the legend of the Holy Grail to which Chrétien de Troyes had just given poetic form. On the lower floors are the staff and supply rooms. In this castle it would have been easy to accommodate five thousand men. The oven, a thing of incredible size, is still there. Whole rows of clay vessels, half sunk into the floor and as tall as a man, were used to preserve enormous quantities of olive oil. The citadel was well organized for a long siege.

The commander lived in a tower room with a flat terrace as roof. Since the ground on which the castle stands is invisible from the terrace, the tower seems to hover in the air. To the north and south one looks out into the bare mountains; to the west, on a clear day, as far as the sea; to the east, into the desert, which extends almost 360 miles to the Euphrates.

The construction of the castle is magnificent, and fantastic. But there is also something barbaric about it. There was a system of such citadels in Syria. The sites were chosen so that at least two citadels were always within sight of each other. It was therefore possible to pass on messages from one to the other by light signals. This strategically well-conceived system dominated the coast road from north to south, the mountain pass running from west to east, from the coast to Homs, and the old caravan route which, coming from Tarsus, Antioch, and Aleppo, amid mountains and desert, runs to Damascus, Jerusalem, and Egypt.

In this fortress European knights lived from 1180 to 1271 —men whose homes were in the Champagne, the Palatinate, Tuscany, Cornwall. What were they doing here? What kind of world was it from which these men came who built such mighty buildings in a land where none of them or their forefathers had been born?

The sudden appearance of the heavily armed armies of European knights in Syria at the close of the eleventh century must have had the effect of a natural catastrophe on the Arabs and Turks. Four and a half centuries previously the Arabs had left their deserts in a similar way and appeared in Europe with powerful armies, though, strictly speaking, it is wrong to say they appeared in Europe. When Mohammed began his teaching, what we now call Europe did not exist. It did not come into being until the period between the military expeditions of the Crescent and the Cross. The feudal system was the first social order that the northern peoples created after their great migrations. A remarkable characteristic of this order is that it was not merely a national one. As a result, the European aristocracy has remained international to this day.

In the period during which Europe was being consolidated, the Arabs, wild Bedouins of the desert, with nothing but their new faith, their imperturbable bravery, and their exquisite language, were producing the finest blossoms in the enchanting garden of Arab civilization. Fiery and sensitive as their horses, and tough and patient as their camels, they conquered the world. The kingdom of the Omayyads, with Damascus as its capital, which lasted from 661 to 750, extended from Spain and France to India and as far as the borders of China and Central Asia. It was greater than the Roman Empire at the period of its greatest expansion. The founder of the dynasty that made Damascus one of the most brilliant metropolises in the world was the Caliph Muawiyah.

Muawiyah was a member of the old family of the Quraish, which had been banished from Mecca by Mohammed, but came to power again during the campaigns that took place after the Prophet's death. Muawiyah once said, "I do not need my sword so long as my whip suffices, and I do not need my whip so long as my tongue suffices. And when but a hair binds me to a fellow man I do not let it break. If he pulls I give way. If he gives way I pull." He was not a politician; he was a diplomat. His path to power was less bloodstained than that of most founders of new dynasties.

During the subsequent centuries the Arab genius blended the legacy of Greek antiquity and Persian culture with the teaching of Mohammed into a fresh unity. The brilliance of this achievement still commands our admiration.

The Knights of the Cross encountered this civilization when they tried to liberate the Holy Sepulcher from the infidels. They came from a Europe that had attained self-consciousness during the three previous centuries. This consciousness had a Christian basis, and was still mindful of the fact that its religion derived from the East.

When the Crusades began, the Normans had just reconquered Sicily from the Arabs. Robert Guiscard, the great Norman Duke, was on his way to conquer Byzantium when he died from the plague. His son, Prince Bohemund of Tarentum, became Prince of Antioch. About this time

Arabic numerals were introduced into Germany. In England the Tower of London was being built as a Norman fortress. Westminster Hall came into being. England had three million inhabitants at this period. In France, Abélard had made the first attempt to prove the harmony of reason and faith. In Spain, Rodrigo Diáz de Bivar, the Cid, hero of the Moorish wars, captured the city of Valencia. At the close of his life, Judah ha-Levi, the Spanish poet who was born in Toledo, a theologian and a doctor, one of the most important Jewish scholars of the Middle Ages, migrated to Palestine—the first Zionist.

When the Crusades were over, Dante wrote his *Divine Comedy*. Giotto, the founder of European painting, painted his devout and tender dreams. Thomas Aquinas, the "universal teacher of Christendom," wrote his main work, the *Summa Theologiae*. Roger Bacon took the first steps into the realm of modern science by declaring experiment and experience to be the bases of knowledge. The Norwegians adopted Christianity. Edward II of England drove the Jews from Ireland and summoned the first citizens to the British Parliament. The Canary Islands were discovered by the Genoese. Marco Polo, the Venetian traveller, described his long sojourn in China. In Peking a Christian church had once again been dedicated to the worship of God.

In the two hundred years in which the Crusades lasted, the Alpine road across the St. Gotthard was built. Florence introduced a gold currency. St. Francis of Assisi sang the praises of poverty. The cathedrals of Rheims and Burgos were built. Moscow was founded. Tannhäuser went to the Wartburg for the minstrels' contest. The Universities of Paris and Damascus were inaugurated. Rudolf of Hapsburg was the first of that dynasty on the throne. The Mongols were waging their war of conquest. Euclid, Aristotle, and the Koran were being translated into Latin.

This is the background against which the Crusades took place. What was their real significance? Are they merely a romantic legend? Were they a splendid manifestation of faith and gallantry? Were they an experiment in imperialism or merely the final marauding expedition undertaken by the peoples of the North who had destroyed the order of the world, the Imperium Romanum, out of sheer curiosity, ignorance, and rapacity?

The Crusades were all that and something more. They were preceded by an age-long theological dispute between Christianity and Islam. When the Prophet's teaching became known, Christians did not begin by regarding it as a new religion but as a sect. Mohammed's teaching is as strictly monotheistic as the Jewish doctrine of God. On the other hand, however, the Moslems never managed to reconcile themselves to the concept of the Trinity. They considered it polytheistic. Islam recognized Jesus as a prophet of the Faith. Mohammed also took over large portions of the Christian as well as the Jewish tradition. The Moslems felt themselves so akin to Christian teaching that a Caliph of Damascus invited an Emperor of Byzantium to ascertain which was the true doctrine. Once when the Sultan Saladin was approaching Jerusalem amid the ups and downs of war, he sent a message to a delegation of Knights of the Cross saying, "I believe that Jerusalem is the House of God, just as you do. I do not want to besiege it or take it by storm." It was not his fault that the unreasonableness of the Christians forced him to take the city by storm after all. The treatment that he accorded to the city was humane, compared with the massacres that the Crusaders had inflicted on heathens and Jews on their first conquest of Jerusalem.

In the romantic world of the exuberant European feudal chivalry the Crusades were conceived as a kind of divine judgment. The time had come to settle the theological dispute by the sword. The romantic eagerness to go to war for the great ideal of the Faith was not disturbed by geographical knowledge. That the verdict was against Christianity upset the minds of the devout for a long time, but in the end it contributed to the process by which the primitive puritan conception, prevalent among the northern peoples, that God owes his children success in this world, gradually yielded to a deeper and more spiritual conception of his relationship to his children.

A final memory of the Crusades survived into our own day. Those of us who were born before the First World War were contemporaries of the last King of Jerusalem. His Apostolic Majesty Emperor Franz Josef of Austria counted among his many titles that of King of Jerusalem.

The Crusades were based on a variety of motives. The penetration of the Seljuks into Anatolia, the danger that resided in the weakening of the Byzantine Empire, the hope that the Italian commercial cities of Genoa, Venice, and Amalfi had of reconquering the coasts of the Eastern Mediterranean and opening up the Near East to commerce again, all helped to bring the Crusades into being. That al-Hakim, the probably insane Caliph of Cairo, had had the Church of the Holy Sepulcher in Jerusalem destroyed in the year 1010 caused tremendous excitement throughout Christendom. The idea of liberating the Holy Places in Palestine from the infidels first appeared at that time.

The decisive personality in the preparation of the Crusades was Pope Urban II, a statesman of the first rank. His plan was to unite the European chivalry under his leadership. If he succeeded he could hope to re-establish the Pax Romana under the rule of the Roman Curia. Hence, the cry for help that the Emperor Alexius of Byzantium, before whose gates the Seljuks were standing, sent to Urban II and the Council of Piacenza, fell on ready ears.

The Pope called a meeting in Clermont. The speech that

he made there was as fire to the dry brushwood of pious resolution. It had world-wide repercussions. There are only a few historical speeches that may be considered historical facts in themselves. This was one of them. So many people had flocked to Clermont from all parts of Europe that the assembly had to be held in the open air in spite of the late season. This is what the Holy Father said:

"The cradle of our salvation, the fatherland of our Lord, the motherland of religion, has fallen into the hands of a godless people. The godless Saracens are oppressing with their tyranny the Holy Places where our Lord went about and are holding the faithful in bondage and subjection. Dogs have entered the sanctuary, the Holy of Holies has been desecrated. The people who serve the true God have been humiliated. The Chosen People is suffering unworthy oppression. Arm yourselves, my brothers, with the zeal of God! Gird your swords! Prepare yourselves and be sons of the Almighty God. It is better to die in battle than to see our people and the saints suffer. Those who are zealous for the Law of God, let them join us. We want to help our brethren. Set out, and the Lord be with you. Turn the weapons with which you are criminally shedding the blood of your own brethren against the enemies of the Christian name and faith. Thieves, robbers, incendiaries, and murderers must not possess the Kingdom of God. Buy for yourselves the grace of God by your well-pleasing obedience, so that he may quickly forgive you the sins by which you have roused his wrath. We, through the mercy of God and supported by the holy apostles Peter and Paul, remit all the punishments which the Church has imposed on them for their sins, for all faithful Christians who will take up arms against the heathen and take upon themselves the burdens of this pilgrimage. And if anyone falls, in true repentance, he may firmly believe that his sins are forgiven him and eternal life is bestowed on him."

In powerful cadence, and in Biblical style, the Pope's address resounded over the heads of his excited audience.

From the crowd the cry rose up, *"Dieu li volt!* It is the will of God!" And the cry was to echo around the world for two hundred years.

Alas, the Crusades began with cruel massacres of Jews, committed by the mob that moved up the Rhine Valley. The Church authorities tried to stop these massacres, but without much success. On the other hand, however, the leaders of the first Crusaders' army were the choice flower of the European aristocracy. The earliest Crusaders included Robert Guiscard's son, Prince Bohemund of Tarentum, his grandson Tancred of Hauteville, the hero of Tasso's *Jerusalem Delivered*, and Raymond, Count of Toulouse. Raymond had already fought against the infidels in Spain. He was an ancestor of the painter Henri de Toulouse-Lautrec. Duke Robert of Normandy and Count Stephen of Blois, whose castle is still one of the most beautiful buildings on the Loire, joined the Crusaders in Constantinople. In Lucca, Pope Urban had entrusted the banner of St. Peter to Count Stephen of Blois. He died a prisoner of the Saracens. The commander of the First Crusade was Duke Godfrey of Bouillon. The ruins of his castle are in a valley of the Ardennes northeast of Sedan. Godfrey's sword and cross still hang in the Church of the Holy Sepulcher in Jerusalem.

The First Crusade led to the capture of Jerusalem. The Second was led by Louis VII of France and the Emperor Conrad III. It ended in complete disaster. It was on the Third Crusade that the Emperor Frederick Barbarossa was drowned in the little river of Salef at the foot of the Taurus. The further course of this Crusade included the more romantic than political dispute between the Sultan Saladin and King Richard Cœur de Lion of England.

The Fourth Crusade led to the capture of Constantinople by the Franks. A final success was accorded to Europe when the Emperor Frederick II set off for the East from Sicily. This ruler had made a Crusader's vow. As he had delayed too long in fulfilling it he had been excommunicated. In the end, however, he set out after all. He surprised the Arabs by his culture and knowledge of Arabic and dumfounded Europe by concluding a sensible treaty with the Caliph al-Kamil in 1229, after a whole century of Christian defeats. The treaty granted Christians free access to the Holy Places. Only the Dome of the Rock in Jerusalem, which stands on the site of Solomon's Temple, was reserved for the Moslems.

Frederick II's diplomatic success did not last long. As a result of the disunity of Christians among themselves and of the violent competition between Venice and Genoa it was impossible to save the European position. In 1291 the last Crusaders were driven out of Syria.

The commander who liberated Syria from the Crusaders was the Mameluke Sultan Baybars, the son of a slave and founder of a powerful Egyptian dynasty. While Baybars was fighting against the Crusaders, the Mongols invaded Syria. In the Battle of Ain Jalut, Baybars annihilated the Mongol general Kitbuqa. Once before on this field near Nazareth an overwhelming giant had been defeated by the courage of a determined man: Ain Jalut is the Pool of Goliath. The Mongol general Kitbuqa was a Nestorian Christian; with him, the faith of the monk Olopoen returned to his Syrian homeland after seven hundred years. Kitbuqa fell on the field of Goliath. It was the first defeat to be suffered by the Mongols. Europe wept and rejoiced. It mourned the defeat of the Crusaders; it rejoiced at the defeat of the Mongols. The Mongols were so dumfounded by the fact that it was possible for them to be defeated at all that they withdrew to Asia again. Probably the Mameluke Sultan Baybars, who drove the Crusaders from Syria, saved Europe from the Mongols.

On the high terrace of the donjon in Krak-des-Chevaliers one can imagine how these knights, after generations of hard fighting in an exhausting climate, enclosed in their mighty fortress, and looking down on the hostile country all around them, were finally seized by a sensation of vertigo. The fortress was surrendered to Baybars without a blow.

The Crusades changed the face of the earth. The historical reality of early Christianity became part of the European consciousness again at the Holy Places. The terrible plundering of Constantinople led, through the influence of the precious objects that were stolen and taken to Europe, to an important revival of European art. The art of making colored glass had been acquired in the East. In the church windows of the Gothic cathedrals Europe created works of sublime beauty and piety in honor of the imperilled Faith.

After the loss of Syria, Count Godfrey of Villehardouin, Marshal of Champagne, a great lord, a master of irony, and a dandy, created a duchy in the Peloponnesus for himself. His castle, on the hill of Mistras in the valley of the Eurotas, was not far from the site of ancient Sparta. This knight left behind a war diary. The dialectical tension that can be proved to exist between his account and the actual events is the same as one finds in all the war diaries ever written: the attempt to honor the truth is impaired by a gift for fiction. The Count of Villehardouin's war diary was the beginning of French prose literature. The literary ancestor of Montaigne, Flaubert, and Proust was a Crusader.

Arabic civilization had proved itself superior to European not only in its culture, toleration, refinement of manners, and the breadth of its horizon, but above all in the art of warfare, always the most impressive achievement in the eyes of Europe. Europe had now come in close contact with this civilization. One of the worthy chroniclers of the time says in his description of Saladin, that distinguished man who was born a Kurd, how astonishing it is that such a false faith should produce such a fine man.

The courtly civilization created by the troubadours of Provence in the thirteenth century was a brilliant synthesis of the chivalrous traditions of Europe and Arabia. The heraldic motto of the troubadours, *"Prou et courtois"*— Proud and courteous—stems from the desert, and is one of Arabia's gifts to Europe. The troubadour tradition was continued by the German minnesingers' immortal songs. Throughout the Middle Ages and right into our own time the ideal of chivalry created at that period mitigated the cruelties of European warfare. It was finally extinguished in the First World War.

The political consequences of the Crusades were far-reaching. The Byzantine Empire was so weakened that it fell a prey to the Turks after little more than two hundred years. The Czars of Russia partook of the religious legacy of the Byzantine Emperors. The power and riches of the French Crown were enhanced. The Order of Teutonic Knights, which was founded in Acre on the Syrian coast, moved to the raw northeast and conquered the Baltic. The most important result of the Crusades is that Arab civilization transmitted to Europe the inheritance of Greek antiquity that it had adopted and preserved. But for the Crusades Europe would never have become what it was intended to be. The mighty walls of Krak-des-Chevaliers, in faraway Syria on the ridge of the hills between sea and desert, were not built without a purpose.

In the Shade of the Lebanon

The cedar of Lebanon is one of the famous trees of antiquity, as historical as Noah's leaf and Athene's olive tree. Because of its rarity and beauty, the cedar, which is an evergreen, has always been a symbol of happiness. In Psalm 92 we read, "The righteous shall flourish like the palm tree: he shall grow like a cedar in Lebanon." Cedar wood was lavished on the Temple of Solomon, whose splendor is described in the Bible and whose fame has endured for three thousand years. The fame of the cedar is older still. King Solomon reigned from 972 to 932. One and a half thousand years earlier, the Pharaoh Snefru adorned the temples and palaces of his realm with the cedar wood of Lebanon. We know this from a hieroglyphic inscription dating from the year 2750 B.C. which also gives us the earliest information about a link between the ancient kingdom of Egypt and Syria. The cedars for the Pharaoh Snefru came from the Biblical Gebal, on the Phoenician coast. This place was later and is still sometimes called Byblos.

For a long period the masts of the ships in the Mediterranean, from the Phoenician coast to the Pillars of Hercules on the Atlantic Ocean, were cedars of Lebanon. And the cedar still sails the seas. The Republic of Lebanon, which was re-established a few years ago, contains the cedar in its flag—the peaceful symbol of a State whose people are one of the youngest and also one of the oldest in the world. The dense cedar forests with which the Lebanon was covered in antiquity have vanished. Only one group of the old trees has survived.

The Lebanese mountains extend right along the Phoenician coast. They begin in the north, opposite Cyprus, and end in the south, on the northern border of the State of Israel. The range is about 180 miles long. Deep valleys cut into its flanks. The rivers on the western side carry water all the year through. In its northern section the mountain ridge rises to a height of ten thousand feet.

East of the Lebanon lies the well-watered and fertile tableland of El Bika, which was known as Coelesyria in ancient times. On El Bika, at the source of the Orontes, stands the tremendous ruin of the Sun Temple of Baalbek. East of El Bika and running parallel to the Lebanon is the Anti-Lebanon. It ends in the south in Mount Hermon, where the Jordan rises. From the summit of Hermon it is possible to see Lake Gennesaret. The Anti-Lebanon is the western frontier of the Syrian Desert.

In order to visit the cedars, I drove one morning from Beirut in a northerly direction up the coast. The well-built, albeit narrow, road runs by the sea. On the right, the sun was rising over the Lebanon. Slowly it warmed the cool morning air. On the left I looked out to the sea, trimmed with small white crests. A few fishing boats, escorted by gulls, were en route, and a white steamer was making its way to the port of Beirut, with a dense trail of smoke and at a good speed. The strip of land that nature has left for man between the mountains and the sea is narrow. Occasionally a valley comes into view. As the Lebanon wards off the cold winds from the north and east, the climate is subtropical. Olives, grapes, and figs grow abundantly. Fields alternate with dense shady orange groves. The fruits shine seductively from the rich green, ripe for harvest. This is the oldest coast in history. Probably olives and figs were cultivated for the first time on this coast. The word for "wine" in ancient Egyptian, at the end of the fourth millennium B.C., was Phoenician in origin.

It was onto this coast that the fish spewed out Jonah. The fishermen of Sidon still show the spot today where this remarkable event took place. From the very beginning the prophet in the fish's belly has been more difficult for zoologists to swallow than for the fish. It is impossible to console the zoologists with the assurance that it is merely a remote legend. The incident occurred at a fairly late point in time. The prophet Jonah lived in the first half of the eighth century. That is quite late compared with the enchanting episode that took place not fifty miles south of Jonah's unusual landing. There, Zeus emerged from the sea in the form of a bull, near a meadow by the shore, where the Princess Europa, daughter of King Agenor of Tyre, was playing with her friends. Europa climbed onto the bull's back and was carried across the sea to Crete. There she gave birth to King Minos. This legend is probably at least two thousand years earlier than the story of Jonah. The legend is concerned fundamentally with the rise of the Minoan kingdom, whose civilization is the oldest known that can be called European. Excavations are constantly bringing new surprises to light, however, and now that scholars have at last succeeded in deciphering Linear B, of the three Cretan scripts, further revelations may be expected. It will not be surprising if the archaeologists establish that the Minoan civilization derives from Syria, as the legend suggests.

After driving for two hours, with constantly changing scenery, we turned off eastward into the mountains. The road ascends through steep gorges, past picturesque villages which, sometimes surmounted by the tower of a Maronite church, lie on the slopes. Glistening and sparkling, the sea rises on the horizon. After another three hours we reached a height of eight thousand feet.

The road follows a river valley. On the mountain slopes every square yard is cultivated, in terraces that are supported by stone walls and, seen from above, provide impressive evidence of the peasants' toil. Occasionally we

Sumerian Mosaic, 2800 B.C. British Museum, London

The Gate of Ishtar of Nebuchadnezzar's Palace at Babylon, Iraq

The Golden Gate as Seen from the Garden of Gethsemane, Jordan

The Damascus Gate, Jerusalem

passed one of the beautiful summer houses of the rich Phoenician merchants from Beirut.

On the lower levels the tree is the mulberry. On the steep slopes of the mountains, oaks grow with beeches and pines between them. Sometimes a wall of rock falls abruptly to the river that rushes along below. Owing to the innumerable bends in the road, deep cool shade alternates with bright warm sunshine. As the heat of the sun increases it compensates for the loss in temperature caused by increasing height. Ingenious irrigation systems distribute to the remotest corner the precious water brought to the Lebanon by the annual snow. The landscape is simultaneously wild and cultivated. The climatic contrasts in this corner of the world are so great that within a radius of fifty miles from the coast, where it is possible to bathe, there are banana plantations, skiing sites, and desert oases.

We met only a few cars, but many donkeys. Indefatigably this faithful animal, man's old friend, bears the burden of commerce, and usually his master or mistress as well, on his patient back, through the dust of the highroad.

The cedars, only about four hundred of them now, which survive under the ridge of the mountain would not exist today if they were not in such an inaccessible spot that it has never been worth anyone's while to fell them.

The cedar of Lebanon does not grow to a great height. Even the oldest are no more than a hundred feet high. The Indian cedar that grows in the Himalayas, the deodar cedar —"tree of God," in Sanskrit—reaches to nearly twice that height. There are still cedar forests in the Taurus Mountains and the Atlas. The cedar, tapering as it rises, spreads its broad fanlike branches in all directions. Its outline is almost that of an equilateral triangle, and it therefore looks like a pyramid. Each tree stands by itself. The largest of the trees overshadows a well of delightfully refreshing spring water. Next to the well is a Maronite chapel, whose priest gave us a kindly welcome. On high feast days he celebrates Mass in the open air at an altar beside the well.

I was unable to discover any reliable evidence as to the age of the trees. On a branch that had been sawn off, the diameter of which was 20 inches, I counted 282 annual rings. As the veteran by the well has a circumference of more than 600 inches, it is possible that it began to flourish in the time of King Solomon. The trees form a dark, solemn-looking group. They stand before a bare, gray, stone-covered slope on which a narrow road winds up to the ridge of the mountain, only a few hundred yards higher. Last winter's snow was still lying on the ridge.

The cedars are contemporaries of a tempestuous period of history in which innumerable wars and religious conflicts were waged and great empires rose and fell. The tide of events washed the flotsam and jetsam of all these disasters into the lonely valleys of the Lebanon. The mountains of Lebanon have been a refuge to many. In the history of the Near East they have given shelter to lost causes.

In the south of the Lebanon there are villages that are still inhabited by Samaritans, the last remnants of the people to whom the Good Samaritan belonged. To this day they have kept to their old religion. The Samaritans play a great part in the textual criticism of the Old Testament. Originally, they formed part of the people of Israel. It is not known exactly when the separation occurred. The Samaritans obtained permission from Alexander the Great to build their temple on the holy mountain of Gerizim, in Palestine. The separation must therefore have taken place some time before 330 B.C. When they were separated from the people of Israel the Samaritans took with them, as their only sacred book, the Pentateuch, the five books of Moses. They have preserved this "Samaritan Pentateuch" faithfully through the centuries. They have also preserved their ancient customs. Up to the First World War they celebrated their religious feasts under a High Priest whose office was hereditary in a family of the tribe of Levi. Every year at the Passover seven white lambs were sacrificed, according to the Law of Moses. I do not know whether this ritual has survived the disturbances of two world wars.

As the Samaritans lived strictly apart from the Jews, the Samaritan Pentateuch was not influenced by the Hebrew scribes. It therefore represents the form that the five books of Moses had among the Jews in the fourth century B.C. Its text provides important evidence of the accuracy of the textual traditions of the Old Testament. There has been an Old Testament as we understand it today only since about the year 200 B.C. From the Samaritan Pentateuch we learn that the canonic form of the books of Moses had already been more or less settled by the end of the Babylonian captivity, that is, around the middle of the sixth century B.C.

There are still a number of Nosairis (the Ansarie tribe) in the Lebanon. They are an Islamic sect who trace their descent from Ishmael, the son of Abraham by Hagar.

In the region of Hermon live the Druses, another Islamic sect. The Druses have made a fanatical cult of the three best things on earth. They are fanatically devout, fanatical lovers of freedom, and fanatically hospitable. A further specialty is that they give divine honors to the caliphs. The prophet Mohammed himself never claimed divine descent.

There are still Assassins in the Lebanon, survivors of that mysterious and terrible sect of murderers from the Taurus who introduced murder into politics more than a thousand years ago. The French and English term comes from the name of this people—a word that flashes like a falling dagger.

Traces of vanished civilizations survive in various place names of the Lebanon of whose existence we know only from the latest archaeological researches.

One of the lost causes has returned to the world from

the mountain valleys of the Lebanon. During the long centuries of Arab rule the Patriarch of the Maronite Church resided in a mountain monastery in a high valley of the Lebanon. This monastery was founded by the Emperor Theodosius I at the end of the fourth century. The head of the Maronite Church bears the title of Patriarch of Antioch. Today the Maronite Church again stands under the sovereignty of the Pope, but it has retained the privilege of celebrating the liturgy in the Syrian tongue, and the priests of the lower ranks may even be married. The Patriarch now resides in Beirut.

North of Damascus, in the Anti-Lebanon, is the village of Ma'lulah. The peasants of Ma'lulah still speak Aramaic, the language spoken by Jesus. I visited this village, which lies away from the road, deep in the mountains. As we approached the center of the mountain chain from the east, from the road that runs from Aleppo through the Syrian Desert to Damascus, the road appeared to end in a steep wall of rock. Close to the wall there was a cleft through which we were able to drive into the small valley where the village lies. At the foot of this great wall we saw a strange sight. The snow-covered Syrian Desert at our feet was wrapped in a surging mist from which, here and there, a chain of hills emerged. The sun shone weakly through the mist in various places, steeping the clouds in purple. The irregular outlines of the purple patches moved across the land like the emanations of invisible spirits. And high above was the deep blue sky of the desert.

The village, with its white houses, towers up on the steep slopes of the valley, crowned with a Monastery of St. Thecla. The peasants, friendly people, offered us mocha. Then they chatted about the strangers in Aramaic, a Semitic language closely akin to Hebrew. Assyro-Babylonic, Canaanite and Phoenician, Arabic and Ethiopian all belong to the same family. Originally these languages were as close to each other as dialects of the same tongue. In the course of the centuries they have become more widely differentiated. Aramaic has played a remarkable role in history. Darius I, whom history calls "the Great," and who was the creator of the Persian Empire, made it the official language of the Empire. From the middle of the eleventh to the middle of the eighth century, there was an Aramaic State with Damascus as its capital.

Damascus was once captured by King David. Two hundred years before Darius, this Empire was destroyed by Tiglat-Pileser III, King of Assyria. Hence a language that had not been spoken originally by the founders of this Empire and that no longer had any imperial power behind it became the official means of communication of the Persian Empire—a unique occurrence.

Some time after the Israelites had returned from the Babylonian captivity, they adopted Aramaic as their everyday language. Hebrew remained the language of the priests and scribes. Parts of the chronologically latest books of the Old Testament, the books of Ezra and Daniel, were written in Aramaic. Hence Aramaic became the language spoken by Jesus, his disciples, and the Jews of his time. The earliest inscription in Aramaic of which we know dates from the ninth century B.C. and was discovered in Tell-Halaf in northern Syria. One of the earliest extant written references to Christians is in Aramaic, but in Latin characters. It is scribbled on the wall of a house in Pompeii in a room that was presumably a domestic chapel. This must have been before A.D. 79, when Pompeii was destroyed.

The first great maritime people in history, the Phoenicians, lived on the coast of Lebanon. In the Bible they are called the Canaanites. They were also the first mercantile people. I have already mentioned that the alphabet derived from them. They discovered the Atlantic Ocean. As early as 1000 B.C. the Phoenicians had already founded Cádiz, on the Strait of Gibraltar, and they followed this, c. 850, with Carthage, on the coast of North Africa. It was from the Phoenicians that Homer learned that the ocean really exists. Palermo in Sicily, Córdoba in Spain, Tarsus at the foot of the Taurus Mountains, stand on the sites of ancient Phoenician cities.

At the time of the Pharaoh Necho, who reigned from 609 to 593, Phoenician sailors circumnavigated Africa for him. They sailed from the Red Sea, by way of the Cape of Good Hope, to the Strait of Gibraltar, then through the Mediterranean and back to Egypt. The journey took over three years. They landed twice, sowed, reaped, and then sailed on again.

How do we know about this? The fact that Herodotus recorded it only means that he wrote down what he had heard. He did not take part in the voyage. But sometimes tradition allows itself the joke of providing evidence for real facts. Herodotus wrote, "And then they related how—and anyone who cares to do so may believe it, but personally I don't—they had the sun on their right on their voyage around Africa." The very thing that Herodotus doubted is proof that the brave mariners really had been in the Southern Hemisphere, where the sun is in the north at noon. Luckily, when they returned home they told the truth, even when they had most reason to fear they would be decried as liars.

Strabo, the geographer of the time of Christ, reports that the Phoenicians had already been in Cornwall in Hannibal's time, to obtain the valuable tin. He records the delightful story of the Phoenician captain who was followed by Roman ships whose owners wanted to discover the sea route to the tin mines. The Phoenician ran his ship ashore on the Atlantic coast of Spain and travelled back to Carthage by land. When he arrived in his native city he asked the Carthaginian Senate to replace his ship and the loss of earnings because he had saved the tin monopoly. His request was granted.

A pair of golden earrings that Flinders Petrie found in a tomb in Gaza are evidence of a very early link with the North. For a long time, the famous scholar carried the earrings about with him in his pocket. He could not assign them to any of the three dozen civilizations known to him. Then one day by a happy chance in his London club he met a scholar who knew as much about the civilization to which these earrings belonged as Petrie himself knew about Egypt. This expert was able to tell him that the earrings derived from the Ireland of the second millennium B.C.—a date that agreed very well with the age of the tomb in which the earrings had been found.

Herodotus also gives some amusing details about the Phoenicians' trading activities on the west coast of Africa. The Phoenicians who rode at anchor off the coast often failed to come into personal contact with the natives. They went ashore in boats, laid their wares on the sand, and then retired to their ships again. After a while the natives would come out of the bush. They would put as much gold by the side of the goods as they were prepared to give, and then they would disappear again. Thereupon the Phoenicians came back. If the gold was adequate they took it with them. If it was not, they left the goods and the gold on the sand and returned to their ships until the natives brought more money. Herodotus notes that neither side cheated the other. Admittedly, he adds, with gentle irony, "it is said."

For a long time all knowledge of the Phoenicians was merely secondhand. Even Egon Friedell described them in his *History of the Civilization of Egypt and the Ancient Orient* as a clever, commercial people with no creative gifts. It is impossible to maintain this view of them. The archaeologists have proved the contrary. In a dozen places on the

Phoenician coast the most incredible things have been retrieved from the earth. In Ras Shamra, somewhat south of the modern port of Alexandretta, the excavators discovered a city that represents a completely forgotten phase of Canaanite civilization. The city was called Ugarit. Hence the whole civilization is called Ugaritic. The city was rich and prosperous from about 1400 to 1200. In Ugaritic the word "Syria" appears for the first time, spelled "Shryn," about 1400. In the architecture of Ras Shamra, Egyptian and Hittite motifs have been discovered. The Hittites had their kingdom in Asia Minor, and their capital was east of Ankara, the modern capital of Turkey. Pottery from the island of Cyprus and even from Mycenae, the kingdom of Agamemnon on the Peloponnesus, was also discovered. This whole civilization of Ugarit, or Ras Shamra, disappeared about 1200. Probably it was destroyed by the so-called maritime peoples of whom we know that even the Egyptians had great difficulty in preventing them from conquering their land. Two traces of the Ugarit civilization have survived. One is simply the name of a village in Lebanon not far from the site of the city of Ugarit, which is called Furzul. Furzul is the Ugarit word for "iron," the working of which must have been known to the Ugarites at a very early date. The other survival are a few pearls of Ugarit literature that have been preserved in parts of the Proverbs and Psalms.

The most impressive of the Phoenician excavation sites is the city of Byblos. This is about an hour's journey from Beirut. On arrival in the small town, on the lookout for the five-thousand-year-old past, one finds first of all a magnificent early Romanesque church, built in the eleventh century by the Seigneurs of Gibelet, the French rulers of Byblos at the time of the Crusades. The church, which has been well preserved, is served by Maronite priests. That is, however, only the beginning of the surprises that await the visitor to Byblos. A tremendous wall surrounded by a deep moat rises up on the seaward side. It forms part of the castle built by the Seigneurs of Gibelet. This Crusaders' castle, with walls several yards thick, is a tremendous fortress that must have had great strategic value. It dominated the harbor as much as the important coast road. Nothing has survived of the minor furnishings, but only a small part of the walls has been destroyed. From the high belfry one can look far out to sea. At the foot of the castle there are a few pillars of a Temple of Jupiter, and a reasonably well-preserved Roman amphitheater on the slope down to the sea. Not far away, a few feet lower down, are the excavated foundation walls of a Phoenician temple dating from the eighteenth century B.C. A hundred yards farther and a few yards lower down can be seen the outlines of a Phoenician temple of the twenty-eighth century B.C. It is still possible to see the altar on which human sacrifices were made to the god the Bible calls Moloch.

On the way down to the excavation sites I came across a few prehistoric skeletons left in the ground. Burials took place in clay vessels. The tombs date from the fifth millennium B.C. While I was gazing at one of the strikingly narrow, finely constructed skulls, the bells of the Crusaders' church began to ring. High above, the regular-service airplane moved across the sky on its way to Istanbul.

Valuable treasures have been found in the Royal Phoenician tombs in Byblos. They are now in Beirut Museum. In the temple from the twenty-eighth century an alabaster vase with the seal of one of the pharaohs was discovered, and it was this that made it possible to assign a date to the building. A gilded bronze statuette dating from about 2000 B.C. reveals a hair style that may still be seen in Lebanon. An ivory relief represents the struggle of a bull with a lion and griffin. A sphinx of gilded bronze has what is called a Semitic profile. In addition to a silver mirror framed with gilded leaves, one can admire fluted golden drinking vessels of classical proportions and a portrait carved from a single rock crystal, the size of an egg. All these objects are exquisitely beautiful. The most surprising thing about them is that they do not seem a bit alien. The weapons were made of gold or electron, an alloy of gold and silver. Among the battle axes with inlaid ornaments are pieces that one is bound to call elegant.

From a thirteenth-century vault that lay at a depth of thirty-five feet, the archaeologists have excavated the sarcophagus of King Ahiram of Byblos, a contemporary of Moses. The sarcophagus rests on four lions and is embellished with reliefs, one of which shows King Ahiram on his throne, flanked by two sphinxes. This representation is important in the history of art. We know that King Solomon's throne was made by Phoenician craftsmen, and may hence assume that it was similar to the throne of King Ahiram.

The side wall of the outer stone covering of the sarcophagus bears an inscription; it is the oldest known inscription using the letters of the alphabet. The alphabet was invented about 1600 B.C. by a Phoenician miner in the turquoise mines of the pharaohs in Mount Sinai. By way of the Greeks and Romans this inspired Phoenician invention reached all the civilized peoples of the West, and by way of the Aramaeans and Persians it reached the Indians. When one thinks of the debt that civilization owes to the alphabet one realizes the significance of this inscription. As it happens, what it says is important too. It reads:

"THIS SARCOPHAGUS WAS MADE BY ITHOBAL, SON OF AHIRAM, KING OF BYBLOS, FOR AHIRAM, HIS FATHER. MAY IT BE MADE FOR ETERNITY! AND IF A KING AMONG KINGS, A GOVERNOR AMONG THE GOVERNORS MAKES WAR ON BYBLOS AND WRESTS THIS SARCOPHAGUS FROM THE EARTH MAY THE SCEPTER OF HIS

Damascus

When I visited Damascus for the first time I came from
Aleppo. I rode in a large American car, and we were making
seventy miles an hour. It was seven in the morning. The
citadel of Aleppo, gilded with a sparkling aura by the sun,
sank below the horizon. There were seven of us in the car.
When we set off, a dignified white-bearded Bedouin had
courteously offered me his seat next to the driver. When
we had gone only a few miles my well-wisher uttered the
only Arabian word that I understand: "Radio." The driver
switched the set on as loud as possible. This was a bit trying for the nerves. A female voice began to sing—a beautiful voice. She sang what sounded to me like a very monotonous Arabian song that went on for hours. I felt that the
singer must have started her ballad at five in the morning,
with Noah's dove, and would begin to tell of Mohammed's
flight from Mecca toward noon. Because of the dust, we
kept the windows of the car shut. To begin with, I thought
the noise would drive me mad. But one does not travel
across Syria to listen to jazz hits. These ballads now sung
over the radio are heirs to an old tradition. Even before
Mohammed's time the poets of the Bedouin tribes competed
against one another in the market places. They sang their
songs accompanied by instruments. The songs that won a
prize were put up in the Kaaba in Mecca painted in gold
on silk. Poetry has given the Arabic language the lightness
and flexibility, the elegance and richness, that enabled the

Arabs to assimilate the civilizations they had defeated in their conquest of the Orient. Nearly always the stronger but less cultured victor will be inclined to assimilate the higher culture of his vanquished enemy, but he will not always be able to do so successfully.

The road on which we were listening to the happy end of the story of Noah's dove runs, perfectly asphalted, through the stony desert. At times a faraway rocky mountain range appeared on the horizon, glittering in the sunshine, behind the sand hills. At one point the snow-covered peaks of the Anti-Lebanon appeared on the right. It was on this road that Sargon, King of Akkad, travelled at the close of the third millennium B.C. In an inscription King Sargon related that his mother was of humble origin and after his birth had exposed him on the Euphrates in a basket sealed with pitch. King Akki, who was called "the Irrigator," took him in and educated him. Three hundred years later, in the middle of the twentieth century B.C., Abraham travelled this road on his journey from Haran in Mesopotamia via Aleppo to Canaan. Around 1500 the Pharaoh Thutmose III took this way when he conquered Syria. One of his obelisks now stands in New York City. Around 1250 Moses came along this road from Sinai. In 597 Nebuchadnezzar took it on his way to capture Jerusalem and lead into captivity King Jehoiakim of Judah and part of his people. This desert road is a highway of history.

After three hours' driving, we crossed the pass that runs over the Anti-Lebanon. A broad plain stretched out before us. Above the horizon snow-covered Mount Hermon rises, on the Palestine border. Plantations of apricot and orange trees, vineyards, cypresses, poplars, and willows give life to the scene. Old farms lie in the shade of the trees. The last roses of the year bloom in the hedges. At one swoop the sterile desert turns into a flowering garden. No wonder that this oasis seemed a paradise to the Bedouin.

When I arrived in Damascus, which has been the capital of so many kingdoms and has been captured, destroyed, and rebuilt so many times, the Syrians were celebrating the anniversary of their liberation from the French mandate. Many Bedouins had come to the city from the desert, wearing their beautiful costume, the burnoose, a white cape that falls over the shoulders and is fastened around the head with a silver cord. It is enchanting to watch three or four young Bedouins, beautiful men with lean faces, bold incisive noses, and dark desert eyes walking hand in hand in the streets. No motorist would dream of trying to break up this chain of friendship. He might well be killed in the attempt. Among the cheerful crowds and the cars, a mass of donkeys make their way with tripping steps and dignified camels amble arrogantly about, contemptuously ignoring the crowd.

British and French rule in this part of the Orient did not last long. As their policy was based on little more than superior gun power, their successes did not even endure a hundred years. The history of man is not the history of his weapons nor the history of his exports, though peaceful commerce has often turned its profits into armaments. The history of man is the history of ideas.

Islam has taken over large areas that were once flourishing domains of Christianity. It was only in Syria that the Maronite and Syrian Churches, and only in Egypt that the Coptic Church, were able to preserve the Christian tradition.

After centuries of glorious, civilized rule, the empire of the Arabs in the East, on the African coasts of the Mediterranean, and in Spain decayed. What we are now experiencing in the Arab countries is a genuine rebirth. The Arab tongue is spoken and understood over an extraordinarily wide area, extending from Mesopotamia to Morocco. In the African interior, Arabic has been the language of commerce since the middle of the eighteenth century. In all the countries where Arabic is spoken the dominant religion is Mohammedanism. This world, which consists on the one hand of numerous national states, and on the other merely has a tradition, a book, and a religion in common, is similar to the world of the late Middle Ages when the Latin language, humanism, and Christianity had created a unity within which nationalism was only just beginning to make itself felt.

In studying this development it is important not to be confused by the fact that the reviving Arab spirit is emerging in the garb of an exaggerated nationalism, after a long period of oppression and foreign influence. Nationalism has proved to be an extremely malignant but nevertheless very effective instrument in politics. The Arabs are now paying back to the West what they have learned from it.

The Damascenes are fond of saying that Damascus is the oldest city in the world. In any case, the name Dimashq is not of Semitic origin. The city of Dimashq must have existed before the time of the Amorites, that is, before the middle of the third millennium, when the Amorites invaded Syria in the first Semitic wave from Arabia. Excavations have confirmed the great antiquity of the place. I stayed in the Hotel Queen Semiramis. From the window of the hotel I could see the Djebel Kasyun, which towers up on the northern edge of the city, 4,300 feet high. According to Moslem tradition, the Djebel Kasyun is the mountain on which it was revealed to Abraham that there is but one omnipotent God. The Arab Mohammedans live in the lands where the story of the Bible was enacted. Hence this intrinsically poetic people has created many fascinating legends, which serve a good purpose. Quite often they throw light on a situation that the Bible fails to clarify, such as Abraham's "illumination."

Halfway up the Djebel Kasyun, Abraham's mountain, there lies the Mastabe el-Imperator, the Emperor's Terrace. It was built by the courteous Damascenes to enable the German Emperor Wilhelm II to survey the city when he visited it during his journey in the Orient, and was intended to accommodate the Emperor and his suite.

The late German Emperor was the last European monarch to undertake a crusade, albeit an extremely peaceful one. On this journey to the Holy Sepulcher, Kaiser Wilhelm travelled in the wake of his forefathers, the Margraves John and Albrecht of Brandenburg, who went on a pilgrimage to Jerusalem from Berlin in 1435. When one stands on the Mastabe el-Imperator, as the sun sinks down in the west behind the Lebanon in great splendor, the deep red disk of the moon rises over the desert, and the lights appear among the white villas in the gardens of the oasis of Damascus, one has cause to praise the beauty of the world.

The Damascus bazaar, which constitutes a whole area of the city with its many streets and alleys, is named after Abdul-Hamid, one of the last Turkish Sultans. The Souk Hamidye is one of the oldest market places in the world. Because of the hot climate, the bazaar is covered. The people crowd there in a lively and cheerful throng. Public scribes sit in corners. These men are masters of the difficult art of writing Arabic script beautifully. One can watch the barbers shaving heads and chins. Baker boys run through the lanes imploring Allah to send them customers: "Allah is the nourisher. Buy my bread!" Haggling is considered one of the pleasures of life in which dealer and customer try to outwit one another in a dozen languages. The carpet on which they all sit together is a tilting ground of wit. To buy a shawl or a copper vessel one must be prepared to conclude a friendship for life. If the next dealer is a piece of silver cheaper one can forget it again. It is pleasant to note that there is no jealousy among the dealers. If one buys from a neighboring dealer and casts an apologetic glance back at the first one, he will come hurrying up to assure you that "Allah has sent my neighbor a good buyer. In time he will send me one too!" How wise! In the Arab countries one gets the impression that the Moslems observe the moral teaching of the Koran more cheerfully than Christians follow the moral teaching of the Bible. If one happens to pass a stall where one has bought something, one is welcomed like a brother from the desert. The Oriental understands something of the difficult art of taking life easily.

The roof over the bazaar comes to a sudden end. Three tremendous Corinthian columns rise far above the roofs. Between the pillars stand the elegant outlines of a minaret, an Arab work of art of the eighth century, framed by a work of antiquity. The Corinthian columns are the remains of the Temple of Jupiter Damascenus. The temple stood on the site of a shrine that was dedicated to the Syrian god Hadad. Hadad's emblems on the ancient reliefs are thunder and lightning. Sometimes Hadad stands on a bull, the Mediterranean symbol of creative force. Hadad was the Canaanite weather god who in later times was merged with Jupiter. The Emperor Theodosius I turned the Temple of Jupiter into a church, which was dedicated to John the Baptist, who, in the Greek Church, is called Johannes Prodromos, that is, the Forerunner. The church was later enlarged and beautified by the Emperor Justinian. It had a noteworthy fate. At the siege of Damascus by the Moslem Arabs, which took place in A.D. 635, the Arab commander Khalid ibn-Walid succeeded in invading the city from the east. When the Damascenes realized this, they hurriedly surrendered the western part of the city to the Arab commander abu-Ubayda, who was on the other side. The Arab leaders met near the Church of Johannes Prodromos. For us who have lived through so much barbarity, what happened sounds almost incredible. The eastern part of the city was regarded as taken and was plundered. The western part was considered to have been surrendered and was spared. The Church of St. John was made available to Moslems and Christians alike. They entered the shrine through the same door. The Moslems prayed in the eastern portion, the Christians in the western. Seventy years later, the Caliph Walid I built the Omayyad mosque in place of the Emperor Justinian's church.

Walid I, in whose reign Spain was conquered in the year 711, and Samarkand in the Asian interior in 712, wrote poetry, composed, and played musical instruments. He listened patiently to the works of other poets, although he was the mighty Caliph. He must have been an exceedingly gifted man.

At this period there lived in the metropolis of the Arab empire the last of the Fathers of the Greek Church, St. John of Damascus. His contemporaries nicknamed him "Chrysorrhoas," that is, "gold-pouring," on account of his eloquence. He was a great scholar and a great theologian; he constructed a theological system based on the teaching of the Fathers and the Councils of the period from the fourth to the seventh century. Thomas Aquinas called him a source of wisdom. John Damascenus was Prime Minister to the Caliph of Damascus until the year 724. This was a world of free minds and spirits.

John exerted an important influence on Islam as well as on Christianity. His system kindled a rationalistic movement in Islam theology, admittedly only of short duration. But the close contact and free discussion between the two religions led to the adoption by Islam of much of the Greco-Christian tradition of the early centuries. John Chrysorrhoas closed his life as a monk in the Monastery of St. Sabas on the Dead Sea and was canonized by the Greek and the Roman Church. Hardly a century after the death of Mohammed, John Damascenus witnessed one of the most fantastic triumphal processions in history: that of the commander Musa ibn-Nusayr, who entered Damascus after the conquest of Spain, with four hundred fair-haired West Goth princes in his train and a silver table adorned with mounds of precious stones in his booty, taken from the Cathedral of Toledo. In the Pyrenees the Arabs came to a halt after they had been defeated in the Battle of Tours and Poitiers on the banks of the Loire.

In the Battle of Yarmuk, a century before, when the Arabs defeated the army of the Emperor Heraclius of Byzantium on a hot August day in the year 636, it had been a sandstorm that enabled the Arabs to win the fight against the Greeks, who did not know how to protect themselves from this natural phenomenon. At Tours and Poitiers it was the wolf's pelts of the Franks that helped Charles Martel, the commander of the Franks, to victory, with the aid of God, in the icy cold to which the Arabs were not accustomed, and which saved France from being conquered by Islam. Sand and cold, burnoose and wolf's pelt, led to two historic decisions at opposite ends of the then known world.

From the Temple of Jupiter I went to the Omayyad mosque, a masterpiece of early Arab architecture. Taking off my shoes, I entered the courtyard, which is 450 feet long and 120 wide, paved with marble and surrounded on three sides by a colonnade. The very proportions of this courtyard evoke a sense of solemnity. The long south side is occupied by the mosque. In one half of the yard there is a stone fountain; opposite, in the other half, a treasure house that stands on twelve columns from the ancient Temple of Jupiter. In the galleries, where scholars interpret the Koran to young people, some early Arab mosaics have survived, landscapes and pictures of cities with tall buildings, reminiscent of Benozzo Gozzoli. The green, blue, and gold are subtly shaded, and the composition reveals great refinement in the draftsmanship; these mosaics are like dreams thrown on the wall, memories of the Fata Morgana of the desert.

Of the three minarets that can be seen from the courtyard of the mosque, one is remarkable as a masterpiece of the Arab-Egyptian style. From the gallery of this tower the muezzin called the faithful to prayer in a sad, sustained song. The minaret on the other side is called Madinet Isa, the Minaret of Jesus. According to Moslem belief, the tip of the Madinet Isa is the spot where Jesus the prophet will enter the world again when the Last Judgment begins.

The mosque itself has an extended, tall, rectangular, central part flanked by two smaller rectangular wings. The structure is 435 feet long and 80 wide. Two rows of Corinthian columns, linked by tall arches, run throughout its whole length. Parts of the ceiling are still inlaid with gold. The floor is completely covered with carpets, said to be three thousand in number. They include magnificent pieces, many hundreds of years old. The total impression is one of space and light. The magnificence and richness of the furnishings are less impressive than the harmony of the whole design. Here and there a believer kneels on the floor, saying his prayers.

Almost at the center of the mosque there is a rectangular chapel with a cupola. Its side walls are slender marble pillars linked by gilded railings. According to tradition, the head of John the Baptist has been preserved in this chapel in a marble sarcophagus, covered with damask brocade, since the time of the Emperor Theodosius.

Damascus is the city where Saul of Tarsus became a Christian. The way to the ancient Jewish quarter of the city runs through innumerable crooked little lanes from the

Mosque of the Omayyads to the Derb-el-Mustakim. This is the street called Straight that is referred to in the Acts of the Apostles. The street called Straight runs through the whole city from east to west. At the time of the Romans it had colonnades, remains of which have been excavated in many places. The Jewish quarter is no doubt still in the same spot as in days of old. The Lord called Ananias in a vision and said to him, "Rise up and go to the road called Straight and inquire at the house of Judas for a man of Tarsus named Saul." A house of the first century that has sunk many feet down in the ground is called the House of Ananias. It is now a chapel. The gate where Straight Street ends also stands on the same spot as in Roman times. Parts of the old Roman city wall have survived. These stones have seen a thousand sights since the day when Paul was struck with blindness. They have seen the arrogance of triumphant armies and the tears of the defeated. Innumerable caravans have passed through this gate, bringing silks and incense, the valuables of the East. They brought slaves for the mines and galleys, female slaves for the harems of the satraps and pashas. These stones have seen the cart with the million pieces of gold with which the Damascenes ransomed themselves from Tamerlane, the Mongol Khan. They have echoed the lamentations of the world-famous armorers of the city, whom Tamerlane deported to Samarkand and Khurasan, to create a new armament center. Army leaders and scholars, slaves and travellers from all over the world have passed in and out of the gate of Damascus since then, for almost two thousand years. Nothing endows these ancient stones with such significance as the fact that they saw how a blind man, led by the hand of a companion, staggered past, scarcely noticed by the haughty Roman sentry. The blind man had had a vision. Jesus Christ had appeared to him, to Saul, who had persecuted with such great anger and zeal those who preached

Christ. What thoughts must have stirred in this ambitious young man's mind as he walked through this gate! The night of blindness surrounded him. Struck down by a supernatural power, he did not yet know how soon he would recover the light of his eyes, and far more than that.

I believe that no one can pass through the East Gate of Damascus without being moved in his heart. Paul did not leave the city by this gate. The Jews banded together to kill him. The disciples let him down by night along the face of the wall, lowering him to the ground in a hamper. At the foot of this wall there began the path that led Paul to Rome, to die there as a martyr after he had preached the gospel to the world.

Ur in Sumer

Ur lies 12 miles west of the lower course of the Euphrates, in the southern part of the Mesopotamian Desert. It is 120 miles from the coast of the Persian Gulf. As the birthplace of the patriarch Abraham, Ur is the earliest site of Christendom on earth.

Our knowledge of history extends far beyond the time of Abraham. Even for the Flood we are no longer dependent on the evidence of the Bible. From the lists of Sumerian kings we know the names of a series of rulers who ruled in the cities of southern Mesopotamia before the Flood. Abraham is the first Biblical personality whose biography, as transmitted by the book of Genesis, can be supplemented by information from non-Biblical sources.

Ur is more than 600 miles from Damascus. It costs much time and money to visit Ur, but the surprises that befell me on this journey were surpassed only by those that awaited me on my visit to Horeb, the mountain of the Law on the Sinai Peninsula.

The bus for Baghdad leaves Damascus at 5 P.M. Shortly before sunset I arrived at the big station where the journey begins. The vehicle that was to take us through the Syrian Desert was a tremendous affair consisting of a powerful locomotive coupled by a movable axis to a Pullman car on tires. The whole "train" was clad in ribbed aluminum. In the prospectus the bus had been lauded as "air-conditioned." It turned out that the more important fact was that it was well heated at night rather than that it was well cooled by day. For sleeping it was possible to make the seats recline, and they were as comfortable as the seats in an airplane.

There was a slight delay before our departure. The bus bringing passengers from Beirut was an hour late, owing to a premature snowfall on the pass of the Lebanon. These passengers from Beirut included a beautiful Indian lady in a silk sari. She was travelling with fifteen suitcases, by the land route through Persia to Karachi, the capital of Pakistan. A distinguished-looking Bedouin in a white burnoose sat down beside her. He was to alight in the desert in the middle of the night. One imagined a few Bedouins of his tribe waiting for their sheik. While the electric arc lamps of Damascus flared up in the distance they would be sitting around a campfire whose red glow under the white desert moon would cast on the sand the ghostly shadows of their recumbent camels.

To begin with, we travelled along a good asphalt road. After an hour on the road we had to stop for the customs and passport formalities. These take place not on the actual geographical frontier, which is an imaginary line in the desert, but on the frontier of the inhabited territory. The desert is no man's land. In the customs house we were given an excellent cup of tea. Then we set off on the road again. Our gasoline-driven monster travelled at a speed of 50 to 60 miles an hour, its wheels whirling up a huge cloud of dust.

The Biblical account of Abraham's life is vivid and full of color. But questions about the degree of truth that may be attributed to the Biblical tradition stirred men's minds even in the time of Jesus. Philo, the Jewish philosopher, who was born in Alexandria about 10 B.C., said, "Everything in the Old Testament is truth. Everything that is true is in the Old Testament." The early Church Fathers attempted to establish the applicability of this assertion to the whole Bible. I am not concerned with the truth of the revelation but with the trustworthiness of the Bible as a source of tradition. The assertion of classical natural science that the truth of revelation is incompatible with the findings of science led imperceptibly to the depreciation of the Bible as a historical source. Now, archaeology and historical research are demonstrating more and more clearly that the Bible is in fact a trustworthy historical source. The number of facts which it records that are being confirmed by research in other fields is growing from year to year. That is not surprising. There is in the whole of human history no document the text of which has been transmitted over such a long period with such exactness as the text of the Old Testament. Textual criticism has been able to establish, as the result of a whole century of scholarly work, that the text before us today has not changed substantially since the time of Jesus. Until quite recently the oldest surviving documentary evidence for this assertion was a papyrus dug out of the sand of Egypt: the famous Nash Papyrus, which is preserved in Cambridge University Library, and was published in 1902. It contains in Hebrew the Ten Commandments and the text of Deuteronomy, Chapter 6, verses 4 and 5. After Alexander the Great's expedition and the establishment of the Ptolemaic dynasty by one of Alexander's commanders, the official language in Egypt became Greek. The dry sand of the desert has preserved a great number of Greek papyri. Hebrew papyri in Egypt, however, are rare. The Nash Papyrus is a rarity of the first order. The two verses of Deuteronomy are words spoken by Moses in explanation of the laws, which he uttered to the people from Mount Horeb before his death: "Hear, O Israel: The Lord our God is one Lord; And thou shalt love the Lord thy God with all thine heart, and with all thy soul, and with all thy might." Not much text there for the scholar to work on, but the writing and the material prove that this fragment of papyrus comes from the second century B.C. It was this that Jesus used in his reply to the scribe who asked him which was the most important of all the commandments.

In 1947, in an out-of-the-way cave by the Dead Sea, Bedouins discovered several scrolls stored away in clay pots wrapped in linen and covered with pitch to protect them against the damp. This complicated form of preservation, which kept these extraordinarily precious scrolls in good condition, is very old. After he had bought the field on his return from Babylon, Jeremiah ordered Baruch to "take these letters, the sealed bill of sale, together with this open address, and lay them in an earthenware vessel that they may long remain."

These pre-Christian scrolls from the cave by the Dead Sea contain, among others, the prophet Isaiah, passages from Daniel, and a commentary on Habbakuk. In 1949 and again more recently further scrolls have been discovered. Unfortunately, the Bedouins have meanwhile learned their value, and they sometimes transfer them to carefully chosen caches in the desert. For the time being some of the scrolls have thus disappeared. But as they are worth a great deal of money they are bound to come to light again in time. One of the two rolls of Isaiah has been published. It consists of seventeen parchment leaves sewn together, on which the whole text of Isaiah is written in fifty-four columns. This text, which is seven hundred years older than the hitherto oldest known texts, found in 1890 during the rebuilding of the old synagogue in Cairo, contains numerous deviations in the choice of words, in the grammar, and above all in the spelling, but there are no major textual differences. The prophet Isaiah lived about 700 B.C. It cannot be established scientifically but it may be assumed that as the inheritance of the past has been treated so carefully in later times, the sacred writings of the prophets were preserved even more faithfully in ancient times.

It is generally taken for granted today that the Pentateuch, the five books of Moses, were first written down in the tenth or ninth century B.C. There are many good reasons for assuming that even this first version was based on earlier written sources. Three thousand of the four thousand years that separate us from Abraham are bridged by a written tradition.

As I pondered on this comforting thought I fell asleep. Toward 2 A.M. we made a stop. One of the tremendous wheels of our monster had to be changed. I got out and walked a few hundred yards into the open country. The full moon was shining. Despite its brightness, the stars were sparkling with a brilliance of which I had never seen the like before. The sky seems higher and wider here than in our latitudes. The sand beneath my feet was hard. Here and there a miserable thistle was growing. The camels eat this dry plant. As it is alive it contains traces of water, but it needs a camel's teeth to find them.

Before me there lay a small chain of sand hills. Otherwise infinity stretched out in a silvery radiance in all directions. From here to the south the desert extends for nearly fifteen hundred miles across the whole peninsula of Arabia to coastal Hadhramaut on the Indian Ocean. It would take more than a hundred days to reach this coast from here on a camel. For many miles around there are at most a few Bedouins who know where the few spots with water are.

Even thirty years ago the journey from Damascus to Baghdad took twenty-three days on the back of a camel. Day after day the grandiose spectacle of the sunrise, the heat of the day. Night after night the coolness, the silvery moon above the silent desert, producing a tremendous tension. The infinity of earth compels man to enter the bridge that leads to the infinity of the other world.

At last the tire was fixed and the men were calling for me with ghostlike, echoless voices as though from afar. I returned to the bus. Tomorrow a vulture would hack to pieces the mangled tube the mechanic had just thrown away. Through the small dust-covered window I watched the desert as it passed by, mile after mile. The empty tin cans that mark the track every hundred yards shine in the beam of headlights. Fancy turns the rocks into wild legendary animals. After some hours the sky brightens. It is like waking from an oppressive dream. The sun rises. The spectacle begins with a first glimmer of pale pink. This pink deepens every minute until it becomes a flaming purple. The first bright hues of blue appear. Then come new colors, gradually intensifying into an intoxicating crescendo of the whole prism. The sun begins to warm the air, to dazzle the eyes. Day has come. How could early man have failed to worship the sun as a deity?

Meanwhile the bus has entered inhabited territory once more. Palms and a few scattered houses come into sight. The bus stops at the passport and customs office of the State of Iraq, and the hot tea we are offered tastes delicious. Then we cross over the Euphrates. At this point a tremendous bridge links the high dams on both sides of the river. Slowly and majestically the Euphrates rolls the silt of the Taurus Mountains down to the Persian Gulf, past innumerable places that are among the oldest sites of history. Punctually at 10 A.M. we reached the Tigris. We were in Baghdad. A triumphal arch, a tremendous gate, stands in an open square. Gigantic winged lions with human heads embellish it. They come from the Palace of King Ashurbanipal in Nineveh. These pieces of sculpture, which are two and a half thousand years old, come from a relatively late period. Not much has survived of the ancient splendor of the city of the Caliph Harun-al-Rashid, the Baghdad of the Arabian Nights' Entertainments. That Baghdad was destroyed by the Mongols in the thirteenth century. Only the hotel where I stayed has preserved in its name the memory of Sindbad the Sailor. But the quay wall still consists of bricks with the stamp of Nebuchadnezzar.

For the visitor to Baghdad the museums are its most remarkable feature. Year after year incredible things from all ages of human history are being brought to light from twenty different sites. The Iraqi Museum is a treasure house of precious objects, overcrowded but admirably organized. Everything is clearly labelled. The building is old-fashioned, however, and quite inadequate for everything the museum possesses today. It has treasures surpassing those of the British Museum and the Louvre in number.

From Baghdad to Ur it is 240 miles in a southeasterly direction. First, an asphalted road runs to Hilla. On the way the road branches off westward to Karbala, the Holy City of the Shiites. In Karbala, Husein, grandson of Mohammed, who was assassinated and buried there, is revered. Even today only orthodox Moslems are allowed to enter the mosque. There is something comforting about the fact that there are still places in the world to which one is not admitted even with a press pass.

A little while later the walls of Babylon appear at some distance from the road. The land is irrigated and cultivated everywhere, though in a very primitive fashion. No one in this land would be in want if the irrigation scheme current in the second Golden Age of Babylon, in the seventh century B.C., were restored.

The Iraqi government has begun the building of a dam in the north, in an irrigation project costing a hundred million dollars. It is estimated that twenty million people can be fed from the soil of the Land of the Two Rivers.

Sixty miles southeast of Hilla we cross the Euphrates near Samawa on a pontoon bridge. On the other side of the river we travel through a narrow, partly covered bazaar street. Here one can only drive slowly. Coppersmiths are working in the road. The tentmakers sit outside their doors. A wether is being killed. Children are playing. Dignified men are drinking their cups of mocha. Veiled women look inquisitively at the car. Strangers are rarely seen here. This bazaar street probably looked more or less the same a thousand years ago. It is cheerful, sociable, dirty, full of life and noise. It is inhabited by Bedouins who have settled down here. This indestructible, patient, and industrious people bears its poverty with dignity. It likes to laugh at itself and at its government. It is helpful and hospitable. From time to time it flares up in sudden revolts. It is a people that history passes over.

The desert then returns again. From here on it is completely flat. As far as the eye can see there is not the slightest undulation. This is the alluvial land of the Euphrates, and we covered sixty miles without meeting another car. Some fifty feet below us was the clay stratum left behind by the Flood. In every century the coast moves two to two and a half miles farther out to sea. In Abraham's time the sea extended as far as Ur. Today the coast is 120 miles from Ur. Abraham was born in Ur, and it was there that he spent his youth, there that he married Sarah.

The family did not remain in Ur. In the eleventh chapter of Genesis we read: "And Terah took Abram his son and Lot the son of Haran, his son's son, and Sarai his daughter-in-law, his son Abram's wife; and they went forth with them from Ur of the Chaldees, to go into the land of Canaan; and they came unto Haran and dwelt there." Haran lies in northern Mesopotamia, exactly midway between the Euphrates and Tigris. Abraham's father died in Haran. When Abraham travelled on to the land of Canaan at God's behest, he went across the Syrian Desert. The continuity of tradition in the East is evident from the fact that there are still innumerable legends about Abraham in Haran. The inhabitants of Ain el-Khalil consider themselves direct descendants of the patriarch, calling themselves "Sons of Abraham." Abraham is venerated as much by the Mohammedans as by Christians. Mohammed once declared that it was the religion of Abraham that he wished to restore, and he called Abraham "Halil Allah, the friend of Allah."

Even Rebecca's well still exists, a memorial of the story of how Abraham's servant sought a wife for Isaac, that enchanting story that is told in all its patriarchal beauty in the twenty-fourth chapter of Genesis.

The most amusing of the Mohammedan legends concerning Abraham is connected with a pond in Urfa, which is not far from Haran. It seems that Nimrod, who was not only a mighty hunter but also King of Assyria, fired glowing charcoal at Abraham with his catapult. Despite Nimrod's skill, however, the charcoal missed the holy man and became a fish pond; the sparks gave birth to fish. To the present day these fish are considered sacred and are not eaten. In Abraham's bosom even a carp can attain blessedness.

During the final part of the journey to Ur a dark line

appears to the left on the horizon: the date palm groves on the banks of the Euphrates. Twelve miles before our destination a jagged outline appears on the completely flat horizon. This is the Ziggurat, the temple tower of Ur.

Ur was a seaport, with more than a hundred thousand inhabitants. It transmitted to Abraham the legacy of a thousand-year-old culture, the culture of Sumer, the Golden Age of which lasted from 3000 to 1900 B.C. The Sumerians had an outstanding knowledge of mathematics and astronomy. The division of the clock into twelve hours was invented in Ur five thousand years ago. The Sumerians' artistic achievements were important. They had a highly developed religion. The written evidence of this civilization can be traced back as far as the year 2000, in other words, as far back as Abraham. Though it is not very likely, it would be quite possible for the brick to be discovered on which the contract regarding the sale of Abraham's paternal house was scratched. An agreement about an ox and another about a field concluded with a namesake of Abraham's and dating from the same period in Babylon, the period of Ammizaluga, the tenth king of the first dynasty in Babylon, have come down to us. It may be asked what degree of reliability could be attached to this brick if it were discovered. It would be interesting to know how the theologians would answer that question.

It is important not to think of Abraham as a vague, legendary figure but as a clearly defined historical personality. He was a great gentleman, admitted to the presence of the Egyptian Pharaoh. King Melchizedek also received him. In the Bible he is depicted with many fascinatingly human weaknesses. He was a living human being.

I climbed up the Ziggurat, the temple tower. Its walls consist of bricks embedded in bitumen. The tower measures about 200 feet by 150 feet; the walls have an inward slope on all four sides, while on the ground plan the wall line curves outward. These calculated curves correspond to an architectural principle that was also applied in the Parthenon on the Acropolis.

A flight of about a hundred steps, reconstructed from the old material, leads, at an angle of 45 degrees, up to the first terrace. Originally the Ziggurat had three terraces. On the highest one stood the temple building. Gardens were laid out on the terraces. The Sumerians came from mountainous land somewhere in Central Asia and were accustomed to worshipping their gods on high places.

Apart from the central flight of steps which led up the Ziggurat, two further main stairways led, at the same angle of 45 degrees and at right angles to the central flight, up to the great gateway on the second terrace. It must have been a picturesque sight when the processions of the priests climbed up and down these steps. Sir Leonard Woolley has made the ingenious suggestion that Jacob's dream of the ladder on which the angels ascend and descend was a memory of his grandfather's stories of his youth in Ur.

The authority of the old Sumerian deities, who represented mythical natural forces, was so great that fifteen hundred years after Ur had lost its political power the gods of Ur were still worshipped in Babylon and Nineveh. Through the centuries Ur was a holy city. The Sumerian tongue was the language used by the Babylonian priests. Thus, it has been preserved for us.

Before the Persian King Cyrus the Great destroyed his Empire in the year 538, King Nabonidus, the last King of the neo-Babylonian Empire, completely rebuilt the holy places of Ur. Hence, the Ziggurat on which I was standing does not date from Abraham's time. The old, original Ziggurat is contained within the new one. It could be laid bare, but that would be possible only if one were prepared to sacrifice the parts that survive from neo-Babylonian times.

The sun began to set. From the height of the Ziggurat

I looked westward into the waterless, uninhabited desert. This view has not changed since Abraham's time. All around the Ziggurat are excavation sites, temple sites from every age, a mausoleum with well-preserved walls, a gigantic cemetery, palaces and houses from various strata and centuries. The two harbor basins of Ur are clearly visible from the somewhat darker coloring of the soil.

It was in the cemetery that Woolley discovered the celebrated royal Sumerian tombs. Some of the tombs had not been plundered. He found splendid gold vessels, headdresses of gold, a beautifully worked gold dagger, harps inlaid with lapis lazuli and white shell, with the head of a bull wrought in gold. He found a small silver boat, an exact model of the vessels the fishermen in Shatt-al-Arab still use today. He found the magnificent gold jewelry of Queen Shub-ad. After Eve, Queen Shub-ad is the fifth woman in world history whose name is known to us. The second, third, and fourth are Lamech's wives, Adah and Zillah, and his daughter Naamah, who are mentioned in the fourth chapter of Genesis.

The beauty of the precious things that have been excavated and are now preserved in the Iraqi Museum in Baghdad testifies to the high level of the civilization from which Abraham derived.

Two hundred yards south of the Ziggurat part of the city from the period around 2000—that is, from the time of Abraham—has been excavated. It consists of paved streets, along which I walked. The houses do not seem to have lacked certain luxuries. Inside they had a gallery. Archaeologists infer this from the charred remains of the wooden beams found in the ground, which supported the galleries. Not far from this site there is a deep pit. Here Woolley, pushing through endless masses of the rubble of thousands of years, dug so far into the depths that finally the workmen came on a clay stratum that appeared to be

The Dome of the Rock. In the Foreground, the Remains of the Walls of Solomon's Temple, Jerusalem

The Monastery of St. Catherine at the Foot of Mt. Horeb

Mountain Desert near Sinai

virgin soil. Nothing would have been more natural than to have laid aside the spade at this point. That it was not done provided a great moment in the history of archaeology. His scientific instinct told Woolley that something was wrong. In the evening of the day on which his workmen had struck the clay stratum, Sir Leonard stood thoughtfully before the almost forty-yards-deep pit. Had he really arrived at the ground soil of history? The next morning he seized the theodolite and established that the bottom of the pit lay several yards above the level that would have been expected geologically at the time of the presumed first settlement. It was only after a great effort that Woolley induced his Bedouins to continue digging, by promising them extra wages. After another one and a half yards they came on a fossilized bone that the river had washed down from the mountains. After a further three yards new strata of settlement came to light, dating from pre-Sumerian times. Here too, however, there were remains of solidly built houses, traces of a civilized people of whom so far we have no precise conception. Perhaps these people belonged to the Hassuna civilization, which dates from 5300 B.C., three and a half thousand years before Abraham. This clay stratum between the settlement strata can have been produced only by a great and long-continuing flood. It is a geological document of the Deluge. For the early Sumerian historians the Flood was a well-remembered historical event, which interrupted the list of Sumerian kings. The ten royal names that the list mentions before the time of the Flood correspond to the ten patriarchs of the Bible from Adam to Noah.

I walked along a street that Abraham knew in his youth. Shortly after Terah had left the city of Ur with his son Abraham, his daughter-in-law Sarah and his grandson Lot, great military events took place. The splendor and grandeur of the ancient kingdom of Ur declined. One is tempted to say that Abraham left Ur just in time to preserve the tradition. It would be wrong to put it like that, however. The golden treasures of the royal Sumerian tombs, the street that Abraham knew, the traces of the Flood—all this Sir Leonard Woolley dug out of the earth. However impressive these revelations are and however much history and archaeology sharpen our view of early Biblical history, one question remains open. The question is: What tradition did Abraham take with him from Ur to Haran and Canaan?

In the fourth chapter of Genesis, at the mention of Enos, who was a grandson of Adam, we read: "Then began men to call upon the name of the Lord." When God made the covenant with Noah and sent the rainbow as a token, it was the last time, before Abraham, that God spoke to a human being. God spoke once again before the confusion of tongues during the construction of the Tower of Babel. It is not stated to whom God spoke the words quoted in Genesis, Chapter 11. But the tradition that "men began to call upon the name of the Lord" must have been interrupted. We know that Abraham's forefathers and even his own father served the gods of Sumeria. This is stated expressly in the Bible. In the twenty-fourth chapter of Joshua we read: "And Joshua gathered all the tribes of Israel to Shechem, and called for the elders of Israel, and for their heads, and for their judges, and for their officers; and they presented themselves before God. And Joshua said unto all the people, Thus saith the Lord God of Israel, Your fathers dwelt on the other side of the flood in old time, even Terah, the father of Abraham, and the father of Nachor: and they served other gods."

The twelfth chapter of Genesis begins quite abruptly with the sentence: "Now the Lord had said unto Abram, Get thee out of thy country, and from thy kindred, and from thy father's house, unto a land that I will show thee."

If we did not know that Abraham's forefathers had served pagan gods our question would not be difficult. Then we might take it for granted that an oral tradition existed even though there is no reference to one in the Bible. But in fact the tradition was interrupted. We know nothing as to how the word of God was transmitted from Noah to Abraham. From Abraham onward the tradition of the revelation was interrupted no more. He is the Patriarch. What enabled Abraham to receive the word of God after possibly many centuries of the worship of pagan gods is a question to which the Old Testament gives no answer. Nor is it presumably a question that scholars will find easy to answer.

By the Waters of Babylon

Babylon is Bab-ilu, the Gate of God. This proud heathen name has acquired a mythical connotation owing to the events that have passed through the Gate of God like a magnificent procession.

I left Baghdad early in the morning, going past the triumphal arch with the winged lion-men from Nineveh. The morning air was still fresh. Reddish streaks of mist were passing across the autumn landscape. This land between the Euphrates and the Tigris is the oldest soil from which man has wrested the fruits of the earth by irrigation and agriculture. Again and again the road crosses the canals, over small, high-built bridges. One of the canals is called "Hammurabi, Happiness of the People," after the man who built it four thousand years ago. A memorial of the gratitude in the heart of the people! From time to time we drove past a piece of land on which thin parallel lines could be seen—the shallow furrows made by the peasant with his wooden plow. This network of thin lines is the geometry of agriculture. The plow was invented in the land between the Euphrates and the Tigris. The peasants' wooden plows still look just as the sculptors carved them thousands of years ago in the reliefs that praise the fertility of the earth.

The fields are full of stones. One imagines that it ought to have been possible in the course of more than a hundred generations to clear all these stones away. My knowledgeable driver, himself the son of a peasant from this district, tells me the peasants leave the stones where they are because their shade retains a little moisture in the soil. The wooden plow quietly rolls the stones out of its way. An iron plow would be so jagged after one furrow as to be quite useless.

The Euphrates is one of the rivers that branched out from the river of Paradise. "And a river went out of Eden to water the garden; from thence it was parted and became four heads." One of these "heads" is the Euphrates.

Babylon is the first city to be mentioned by name in the Old Testament. In the genealogical table in the tenth chapter of Genesis it is said of Nimrod that "the beginning of his kingdom was Babel, and Erech, and Accad, and Calneh, in the land of Shinar." These places are the names of cities of extreme antiquity, and we now know where they were situated. The story of the Flood is followed by the story of the building of the Tower of Babel and the confusion of tongues, which was not resolved until the outpouring of the Holy Spirit. The date of the foundation of Babylon is hidden in the mists of an impenetrable past.

Babylon lived through two Golden Ages. The ancient Babylonian Empire lasted from 1830 to 1550 B.C. King Hammurabi, the first great legislator in history, was its first important ruler. He calls the second year of his reign "the year in which I established justice." His legislation was based on ancient Sumerian traditions. It remained in force in Babylon for a thousand years. In 1901 a diorite column was found in Susa on which Hammurabi's laws are carved in a calligraphically perfect cuneiform script. This column bears the statement that the legislator's duty is to protect the weak from the strong. There are many detailed points of agreement between the Codex of Hammurabi and the later laws of the Hebrews.

Babylon's second Golden Age began with King Nebuchadnezzar II. It went on under Cyrus the Great, the first King of the Persian Empire, and lasted until Alexander the Great. Alexander established his residence in Babylon after his brilliant campaigns. He died of tropical malaria while preparing a campaign for the conquest of Arabia. This second Golden Age lasted for three hundred years.

We have a description of Babylon's second Golden Age from the pen of an excellent writer, Herodotus, who visited Babylon in the middle of the fifth century. There are many references to Babylon in inscriptions and records on brick.

Excavation of the ruins of Babylon was begun around the turn of the century by the German Oriental Society under Robert Koldewey. Today, we may plainly see what the prophet Isaiah foretold of this wonderful site of human history.

"And Babylon, the glory of kingdoms, the beauty of the Chaldees' excellency, shall be as when God overthrew Sodom and Gomorrah. It shall never be inhabited, neither shall it be dwelt in from generation to generation: neither shall the Arabian pitch tent there; neither shall the shepherds make their fold there. But wild beasts of the desert shall lie there; and their houses shall be full of doleful creatures; and owls shall dwell there, and satyrs shall dance there. And the wild beasts of the islands shall cry in their desolate houses, and dragons in their pleasant palaces; and her time is near to come, and her days shall not be prolonged."

This prophecy, which Isaiah made at a time when Babylon was the most powerful city on earth, has been fulfilled in the most terrible fashion. The excavations are a bewildering and almost impenetrable field of ruins.

The Bedouin who had relentlessly attached himself to me could only speak a few scraps of English. He had not much idea of things. After I had rid myself of him by giving him a reasonable tip, I climbed, laden with map, compass, Baedeker, plans and drawings of reconstructions, up hill and down, in the ever growing heat, across the extensive terrain.

Herodotus says that in his time the circumference of the city was 480 stades—i.e., about 56 miles—which would correspond to the size of Paris today. According to Herodotus, the height of the walls was about 335 feet and their width 85 feet. At the time of Alexander the Great, about a hundred years later, the inhabited city had shrunk to a circumference of 20 miles, which is the distance around the present excavations. Imagine what still lies under the earth!

Amid the remains of brick walls and ancient towers rises a remarkable pagan symbol of masculine power over the female earth, a tremendous stone monument on a new pedestal: the celebrated Babylonian lion which stands over the recumbent figure of a woman.

The monuments excavated in Mesopotamia are not so impressive as those of Egypt or Greece. All through the centuries in this land without stone, wood, or metal, the building material has always been the unassuming brick, which was simply baked in the sun. After destruction had taken place, the ruins were levelled to the ground and the new buildings erected on them. Hence, in the course of thousands of years, these Mesopotamian cities grew into hills more than 300 feet high. What the archaeologists are able to expose are nearly always merely foundations. To penetrate to older strata the later have first to be destroyed. Moreover, for centuries the peasants have used the bricks from these ruined sites for their own buildings. It needs an experienced eye to reconstruct a picture of the ancient days on the basis of the ruins and the maps.

The first Babylon, the Babylon of Hammurabi, in the first half of the second millennium, is of exceptional importance in the history of the origins of the Old Testament. This first Babylon, with all its treasures and temples, was completely destroyed in the year 689, shortly before the establishment of the neo-Babylonian Empire. Its destroyer was the Assyrian King Sennacherib.

The Assyrians must have been a terrible people, violent, wicked, tyrannical, without a trace of humor. Like all tyrants, they had a liking for abnormally large buildings. Even in antiquity they had a bad press. It was they who introduced the deportation of whole nations as a means of instilling terror into politics.

At the time of the Kings, in the year 932, the Jewish people had divided into two kingdoms: northern Israel, with Samaria, and southern Judah, with Jerusalem as the capital. Israel was conquered in 722 by the Assyrian King Shalmaneser, rather more than a hundred years before the Babylonian captivity. His successor Sargon captured Samaria. The method of transplanting a whole population was applied so successfully in this case that Israel, the second Jewish State, and its inhabitants who had been deported from Syria, vanished without a trace. That the other Jewish State, the kingdom of Judah, which was only once a great power, under David and Solomon, did not, in spite of its numerous wars with almost all its neighbors and in spite of its passionately heedless revolts against the powerful rulers of Nineveh and Babylon (follies against which the politically clear-sighted prophets warned again and again)—that it did not meet the same fate as its northern brother State of Israel, that this Judah survived all the ups and downs of history right up to the birth of Christ, is a phenomenon without parallel in history. It cannot be explained in terms of the usual processes of history.

The destruction that Sennacherib wrought was so thorough that the excavations have brought to light only slight traces of the Babylon of the ancient Empire. What we know about ancient Babylon is derived mainly from the library of King Ashurbanipal, who ruled in Nineveh in the year 700. This king was a lover and student of literature. The deciphering of the cuneiform tablets in his library has shed new light on the history of the origin of the epic of creation.

The Chaldeans, as the Babylonians are called in the Bible, had a story of creation based on Sumerian traditions that agrees in many important details with the Biblical version. As Europe was dependent on the Bible for its knowledge of the people of Israel until the archaeological discoveries of our own time, it saw the history of the Jews simply from the Biblical point of view. The archaeologists have shown that Hebrew civilization was deeply rooted in the spiritual world of western Asia, that the Jews shared in the traditions of Babylon and Sumer. The tendency of the Jews to desert Yahweh and serve foreign gods is therefore historically understandable. Where the Jews differed from their neighbors was that from the very beginning—and this is the fact that eludes explanation—they had the idea of an omnipotent God. The attempt to prove that the Jewish idea of God was based on a Bedouin tribal god and evolved into the conception of a transcendent God not only leaves out of account the evidence of the Bible itself but is bound to fail by the very nature of things. An idea of such loftiness as that of God as a being who is invisible and unknowable, a being whose qualities are not merely unknown but who cannot have qualities of the kind that earthly man and earthly things have, does not come to man in a process of gradually developing knowledge. However advanced man's knowledge is, it will never comprehend this divine being. Man cannot fathom the mystery of his existence by purely rational means. God has created man, and it is he who reveals the mystery of his existence to man. The attempts of early civilizations to explain the mystery of human existence mythologically satisfy us with their poetry. The attempts to explain the transcendence of human existence scientifically fail so completely to satisfy the most elementary intellectual requirements that the hypothesis of a *Creatio ex nihilo* is, by comparison, a simple and convincing affair.

It is perfectly in keeping with the imperfections of human nature that God reveals himself again and again. The Bible tells the story of the prophets, the men who were chosen to proclaim new revelations in historical time. Peter in his Pentecostal sermon even calls David a prophet. There has been nothing else quite like the prophets of Israel in human history. The prophets maintained the idea of God as creator of heaven and earth among the people of Israel, a people constantly threatened physically and spiritually throughout its history and constantly surrounded by dangers, until the time was fulfilled. The final dramatic climax in the history of the knowledge of God in the people of Israel came during the brilliant period of the second Babylon. The Babylon that was brought to light by the excavations of Koldewey is the Babylon of the Jewish exile.

The founder of the second kingdom of Babylon was King Nebuchadnezzar, with his father Nabopolassar. As Crown Prince, Nebuchadnezzar defeated the Pharaoh Necho, who had advanced to the Euphrates through Syria, in the famous Battle of Carchemish. It was this same Nebuchadnezzar who defeated King Jehoiakim of Judah and led the Jews into captivity in Babylon. It was not the whole Jewish people that was led away but only those we should now call the "upper ten thousand." The shrewd Babylonians left the vinedressers and peasants where they were. They had to meet the costs of occupation.

The Babylonians treated their enemies humanely. In a letter to Babylon Jeremiah wrote:

> "Thus saith the Lord of hosts, the God of Israel, unto all that are carried away captives, whom I have caused to be carried away from Jerusalem unto Babylon: Build ye houses, and dwell in them; and plant gardens, and eat the fruit of them. Take ye wives, and beget sons and daughters . . . and seek the peace of the city whither I have caused you to be carried away captives, and pray unto the Lord for it: for in the peace thereof shall ye have peace."

On express instructions from Nebuchadnezzar, Jeremiah was allowed to decide for himself whether to stay in Judah or go with the others to Babylon. He decided not to abandon the poor folk left behind in the occupied territory. He became adviser to Gedaliah, the Babylonian High Commissioner in Jerusalem. From Daniel we know that the young Jewish men served the King. Nehemiah was an official at the court in Susa. He occupied the position of royal cupbearer. King Jehoiakim was pardoned, but only after he had suffered imprisonment for thirty-seven years. From then on to the end of his life he drew a pension.

On entering the excavation site one first comes on the celebrated Gate of Ishtar. Ishtar was the goddess of fertility. She later fused with the Greek Demeter. The Gate of Ishtar is an extensive structure deeply embedded in the earth. I passed between high brick walls, fifty feet high, on which one can still make out the shapes of enormous bulls, dragons, and lions, which were distributed at regular intervals. The reliefs were composed of brilliantly colored glazed tiles. All this magnificent work was taken to Berlin fifty years ago. Part of the Gate of Ishtar was filled up by Nebuchadnezzar himself in order to build a processional avenue on a higher level. The splendid glazed reliefs of the sacred dragon, bull, and lion were carefully walled in; as a result they have been preserved in good condition. This is a case where piety has served the ends of scholarship.

Most of Nebuchadnezzar's processional route, which was paved with great stone slabs, has been laid bare. It is several miles in length. It begins at the Gate of Ishtar and ends at the Ziggurat, the tower on the summit of which stood the Temple of Marduk, the god of Babylon. In solemn processions the statues of the gods were carried by the priests along this road. The sacred route was lined with palaces on both sides, and the foundation walls that have been excavated still give one an idea of their grandeur. The road must have looked rather like the Champs Elysées in Paris, between the Louvre and the Arc de Triomphe.

Herodotus describes the Temple of Marduk on the Ziggurat. The tower had seven stories. The path that led up to the temple wound its way around the tower. On the garden terraces were seats where the visitor could rest. In the temple, alongside the image of the god, was a richly ornamented couch and a table of pure gold. Admission appears to have been free to all.

On the great feast days the Jews in exile in Babylon lined the edge of the sacred route while the foreign gods were borne past them in their golden splendor. They were not allowed to display their mourning amid the general jubilation. It was on these great festivals, while the whole people rejoiced, that the Jews went down to the silent, forsaken banks of the Euphrates and sat by the waters of Babylon and wept. It was a great affliction that Yahweh imposed on the Jews. It was also a great temptation. The foreign gods had given their followers the power to capture Yahweh's Holy City of Jerusalem, to destroy his Temple, and to lead the Chosen People captive. They had the power to make their people rich, free, and happy. They were older than Moses, older than Abraham. The Babylonians had a holy city, Ur, that was already a thousand years old in Abraham's time. The Babylonian epics of creation went back, like the account of creation in the book of Genesis, to the beginning of the world. We know how susceptible the Jewish people always were to foreign idols. Even after the miracles that God had performed for the children of Israel on their departure from Egypt, they made sacrifices to the golden calf on Mount Sinai. Even Aaron, the brother of Moses, a member of the intellectual elite, was not entirely innocent of this apostasy. Furthermore, the blatantly decadent civilization of the metropolis must have exerted a deep influence on such an intellectually receptive people as the Jews. Babylon had always been a center of learning, religion, and philosophy. To the religious temptation of worshipping the foreign gods there was added a no less dangerous intellectual temptation.

In Babylon, at the time of King Nebuchadnezzar, there took place the first encounter of two powers that have never since ceased to quarrel with one another. Here in Babylon the Jews met the advanced scholarship of the Chaldeans. Here for the first time faith and learning collided. The Babylonians were very advanced in mathematics. They were outstanding astronomers. The stars were, in their view, not moved by God at all. They moved according to rigid mathematical laws, some of which had been discovered by a Chaldean Galileo. These laws made it possible to calculate the movements of the stars. Chaldean astrology was far superior to modern astrology. We have every reason to assume that the Chaldeans had knowledge of ancient wisdom that has since been lost.

The centers where science was taught were open to young educated Jews. A few centuries later on the Jews possessed themselves of Greek learning with eagerness and success. In the Babylonian exile they withstood this temptation.

Somewhat south of the great processional route the palace of Belshazzar has been excavated. Belshazzar was the grandson of the great Nebuchadnezzar. I stood on the great smooth stone slabs in the hall where the famous banquet took place that is described in the fifth chapter of the Book of Daniel. Belshazzar had had the golden vessels from Solomon's Temple, which Nebuchadnezzar had stolen from Jerusalem, brought in to adorn the table. Letters of flame appeared on the wall of the banqueting hall. The King went pale. The rowdy company became silent. None of the Chaldean wise men was able to interpret the writing. Then Daniel was sent for. He, the powerless captive Jew, addressed the mighty King of Babylon in words that echoed something of the sound of Moses's wrath. Daniel held before Belshazzar the example of the great Nebuchadnezzar, who had humbled himself before God.

"And thou his son, O Belshazzar, hast not humbled thine heart, though thou knewest all this; but hast lifted thyself up against the Lord of heaven; and they have brought the vessels of his house before thee, and thou, and thy lords, thy wives, and thy concubines, have drunk wine in them; and thou hast praised the gods of silver, and gold, of brass, iron, wood, and stone, which see not, nor hear, nor know: and the God in whose hand thy breath is, and whose are all thy ways, hast thou not glorified: Then was the part of the hand sent from him; and this writing was written. And this is the writing that was written: MENE, MENE, TEKEL, UPHARSIN. This is the interpretation of the thing: MENE: God hath numbered thy kingdom and finished it. TEKEL: Thou art weighed in the balances, and art found wanting.

PERES: Thy kingdom is divided, and given to the Medes and Persians."

The King was magnanimous enough to reward the interpreter with a golden chain and to declare that he should be the third ruler in the kingdom. A single sentence follows in the Bible: "In that night was Belshazzar the King of the Chaldeans slain."

Not much later Cyrus the Great occupied Babylon. Cyrus strode along the processional route to the temple of the god Marduk and there grasped the god's hands. The people were convinced that Marduk himself had decided that Cyrus should be King of Babylon.

The Persians were not Assyrians. The aristocratic Iranian civilization was more humane even than the Babylonian. Cyrus sent the deported people back to their own country. He even gave orders for the sacred vessels from Solomon's Temple to be returned to Jerusalem. There they remained until the Roman commander Titus destroyed Jerusalem in A.D. 70. Some of the vessels are reproduced on his triumphal arch in the Forum in Rome. We therefore know what Solomon's seven-branched candlesticks looked like.

Since the time of Titus no orthodox Jew has gone through the triumphal arch of the man who destroyed Jerusalem. The vessels that were taken to Rome from the Temple in Jerusalem did not disappear until Rome was plundered by the Vandals. Possibly the Coptic Church still possesses some of these treasures. It is said that until recently some of King Herod's treasures, including the last surviving vessels from Solomon's Temple, were kept in the vaults of the Church of the Holy Sepulcher in Jerusalem. It is not known where these objects are today.

The magnanimity of the Persian King Cyrus did not alter the fact that for centuries the State of Judah was unable to recover from the effects of Nebuchadnezzar's conquest. The Temple as reconstructed under Zerubbabel fell far short of the splendor of Solomon's Temple. As in every age, the older people spoke sadly of the brilliance of the past.

Exile forced the Jews to recollect their real task in the world. Only in their Babylonian captivity, when they had lost home, possessions, fatherland, and the Holy Temple, did the Jews finally take a firm hold on that which it was their historic mission to transmit to the whole of civilized humanity—their traditional faith in the one omnipotent God. The only thing they had been able to take with them into exile was this faith and the Law of Moses. They were not able to observe their festivals. They were not able to make sacrifices. Yahweh only accepts the gifts of the Promised Land. It was at this period that the Sabbath acquired for the Jews the significance it has had for them ever since. They became the "people of the Book," as Mohammed called them. The beginnings of the Talmud, the great theological commentary on the Old Testament, also go back to this period.

By the waters of Babylon one of the great battles in the history of the human spirit was fought out. Though deprived of their homes, property, and freedom, even in disaster the exiled Jews did not abandon the hope that the old prophecies would be fulfilled. While Babylon became the inheritance of the hedgehog and turned into a swamp, the human race entered into the inheritance of this hope.

The Way to Jerusalem

Snow had fallen during the night. It was the end of November. The Djebel Kasyun, Abraham's mountain on the northern border of Damascus, was sparkling in the morning sun. The day, the incomparable day on which I was to see Jerusalem, had come.

On my departure from Damascus it was uncertain whether I would reach my destination. There was and is war in Palestine. The armistice was in constant danger. Only a few days previously there had been a serious incident on the United Nations demarcation line.

The front runs through Jerusalem. The ancient Jerusalem, which is enclosed by the city wall of the Sultan Suleiman, and which contains Golgotha and the Holy Sepulcher, is in Arab hands. The modern part of the city is in Israeli hands. The soldiers of the Arab Legion stand on the western city wall, looking out into the no man's land that separates them from their enemies.

It was quite difficult to get the Jordan visa, though I did not feel that this was due to a lack of hospitality. A foreigner who wants to go to Jerusalem from Damascus by land has to travel through the Arab base. Even if he is a pilgrim, he cannot prove that he is not interested in military matters. The passions of the belligerents run high. On both sides there is sinister, pitiless hatred. If there had been a sudden change in the situation I might easily not have been allowed to cross the frontier, in spite of my visa.

We drove through the gardens, palm groves, and fields of the oasis of Damascus. Then the desert began. The well-asphalted road links Damascus, the capital of Syria, with Amman, the ancient Philadelphia, capital of the Hashemite Kingdom of Jordan.

Even at the Syrian frontier the examination was thorough, albeit polite. At the Jordan frontier post I went into the building where the passports are inspected. A stout, friendly man, the sergeant type, was sitting in the office, in the uniform of the Arab Legion built up by the Englishman Glubb Pasha. Every sergeant in every army in the world enjoys being called "Captain." The fat, friendly man jumped up and greeted me with a cordial "Morning, sir!" He really was in fact a captain, though usually addressed as a sergeant. He offered me a cup of mocha. I got my stamp.

Before we got to Amman, we passed one of the many camps where the Arab refugees live. The United Nations provides four dollars apiece per month for their upkeep. The refugees' quarters are made of the tin of empty gasoline containers, the outer shell of what constitutes the wealth of the Near East.

Amman is situated in a deep valley. Alongside the Roman amphitheater of the ancient city of Philadelphia skyscrapers stand on the edge of the desert. On the mountain slopes the villas of the well-to-do alternate with caves where the poor dwell as in the Stone Age. Hundreds of cars are parked on the main road, mostly large American cars. Newspaper boys, street vendors, porters, and those Oriental types who always have time to praise the joys of being alive jostle with horses, donkeys, and camels in front of the cafés. The noise is indescribable, but it is a cheerful, exuberant noise. It seems as if these ancient people have no nerves. Gradually even the visitor from the West forgets he has any nerves. The car I came by had vanished, with its driver. I had no idea whether and how the journey would continue. In my pocket I had a scrap of paper with a few lines in Arabic, which I could not read. I had time, therefore, to look at the narrow, sharp-featured faces of the Bedouins who were leading their camels up the street. I wondered whether it would be possible for a Bedouin to get a neurosis. What an absolutely ridiculous idea!

At the end of an hour a friendly man I had never seen before tapped me on the shoulder and pushed me into a car. It appeared that we had had to wait until there were seven paying passengers. The journey is worth while only if every seat in the car is taken. One of the Bedouins in the car had a tiny lamb on his lap. If I had had to wait any longer, I might have had to make the whole journey through the Jordan Valley in the dark. I was lucky.

Outside Amman there began the painfully familiar sight of the base with armed sentries, concrete bunkers on the arterial road, barbed wire, supply depots, field kitchens, and soldiers hanging around. Many men; only one or two women.

As the car climbed out of the valley of Amman, a chain of hills appeared on the horizon: the hills of Moab, the main defense line of the Arabs east of Jordan and the hills from which Moses glimpsed the Promised Land before he died.

Jerusalem is a very old city. In Ezekiel, Chapter 16, verse 3, the Lord says of Jerusalem, "Thy father was an Amorite, and thy mother an Hittite." The earliest historical information we have of Jerusalem goes back two hundred years before its conquest by the Jews. This reference is to be found in the letters that Abdi-Hiba, a princely vassal of the Pharaoh Amenhotep IV who resided in Jerusalem, sent to the Egyptian court. Amenhotep IV, or Ikhnaton, was the founder of sun worship in Egypt. His wife was Queen Nefertiti. These famous letters were discovered in the archives of the Pharaoh in Tell el-Amarna, and are therefore known as the Amarna letters. They were written in cuneiform script in the Babylonian language at the turn of the fifteenth and fourteenth centuries B.C. In these letters Abdi-Hiba continuously begged for help against the enemies of the Pharaoh. It does not appear to have been granted. The first half of the name Abdi-Hiba is the Semitic word for slave, and the second half is the name of a Hittite deity. There are good reasons to suppose that Abdi-Hiba was the representative of a Hittite aristocracy that was then ruling in central Palestine. King David's "mighty men" included two Hittites. The statement contained in Ezekiel 16, 3, may be taken as literally true.

Even at the time of Abdi-Hiba, Jerusalem was already an ancient city. In the Amarna letters Jerusalem is called Urusalim. The name is half Sumerian, half Semitic. It means "the city of peace." When the Jews came into the country, Jerusalem was a fortress of the Jebusites, who were Semites.

The conquest of Canaan by the Jews was a process that extended over more than two hundred years. It was not a purely military conquest. For long periods the Jews lived comparatively calmly among the previous inhabitants, even outnumbering them. It was only after the capture of Jerusalem by King David that the Jews took full control. King Solomon built the Temple in Jerusalem. The Ark, which had been borne so long through the desert, achieved a final resting place. Beside the Temple, Solomon built his magnificent palace. Under him the city flourished. It was the period in which the Jews who had come to Canaan as wanderers adopted the superior Phoenician culture.

Jerusalem has been captured countless times in the course of its history, and destroyed many times. Its golden ages were brief, its periods of distress long and terrible.

Today the city is sacred to three world religions. Since its conquest by David and the building of Solomon's Temple, Jerusalem has been the Holy City of the Jews. It will always remain so. Since the Messiah was crucified on Golgotha Jerusalem has been sacred to Christianity. Since its conquest by Islam and the building of the Dome of the

Rock Jerusalem has been a Holy City of the Mohammedans, second only to Mecca.

To reach the ridge of the hills of Moab, the road only has to rise a few hundred feet. Then it descends again into the Jordan Valley. It follows the course of a small winding river. Willows and beech grow by the leaping waters of this little river. Despite the lateness of the year, they are green. The slopes are bare and stony, and the whole scene is reminiscent of the valleys that lead down from the crest of the Alps. By the roadside there is a big sign with the words "Sea Level." From this point on one feels as if the road is plunging down relentlessly into the depths of the earth. Within half an hour it is hot in the car and we open the windows. The air that streams in is warm. Willows and beech vanish. Palms make their appearance. This is the only spot on earth where an inhabited countryside lies twelve hundred feet below sea level.

The car rounds a spur of the mountain, and the Jordan Valley extends before my eyes. On the left is the dark blue shining surface of the Dead Sea.

Where the Jordan flows into the Dead Sea mountains press down on both its banks. The Dead Sea is 46 by 10 miles—as big as the Lake of Geneva. In the steep ravines on the west bank of the Dead Sea lies Mar Saba, a monastery where St. Sabas lived and died. His remains were taken to Venice by a Venetian who was anxious to enhance the reputation of his native city. There they rest beside the mortal remains of the apostle Mark, which were brought to Venice from Alexandria. In the Monastery of St. Sabas the story of the Indian Prince Josaphat was recorded. It was here that St. John of Damascus—Chrysorrhoas—died and was buried.

We were approaching the Jordan, a narrow river whose course is accompanied by gardens, fields, and palm groves. On the other bank there is a little country town. Behind it the western edge of the Jordan Valley rises up steeply. And behind these bare, wild hills lies Jerusalem.

The sun was about to set behind the hills. The jagged rocks of the eastern slopes were beginning to be colored with a first glow of evening. While I was still absorbed in the scene before me my friendly Syrian neighbor gave me a nudge. He appeared to be well versed in the Bible. He pointed to the little town and said with a smile, "Jericho!"

Nothing can be more moving than when a name that has occupied one's imagination since boyhood suddenly becomes a geographical reality. What a splendid story the Bible tells about Joshua's capture of the city! For six days the Jews paced around the impregnable walls once a day, the armed men in front followed by the priests with trumpets, and these in their turn by the Ark of the Covenant, with the people all behind. From the walls the enemy scoffed at this incredible procession. On the seventh day the procession went around the city seven times. Then the trumpets were blown. The people raised a war cry and the walls of Jericho fell down.

Although it is one of the earliest recorded musical events in the history of the world, Joshua's trumpet recital took place in a late period in the history of Jericho. During the excavation some of the stones of the walls that collapsed before Joshua's eyes have come to light.

Jericho is the oldest city in the world. Archaeology has established that this site has been inhabited without interruption from the tenth millennium B.C.

We stopped at the bridge. After the soldiers who guard the bridge had laboriously examined our papers we drove on across the Jordan. At this time of the year the river does not have much water, but the current was still quite rapid. Not far from this bridge is the spot where Jesus was baptized by John. During our short stop in Jericho the Arab Legionaries came out of the base movie where they had been enjoying the sight of Marilyn Monroe. We drove on into the hills again.

On the constantly winding road from which we had repeated glimpses of the Jordan Valley, we climbed as quickly as the sun set. The rocky walls of the east bank had turned into a glowing red ribbon. The surface of the lake had sunk into a deep black. Half an hour later the road reached the crest of the hills, south of the Mount of Olives.

Before me lay Jerusalem. From this point it is possible to see the whole of it as in a picture. It makes a simple and sublime impression. It looks just like its representation in early medieval paintings. Situated on a rocky plateau surrounded by deep valleys with steep gray slopes, enclosed by a tremendous city wall, intercepted by great gates, crowded with palaces and houses, churches with mighty cupolas, towers and minarets, a human achievement rising out of a wild, riven landscape of hills, silhouetted against the horizon by the last rays of the setting sun, the ancient Holy City towers up to the sky.

However much this picture may have changed in the course of history, even as a mere heap of ruins Jerusalem has never, since King David's time, ceased to be Mount Zion on its rocky eminence—Mount Zion, where, Isaiah says, is the dwelling place of the Lord. As one gazes at it it is quite easy to imagine that this earthly city is the image of a heavenly Jerusalem.

For many, many centuries pilgrims have stood moved in their hearts by this stirring sight after the hardships of their journey to the Holy Land. As the beauty of the earthly Jerusalem rose up from their memories in their final hour, some devout souls must have cherished the hope of now seeing the beauty of the heavenly Jerusalem.

Later, when I flew back, I saw Jerusalem again as the eagles have always seen it. From this point of view Jerusalem is a menacing fortress in a riven moonlit landscape of sublime solitude—a work of man in the midst of creation. One can imagine no more fitting setting for the events that brought about the turning point of history two thousand years ago and that will not cease to influence the world as long as it endures.

The journey closes in the dusk at the Gate of Damascus, the north gate of the city wall of Jerusalem. Immediately alongside the entrance to the gate, the barbed wire begins.

The Holy Places

The following morning I entered the city of Jerusalem by the Gate of Damascus. The day was dull and cold, and it was raining. The lanes are dark and narrow. The houses are built of stone, a stone of a pleasant dark gray. Here and there the road is spanned by a stone arch. Artisans and tradesmen sit under the arches. The streets are frequently interrupted by flights of steps. That is why there are no cars within the city wall. One has the sense of being carried back many centuries into the past.

At present there is not a single Jew in the whole of old Jerusalem. This has occurred several times before. After Titus's capture of the city and also after Hadrian captured it, Jews were forbidden to enter it on pain of death.

After the final reconquest of Jerusalem by the Arabs at the close of the Crusades, in 1291, the Christians were very soon allowed access to the Holy Places. Only the Roman Patriarchate abolished by the Arabs was not allowed again. From 1291 on, the Roman Patriarch of Jerusalem resided for five hundred years in Rome. In 1847 he was reinstated in Jerusalem. The office of Patriarch is associated with that of Guardian of the Holy Land. It is held by the head of the Franciscans of Syria, Palestine, and Egypt. The Franciscans are the only order that has been working in the Holy Places uninterruptedly since the Crusades.

As I walked thoughtfully along the streets, amid tradesmen, donkeys, and soldiers, Bedouins and Armenians, Abyssinian and Greek monks, I saw a nun and a young girl kneeling at a corner of the road. They were praying in front of a marble tablet inscribed with the words:

HIC CRUX AD SYMONEM CYRENAEUM IMPONITUR

It was on this spot that the Cross was laid on Simon of Cyrene. It is the fifth Station of the Cross, the Way of Sorrows that ends at the Church of the Holy Sepulcher.

Since the days of Jesus, Jerusalem has been captured ten times and completely destroyed five times. During the siege to which it was subjected by Titus in A.D. 70 the city and the Temple went up in flames. Sixty years afterwards, Hadrian founded on the ruins a new city that he called Aelia Capitolina, a blending of his own name, Aelius, with that of the god Jupiter Capitolinus. A terrace was built above the Holy Sepulcher and on this terrace was built a Temple of Venus.

Shortly after this, however, the city was completely destroyed again, during the suppression of the rising of Bar Cocheba, whom Rabbi Akiba had declared to be the Messiah. Thereafter the story of Jerusalem sinks into impenetrable darkness for two centuries.

Then the Empress Helena came to Palestine. She built churches in all the places connected with the life and death of Jesus. The Holy Sepulcher was rediscovered. Eusebius of Caesarea, the Church historian, who was living at that time, wrote with the natural skepticism of the scholar that the Holy Sepulcher was discovered "contrary to all expectation." This statement initiated the scholarly dispute concerning the authenticity of the Holy Sepulcher that has never been settled.

The idea that the only surviving witness of the death of Jesus, Ahasuerus, the Wandering Jew, appeared to the Empress Helena in a dream and showed her the site of the tomb is no less ingenious than the suggestion of the Hon. Rev. George Finlay that it must have been an easy matter for the Emperor Constantine to ascertain the site of the tomb from the lists of the Roman census. The tomb had been the private property of Joseph of Arimathea. In its survey and taxation of land the Roman revenue department was quite modern. Ahasuerus cannot, however, be adduced as archaeological evidence, and Suetonius and Tacitus assure us that the Roman census lists were destroyed during the fire that occurred in Rome under Nero and Vespasian.

In the year 614 Jerusalem was destroyed by the Persian King Khosrau II; in 637 it was captured by the Caliph Omar; in 1072, by the Seljuks; in 1099, by the Crusaders. In 1187 the Sultan Saladin captured it from the Franks again. In 1617 it fell into the hands of the Osman Turks. In 1917 the British army entered Jerusalem. In our own time the Arabs have taken it from the Israelis. Even this list of horrors does not include all the disasters that have befallen the city since the death of Jesus. According to the archaeologists, the city of Jerusalem in which Jesus lived lies under at least sixty-five feet of rubble.

Now, however, Jerusalem is built on a rocky hilltop cleft by gullies. It is true that these gullies have occasionally been filled with debris in the wake of military events, but some of the hilltops rise up out of the masses of rubble. These rocky hilltops are historically important sites, but a few archaeological points still remain to be decided.

We know the site of David's fortress. We know where Solomon's Temple stood. We know that the Church of the Holy Sepulcher stands on the site on which the Emperor

Constantine built the first basilica. We even know what this basilica looked like. It has been reconstructed by the archaeologists. The rotunda adjoining the nave, in which the Chapel of the Holy Sepulcher stands, has been copied in St. Michael's, Fulda (Germany). Even now the archaeologists and historians are overwhelmingly of the opinion that the rock on which the Church of the Holy Sepulcher stands is, in fact, Golgotha.

Golgotha lay "outside the wall, near the city." The archaeological problem is whether the wall built by Nehemiah after the Babylonian captivity in the Roman period was still the city wall. The course of Nehemiah's wall is known. It runs south of Golgotha. If Nehemiah's wall was still the city wall in Roman times the rock below the roof of the Church of the Holy Sepulcher is the historical Golgotha.

Archaeological studies of Jerusalem fill whole libraries. No subject is more exciting or more important. Some points remain unsettled, however, and it would be wrong to dismiss as pious deception beliefs that the archaeologists have so far been unable to confirm. The understanding of symbols is beyond the ability and competence of science. It is clear from pilgrims' reports that the Via Dolorosa has changed several times in the course of the centuries. But the Passion took place in Jerusalem. One and a half thousand years of worship are a historical fact. There is no reason to suppose that worship is less pleasing to God than scientific controversies. An excellent nineteenth-century archaeologist said: "In Jerusalem everything is historical."

In its present shape the Church of the Holy Sepulcher derives from the period of the Crusades. Since that time it has often been damaged. It is constantly threatened by earthquakes. In 1808 it was damaged by a serious fire. The actual Church of the Holy Sepulcher lies at the center of the extensive site, surrounded by a garland of chapels all of which have associations with the Gospel story. One of the chapels is built on the rock of Golgotha. The cells of various monastic orders, the offices of the various Christian denominations, the residence of the Greek Orthodox Patriarch, and a number of other chapels, including that of the Finding of the Holy Cross, are grouped around the central building. All told, there are about a hundred buildings. All the Christian denominations are united under the roof of the Church of the Holy Sepulcher. This is the one place in the world where they are not divided. The squabbles that have broken out among them from time to time need not be taken too seriously. The motive behind them was an exaggerated sense of piety. It is true, however, that these disputes have often made Christians the laughingstock of the Moslems.

It is impossible to survey the whole of the church from any one point. The only open space is in front of the south portal through which one enters the church. The impression made by the façade of gray stones is that of an early Romanesque church. At the entrance one has to pay tribute to the Sultan Saladin. Since the end of the Crusades the guardianship of the Church of the Holy Sepulcher has been a privilege transmitted from father to son in a Moslem family.

In the great anteroom of the church proper lies the stone on which Joseph of Arimathea and Nicodemus anointed the body of Jesus and wrapped it in linen cloths. In the fifteenth century the stone belonged to the Copts, in the sixteenth to the Georgians. Later on it came under the protection of the Greek Orthodox Church.

Following the last five Stations of the Cross I turned right, climbed up about twenty steps, and came into a double chapel. The first encloses the site where Jesus was nailed to the Cross. The second is built on the rock of Golgotha. A hole in the rock is the hole in which the Cross was fixed.

Under the Chapel of Golgotha lies, hewn into the rock, a cave in which, according to tradition, Adam was buried. When the Savior's blood flowed down onto Adam's corpse through a chink in the rock, he rose from the dead: "And the graves were opened, and many bodies arose out of them, bodies of holy men gone to their rest: who, after his rising again, left their graves and went into the holy city, where they were seen by many."

The interior of the Church of the Holy Sepulcher is gloomy. As a protection against possible bombardment, the arches and walls are shored up with powerful wooden supports. Under the cupola of the church is a marble chapel with a small anteroom, the Chapel of the Angels. It contains the stone the angels rolled away from the entrance to the tomb. Behind it lies the Holy Sepulcher. The doorway is low. To enter one must bow the head. The walls are of marble. Incense fills the room. Forty-three lamps hang from the ceiling. Members of every Christian denomination tarry in adoration before the stone on which the Savior's body lay in the grave. Monks and nuns kneel before it or lie prostrate on the ground absorbed in prayer. No place in the world has survived in human consciousness so long and so continuously; in no place on earth have so many prayers met as here at the fourteenth and final Station of Christ's Way of Sorrows.

While his body was lying here he descended to the realm of the dead. And it was here that he rose from the dead. Even the disciples were not prepared to believe in the miracle. Their unbelief is the origin of an ancient custom. When on the Day of the Resurrection the priests cry "*Christos aneste*" to the faithful gathered round the Sepulcher, the congregation replies: "*Alethos aneste.*"

"Christ is risen! Truly, he is risen!"

At the foot of the Mount of Olives, on the other side of the Kedron Valley, lies the Garden of Gethsemane, surrounded by a wall, and beside it a church and a Franciscan monastery. We know from pilgrims' reports that Gethsemane was assumed to lie here even in the fourth century, and the site corresponds to the description given in the Bible.

Jerusalem can be seen from the Garden of Gethsemane. Seen from this level, it seems to tower up menacingly into the sky. In Jesus's time the Temple rose up above the city wall. Through the Golden Gate Jesus had entered the city on Palm Sunday to the cries of the cheering crowd. They cried: "Blessed is the king who comes in the name of the Lord." The Jews still believed that the kingdom that Jesus would establish was a kingdom of earthly power and glory. Every year until the eighth century the Greek Patriarch of Jerusalem used to enter the city through the Golden Gate on a she-ass. In the year 810 it was walled up by the Arabs. They had an old prophecy that a Christian conqueror would enter the Holy City on a Friday through this Golden Gate. These simple souls thought they could arrest the course of history by building a brick wall.

There was no need for the disciples to be surprised by the fact that Jesus, who was being sought for by the High Priest's police, stayed so close to Jerusalem. Incredible masses of people must have crowded into Jerusalem for the Passover. A Roman governor once had the paschal lambs counted. According to Josephus they numbered 270,000.

There are eight olive trees in the Garden of Gethsemane, their vast old trunks furrowed by deep clefts and crevices. They have probably often been struck by lightning. They look like weather-beaten rocks, except that fresh shoots with smooth, blue-green lanceolate leaves still spring out of the wood. The trees are extraordinarily old. The girth of the oldest of them is greater than that of the famous historic olive tree of Plato on the road from Eleusis to Athens. It is therefore possible that this gray old tree witnessed the events of that night in which Jesus succumbed to the most human of his temptations, anguish.

It takes about two hours to get to Bethlehem from Jerusalem. Bethlehem is the town where the era in which we are still living began. The name "Bethlehem," which is very old, means "the place of bread." For thousands of years the name has survived unchanged. When Jesus said of himself that he was the "bread of life" his disciples may have been reminded of his birthplace. It was in Bethlehem that the love story of Ruth and Boaz, which is recorded so enchantingly in the Book of Ruth, took place. Ruth's and Boaz's son Obed was the grandfather of King David. Since Joseph was of David's clan, Bethlehem was the place where he had to go for the census enjoined by the Emperor Augustus. Thus it came about that Jesus was born while Mary and Joseph were away from home.

Bethlehem is an unassuming little country town. Since the road from Jerusalem to Bethlehem runs through Israel, the Jordan authorities have built a by-pass. Today, therefore, one approaches the town from the east, from the valley.

Bethlehem is a pleasant little town, spread out over a projecting ridge whose gentle slopes are planted with gardens and olive groves. Thanks to the pilgrims who come here from all parts of the world, the town is comfortably affluent. Its inhabitants are peasants and shepherds.

The Emperor Constantine had a magnificent church built in the year 330 over the grotto where Jesus was born. In spite of the fact that Bethlehem has been destroyed several times, the church has survived. It is one of the oldest in Christendom. In the course of the centuries numerous

buildings have been added to Constantine's basilica. It is
therefore impossible to make out the original outward
shape of the church today. The interior has survived very
largely in its original form. The question that fascinates
the minds of scholars and the heart of the pilgrim is
whether this is in fact the birthplace of Jesus. It is not so
complex as similar questions in Jerusalem. It is true that
there is no mention of a grotto in the Gospels. Luke says
that Mary laid the child in a manger because there was no
room for them in the inn. It is quite possible that this manger was in a grotto. There are many such caves around
Bethlehem. In sudden storms the shepherds take shelter in
them with their sheep and goats. Today these caves are inhabited by Arab refugees. We owe the first reference to
the grotto of the Nativity to Justin the Martyr, who mentioned it in the year 155. Ordinarily 150 years can easily
be bridged by a purely oral tradition. It is only a matter of
three generations. Around 250 Origen discussed the question of the authenticity of the site in great detail. He said
that even the enemies of the Faith admitted that this was
the grotto of the Nativity. St. Jerome lived in Bethlehem
from 386 until his death in 420. He translated the Bible into
Latin. In the well-known engraving by Dürer a lion lies
at the saint's feet. There has never been such a friendly-
looking lion as the amiable cell companion of St. Jerome.
The early Father assures us that the site is historically authentic. Anyway, this tradition is one of the oldest in Christian history.

In the year 614 the Persian King Khosrau II laid waste
the whole of Palestine. The Church of the Holy Sepulcher,
in Jerusalem, went up in flames. Khosrau came to Bethlehem to destroy the Church of the Nativity too. In a mosaic
on the outer wall of the church depicting the Adoration of
the Wise Men from the East, Khosrau discovered that the

Magi were dressed in Persian garments. He left the church unscathed.

In front of the Church of the Nativity there is a wide, open square paved with stone slabs. On the longer side fortresslike walls tower up into the sky. The narrow side is taken up by the façade of the covered portico of the church. Except for a low door, the portals have been bricked in. The longitudinal axis of the church runs from west to east.

The Church of the Nativity is the common property of the Greek, Armenian, and Latin Churches. On its north side there is a Latin church dedicated to St. Catherine and connected with a Franciscan monastery. On the south side the church is adjoined by the Armenian and Greek monasteries.

The interior of the Church of the Nativity is beautifully simple. The ground plan is a cross. The longitudinal body has five naves. The central nave is lined by two rows of ancient pillars with Corinthian capitals. There are traces of medieval paintings on the pillars. High up, on the walls above the pillars, some mosaics from the twelfth century have survived, on which the apostles are depicted without halos. The grotto of the Nativity lies underneath the richly decorated altar. Two flights of steps on the left and right of the altar lead through marble doors down to the cave where Jesus Christ saw the darkness of the world.

The actual grotto is small and low. The walls and floors have been lined with marble. In a niche, an altar has been erected on the site of the Nativity, beneath which a silver star has been set in the floor with an inscription running around it:

HIC DE VIRGINE MARIA JESUS CHRISTUS NATUS EST

As in the Chapel of the Holy Sepulcher, precious lamps hang from the ceiling, the various Christian denominations

haring in their upkeep. Two nuns were kneeling in front
f the silver star and beside them a Bedouin, also praying.

From the grotto of the Nativity there is a passage lead-
ng westward and at the end of it an excavation in the rock
rom which a spring of water rose for the use of the Holy
amily. Since the fifteenth century it has been said that the
tar that led the Wise Men from the East fell into this
pring but can be seen only by virgins. Whatever the skep-
ics may say, for five hundred years no devout virgin has
ooked into the spring without seeing the star.

The passage then turns westward to the place where the
ngel of the Lord appeared to Joseph in a dream and said,
Rise up, take with thee the child and his mother, and flee
o Egypt." There is something touching about the simple
vay in which every single event mentioned in the Bible has
een assigned its place in the grotto.

In another of the passages lies the tomb of St. Jerome and
ehind it the cell where, guarded by his lion, he translated
ne Bible and wrote his many letters. The whole subter-
nean area lies under the choir.

From the churchyard one looks down into the valley
vhere the birth of the Savior was proclaimed to the shep-
erds.

From the time of the Emperor Constantine building has
een continuous in Jerusalem. Through all the centuries
Christians have never ceased building churches, monas-
ries, hospices, and inns in this city. At the time of
ne Crusades fortifications were built too. Again and again
ne buildings have fallen prey to destruction. In some
laces a new church has been built several times in succes-
on on the same site, on the ruins of the old one.

In a city that is sacred to so many religions, archaeologists
e confronted with a difficult problem. They are only

rarely allowed to dig where they want to. On one site, how
ever, they have made an excavation which, simple thoug
it may appear amid the splendor and grandeur of the build
ings of Jerusalem, is remarkable and exciting. It is the stair
way leading down to the Pool of Bethesda, which is men
tioned in the fifth chapter of St. John's Gospel:

"After this came a Jewish feast, for which Jesus went up t
Jerusalem. There is a pool in Jerusalem at the Sheep Gate
called in Hebrew Bethesda, with five porches, under which
multitude of diseased folk used to lie, the blind, the lame, th
disabled, waiting for a disturbance of the water. From tim
to time, an angel of the Lord came down upon the pool, an
the water was stirred up; and the first man who stepped int
the pool after the stirring of the water recovered from what
ever infirmity it was that oppressed him. There was one ma
there who had been disabled for thirty-eight years. Jesu
saw him lying there, and knew that he had waited a lon
time. Hast thou a mind, he asked, to recover thy strength
Sir, said the cripple, I have no one to let me down into th
pool when the water is stirred; and while I am on my way
somebody else steps down before me. Jesus said to him, Ris
up, take up thy bed, and walk. And all at once the man re
covered his strength, and took up his bed, and walked.

It is this pool and the steps leading down to it that have bee
excavated. As was to be expected, the pool lies 65 feet be
low the surface of the modern city. Difficult though it
to find a spot in Jerusalem that can be regarded as histor
cally authentic, there is no doubt about it in this case. Her
is a spot where the Gospel narrative, tradition, and archae
ology are really at one.

Three steps of the flight leading to the Pool of Bethesd
are made of mortar mixed with large, smooth pebble
These three steps certainly form part of the original fligh
of steps that led down to the Pool of Bethesda in Jesus

time. The three ancient steps, shining in the rain, polished over a very long period by thousands of feet, were trod by Jesus Christ, the Son of God.

Haram es-Sherif

When Abdi-Hiba, the prince of Urusalim, wrote his courteous letters to the mighty pharaoh Amenhotep IV in Tell el-Amarna, the Jews were in the Nile delta in the land of Goshen. This was the period when the ancient privileges of the Jews from the time of Joseph and his brethren were slowly falling into oblivion. The slavery from which Moses freed the people of Israel had begun again.

Today, Tell el-Amarna is a place of ruins and jackals like Babylon, while Jerusalem is as alive, as fascinating, as passionately contested as ever. In the struggle between the Arabs and Israelis that has broken out in recent years what is at issue is not the political ownership of some place or other. It is still the Holy City that is the object of the dispute.

Just as the Jews, embedded in the spiritual world of western Asia, with its countless traditions, adopted a wealth of elements from the Sumerian, Egyptian, Babylonian, and Phoenician civilizations, so Islam, which arose in the Arabian Desert toward the end of the sixth century, was forced to come to terms with the Greek, Jewish, and Christian worlds. This new world religion encountered civilizations that were no longer primitive magical worlds like the civilizations the Jews had come up against. The Jews came to Syria eighteen centuries earlier than Islam. What Islam encountered when it conquered the Near East was a world of late, mature, enlightened civilizations. This may be one of the reasons for this religion's practical realism. Mohammed took the metaphysical mysteries, without which no religion can win men's hearts and minds, from the Jewish and Christian traditions.

The cry with which the muezzin summons the faithful to prayer from the top of the minarets begins with the formula *"Allah akbar!"* (The prophet's first muezzin was a Negro, incidentally—a happy circumstance that enriched Islam with an element of tolerance.) *"Allah akbar!"* does not mean, as it is usually rendered, "Allah is great." It means "Allah is greater." Whatever you may think—Allah is greater. Whatever your eyes may see of the splendor and glory of the world—Allah is greater. However you may conceive him—Allah is greater.

Mohammed understood the sublimity of the Jewish conception of God. He tried to emulate it with his own idea of God. In his time there was a large and rich Jewish colony in Medina, which became his refuge after his flight from Mecca. Mohammed therefore had opportunity to become acquainted with the Old Testament. He based his teaching on the Jewish tradition of the patriarch Abraham and King David. From the New Testament he adopted John the Baptist and Jesus as prophets. Near the Golden Gate of Jerusalem a pillar has been built into the city wall from which, according to Moslem belief, at the Last Judgment a rope will be stretched to the summit of the Mount of Olives. Jesus will sit on the pillar and Mohammed on the Mount of Olives. Those who have risen from the dead will have to walk along the rope. Protected by angels, the just will hasten along it with ease while sinners will fall into the abyss of hell. The earliest reference to this kind of "bridge of decision" is found in the ancient Persian religion.

The city of Jerusalem was so fascinating to the Bedouins of the seventh century that Mohammed ordered the faithful to turn their faces to Jerusalem when they prayed. It was only later that he changed his mind and decided to make Mecca the place to which the faithful were to turn. During the dispute among his first feudal followers the point was reached when the Caliph of Damascus was refused admission to the Holy City of Mecca. At that period the Omayyads very nearly made Jerusalem the headquarters of Islam.

The great shrine of Islam in Jerusalem is the Dome of the Rock. It stands on the Haram es-Sherif, the "place of the Temple." The Haram es-Sherif is a holy place of the Mohammedans in the southeast corner of old Jerusalem. To enter this place special permission has to be obtained from the religious authorities. On high festivals only faithful Moslems are allowed in. The Haram es-Sherif is a large open square, confined in the south and east by the city wall of the Sultan Suleiman and surrounded on its northern and western sides by buildings and colonnades. From north to south it measures some 325 yards, and from east to west about 220 yards. In the center, on a raised stone platform that is approached by a broad flight of steps, stands the Dome of the Rock. It is surmounted by a tremendous cupola. Up to the height of the windows its exterior is lined with slabs of marble, and from that point with porcelain tiles in the Persian style. The brilliant colors of the tiles, blue and white, and green and white at the corners, give the building a festive air. The Sultan Suleiman, who supplied the Dome of the Rock with this embellishment, did honor to his title: "the Magnificent."

The Moslems have reason to be proud of the beauty of the Dome of the Rock, which is second only in importance to the Kaaba built by Abraham in Mecca. The Dome of the Rock stands on the site from which Solomon's gilded Temple radiated its splendor.

On the south side of the square stands a second great

mosque, the Mesjid al-Aqsa. The Golden Gate lies roughly
in the middle of the eastern wall, from which the Mount
of Olives may be seen. To the south stands the stump of
the pillar of the Last Judgment.

The Dome of the Rock was built about 700. It is sometimes called the Mosque of Omar. Omar, the conqueror of
Jerusalem, did not build it. It was built by Abd-al-Malik,
the "father of Kings," Caliph of Baghdad. The influence
of the Hagia Sophia on the construction of this edifice is
unmistakable. Its furnishings also evince the Byzantine
style. About this period the Arabs were still dependent on
Greek architects in buildings of these dimensions.

The ground plan of the Dome of the Rock is a regular
octagon. The interior is of great splendor. A high gallery
supported by pillars runs around the whole structure. The
pillars are linked by a wrought-iron railing, made by the
French in the twelfth century. When they took Jerusalem
the Crusaders believed that the Dome of the Rock was the
ancient Temple of Solomon. At the time of the Latin Kingdom of Jerusalem the Dome of the Rock was transformed
into a *templum Domini*, a temple of the Lord. The Knights
Templar built churches in London, Laon, and Metz on the
model of this Arab mosque. The glass windows of the
Dome of the Rock, which also date from the time of Suleiman, veil the interior in a dim, religious light. The cupola
spans the central section of the mosque. In one place the
sky peeps through a hole made by a shell that recently hit
the cupola. Around the gallery is a broad blue band with
golden letters in the ornamental Kufic script, representing
lines from various suras of the Koran. Here, under the crescent moon on the cupola of the Dome of the Rock, which
looks out across to the Cross on the Church of the Holy
Sepulcher, the inscription from the Koran states that
though Jesus is the word of truth he is not the Son of God,
only the Son of Mary, and the ambassador of God and of

his Word. Mohammed did not attain to the goal of the faith of the Old Testament, the message of the Messiah.

One of the portals of the Dome of the Rock is called Bab el-Jenneh, the Gate of Paradise, and another the Bab el-Daud, the Gate of David. In the center of the mosque a natural rock projects a few feet above the ground. It measures about 60 by 50 feet. This is the holy rock from which the mosque derives its name. It is covered by a thick veil of history, tradition, and legend woven by thousands of Hebrew and hundreds of Arab years. According to the Talmud, the rock lies over the entrance to an abyss where the waters of the Flood rush and roar to this day. It is said that this is where Abraham set up the altar on which he intended to sacrifice his son Isaac. King Melchizedek is said to have offered sacrifices here, and Jacob to have anointed the stone. Jeremiah is said to have hidden the Ark under the rock when Jerusalem was destroyed. According to Hebrew belief, it is still on this spot.

The Moslems believe that the Bir el-Arvah is underneath this stone: the pit where twice a week the spirits of the dead meet for prayer. Jesus is said to have discovered the great ineffable name of God inscribed on this rock, and it was this that enabled him to work his miracles. Mohammed once said that a prayer spoken by this rock is worth more than a thousand prayers anywhere else in the world. He himself prayed here. From here he rode to heaven on the back of his wonderful horse Burak. The place on the rock where he laid his head is still shown to visitors. On another spot is the impression made by the hand of the angel who held the rock down when it was about to follow the Prophet on his way to heaven. Here, it is said, the trumpet will be sounded at the Last Judgment and God's throne will stand on the rock.

A piece of jasper, the lid of King Solomon's tomb, is let into the ground. It is said that the Prophet cast nineteen golden nails into this tomb. At the end of every epoch one nail falls out. When they have all fallen out the end of the world will have come. One day the devil broke open the tomb and began to destroy the nails. When only three and a half nails were left the angel Gabriel is said to have discovered the devil at his work and driven him away.

With great reverence my Arab guide showed me the place where the Prophet's green flag is kept. Rather skeptically he then showed me the gigantic casket in which, as he put it, that is kept on which most of the perjuries of the world have been sworn. The gigantic casket contains three hairs of Mohammed's beard.

This fascinatingly poetic tangle of legend, tradition, and history defies critical evaluation. The certain facts of history that are associated with this place are more exciting. There is reason to assume that the rock formed part of the threshing floor of Araunah the Jebusite on which, according to II Samuel, 24, David built an altar. It is known that this was the site of the Temple of Solomon and that the magnificent later temple built by Herod was also situated here.

Nothing has survived of Solomon's Temple. There is, however, hardly an ancient building we know so well from its description in the Old Testament. The foundation walls might be laid bare if archaeologists were allowed to excavate in the Haram es-Sherif. That being impossible, the question is whether it is not a good thing that there are still a few places in the world where limits are imposed on scientific inquisitiveness.

The Temple of Herod was described by Josephus. There is also a description of it in the Kodashim of the Babylonian Talmud from the second century. Probably the altar stood in front of the Temple on the holy rock. The shrine itself was made of white stone. Josephus states that the single stones measured 35 by 6 by 18 feet. The front was as broad as the building was high—about 160 feet. It was entirely inlaid with gold. As the first ray of the sun rising above the hills of Moab caught the golden roof of the Temple the sight must have been magnificent. The whole roof was covered with golden spikes, to prevent birds from soiling the building.

The Holy of Holies was entered only by the High Priest once a year on the Feast of the Atonement. When Pompey captured the city, to the horror of the Jews, he entered the Temple area straight away. This was forbidden under pain of death to all who were not believing Jews. A tablet on which the prohibition is inscribed in Greek has been preserved and is now in the Museum in Istanbul. The Jews' horror turned to utter bewilderment when Pompey entered the shrine itself. The episode symbolizes the clash of two eras in the world's history. The great Pompey, master of the East, who, with Caesar and Crassus, was to rule the Roman Empire, who had the genius but not the good fortune of Caesar, a highly cultivated man, deeply impressed by the incredible bravery of this small Jewish people that had rebelled against the Empire, had become convinced, during the siege, that it was their faith in the God Yahweh that gave this people the strength to hold fast to its Law, the Torah, in the face of all opposition. Pompey wanted to know who this God was. In the shining armor of a Roman patrician he strode through the ragged, shabby, half-starved crowd of defeated Jews, his stern face furrowed by Saturn. Amid the silent consternation of the Jews he entered the Temple building and lifted the curtain before the Holy of Holies. The Holy of Holies was empty. God is unapproachable, inviolable, inexpressible, unimaginable, invisible.

Yahweh's lightning did not strike, but the Roman commander in his shining armor who left the shrine in silence, passing through the silent crowd, was no longer Pompey the victor. Long before the Roman Empire had attained the climax of its power he was the first Roman dimly to realize that a new age was dawning. The first shadow had fallen on the splendor of his fame. Pompey was so much impressed by this experience that he left the treasures of the Temple untouched. Shortly afterwards, the efficient and covetous Crassus appeared in Jerusalem. He pillaged the Temple. A little while later Crassus lost his war against the Parthians, and also lost his life.

A hundred years later the Temple built by Herod was destroyed by Titus. Since then no orthodox Jew has entered the Temple area lest he desecrate the spot where the Holy of Holies once stood. In the consciousness of faithful Jews the Holy of Holies continues to have a real existence.

One fragment of the foundation wall of the Temple, on the side facing the city, has remained standing. This is the Wailing Wall, where for centuries the Jews have bewailed the fate of Zion. A pilgrim of Bordeaux who was in Jerusalem in A.D. 333 already noted this custom. The old stones have been polished by the hands that have stroked them, by the lips that have kissed them and the brows that have leaned against them in grief. Today the wailing of the Jews for Zion is no longer heard by these last stones to survive from the glorious past.

A Monastery in the Desert

Certain names acquire a patina. They shine with the gleam of the centuries that have passed over them. Sinai—what a name! This mountain emerged but once in human history from namelessness into renown. A single event gave

234

to Sinai the dark splendor with which it has shone through the millennia.

God spake to Moses . . . On Sinai the human race was given the Commandments which it is still its unfinished task to fulfill.

The Sinai Peninsula lies between Africa and Arabia. The Gulf of Suez separates it from the African mainland. The Suez Canal links the northern end of the Gulf with the Mediterranean, while the Gulf of Aqaba divides the peninsula from Arabia. It forms a triangle, the apex of which points south to the Red Sea. Mount Sinai lies almost at the apex of this triangle. It is actually a massif with three summits—the Gebel Serbal, the Gebel Musa, and the Gebel Katherina. The highest of the three is the Gebel Katherina, which has an elevation of 8,652 feet.

Sixty miles south of the spot where we were waiting for the ferry to take us across the Canal to the Sinai Peninsula there is a Coptic monastery in the desert mountains between the Nile and the Gulf of Suez. It was founded at the end of the third century.

The Coptic Church traces its history back to the apostle Mark. The Copts are the authentic descendants of the Egyptians of the time of the pharaohs, and their language is an offshoot of the ancient Egyptian language. Severus ibn al-Muqaffa, a Coptic scholar who lived in Egypt at the end of the tenth century, described the origin of the first Christian church on the Nile.

When the apostle Mark landed in Egypt he came into a prosperous metropolis famous for its learning. As he walked through the crowded streets of Alexandria there was only one Christian besides himself in the city—the apostle Peter. Mark split his shoe and went to a cobbler. The cobbler mended the shoe. In doing so he pierced his hand with his awl. Frightened, he cried, "Praised be God." The apostle, surprised and delighted to hear the name of God in the heathen city, healed the cobbler's hand and decided to stay in Alexandria. The cobbler Annainos, the first Christian Egyptian, the first Coptic Christian, became Mark's successor on the Bishop's throne in Alexandria.

Christianity spread rapidly in Egypt. The Egyptians had always believed in a life after death. From the earliest times they were a people of high moral standards and great austerity. The strictness enjoined by the new religion was therefore nothing new to them. The wonderful clarity of the new gospel must have seemed to them like a radiant light that put the confusion of the old order of gods in the shade.

In the year 451 the famous fourth Ecumenical Council of Chalcedon took place. It had to decide whether the teaching of Eutyches, a Coptic Christian, was to be accepted or rejected. Eutyches taught that the human nature of Christ cannot be separated from his divine nature, and that Christ therefore has but one nature: *monen physin*. Hence the name Monophysite. The Council decided that the doctrine should be rejected. Christ has two natures, the divine and the human, which are united. The Copts held fast to the teaching of Eutyches. Since that time they have formed a church on their own, which has been joined by the Abyssinian Christians.

The founder of the Coptic monastery in the desert by the Red Sea was St. Anthony. There have been anchorites and hermits in the Egyptian Desert from the earliest times. St. Anthony was the first Christian to withdraw from the world in order to devote himself to the contemplation of God. Other hermits gathered round him. This led to the foundation of the first Christian monastery. Anthony was 104 when he died in the year 356. Other monasteries were founded. Some sixty miles north of Luxor, Pachomius founded the monastery of Tabennisi. Ever since the year

323 the monks of the Coptic Church have met there twice
a year. It was in Tabennisi that Pachomius issued the Rule
for the Egyptian monasteries—an austere, ascetic Rule.
Athanasius, Patriarch of Alexandria, introduced to the
West the monastic system of the East on his journey to
Rome in the year 340.

St. Anthony's monastery has flourished without the
slightest interruption since its foundation in the third century. St. Anthony could not have done more to change the
world than what he achieved by renouncing a life of action in the world; "he became, though childless, the father
of an immeasurable family."

We crossed the Canal. On the other side is an Egyptian
customs and passport office. Here begins the desert, of
which even today no one is master. We had to state on
what day we intended to make our re-entry from the desert. If we were twenty-four hours overdue a search party
would be sent out. A detachment of the Egyptian camel
corps is billeted opposite the customs house. Twenty of
the purebred gray riding camels lay resting in the sand.
With their magnificent arrogance, so suited to the desert,
they did not deem our car worth even a casual glance.
We had to take with us for the five-day journey not only
gasoline and food but also water, but if we had bad luck
and got stuck these camels would come and search for us.

The journey proceeded along the shore of the Gulf of
Suez on quite a good asphalt road. After travelling about
35 miles we came to a small harbor. It is used for loading
the manganese ore that is now extracted in the Peninsula.
At the time of the pharaohs turquoise was the geological
treasure of Sinai. Behind the harbor the road becomes a
mere track in the desert. Quite unexpectedly the driver
turned aside from the track to the left and made for the
mountains across open country. For the 40 miles from here

to the Monastery of St. Catherine at the foot of the Gebel Musa the car took nine hours. The driver was a Sudanese, a splendid, reliable fellow. Two even scars cut across his left cheek. They are the marks of his tribe. We rarely exceeded a speed of 15 miles an hour. Occasionally the Sudanese accelerated and whisked across a stretch of quicksand at 80 or 90. These tiny pockets of quicksand are like bogs where a car can get hopelessly stuck when travelling slowly.

The monastery for which we were making lies at the foot of the Gebel Musa, on the place where Moses saw the thorn bush burning. The Gebel Musa, the mountain of Moses, is Mount Horeb. As early as the third century Christian hermits lived in this desert. The first of these hermits known to us by name is St. Onophrios. The Empress Helena, who founded so many churches in Jerusalem, also built a church on Horeb. In addition, she had a watchtower built where the hermits could take refuge from the Bedouins, their enemies.

In the year 460 a Spanish nun, Etheria, was on Sinai. Her diary has been preserved, and from it we learn that there was already a monastery here at this time. The nun must have been a very energetic lady. She describes most vividly in a letter to her sisters in the convent at home the difficult ascent to one of the peaks of Sinai.

In the year 561 the Emperor Justinian built a new church on the site of the burning bush. He also built a solid wall around the church and the watchtower. Less than a hundred years later, in 630, the Abbot of the monastery assumed the title of Bishop of Sinai. The whole Peninsula is now an archbishopric of the Greek Orthodox Church, with the archiepiscopal see in Cairo. On high festivals the Archbishop visits the monastery to celebrate Pontifical Mass.

On the return journey, at the Abbot's request I took a

letter to the Archbishop at Cairo. For a whole fortnight no camel had gone there. The address ran:

A sa Béatitude
L'Archevêque du Couvent de Ste. Cathérine
Monseigneur Porphyrios III

St. Catherine, after whom the monastery is now named, was a Christian from Alexandria who suffered a martyr's death under the Roman Emperor Maximinus at the beginning of the fourth century. According to tradition, her mortal remains were taken to Mount Sinai by angels, where they were discovered about five hundred years later. Relics of the saint are still preserved in the monastery in costly Byzantine shrines.

We travelled through dried-out river valleys deeper and deeper into the mountains. The monastery lies 4,000 feet above sea level. The cool of the morning had gone now. It was getting hot. The landscape has a wild grandeur. Only occasionally does a man or camel leave a swiftly vanishing track in the sand. The geological formations change rapidly. Sometimes we passed under jagged, broken rocks, then came steep hilltops crossed for miles on end by black strips looking like walls—layers of asphalt interspersed in the rock. Gradually the valleys became narrower. At times we drove toward a high wall of rock with a small passage through appearing only at the very last moment. Suddenly, at the end of one valley, there appeared a row of twenty shapeless columns, perhaps 150 feet high, looking like the ruins of a shrine built by Cyclopes. They had been exposed by the erosion of the rain in the course of half a million years. Tremendous fragments of rock lie in the valleys like huge forgotten toys. Sometimes we drove across great slabs of rock that the sand has polished bright and smooth. The landscape, which is almost entirely lacking in vegetation, is steeped in vivid colors. White lime, gray granite, black asphalt, and green porphyry alternate. And over all the cloudless sky from which the sun burns down. Hour after hour we travelled upwards through ever-changing valleys. It was through this country that Moses led the children of Israel to Mount Horeb.

The desert mountains are not entirely bereft of life. Here and there there are a few thorn bushes and occasionally a half-withered tree. From a rock a solitary camel gazed across at us.

During a short stop, asked for by the driver, I looked up to the sky. A snowdrift with a hundred thousand lights was sparkling in the sun—the wings of an invading swarm of locusts. For many miles we travelled across the bodies of countless locusts. The swarm came from southern Arabia, the Sudanese driver informed me, and here, far from human settlements and far from any kind of food, the creatures would starve.

Toward noon we saw a solitary Bedouin on a near-by hill. Despite its relentless inaccessibility, the desert is still a humane landscape. When after many miles and many hours in this incredible solitude one meets a human being it is impossible to drive past him. So we stopped. The Bedouin came slowly toward us. We greeted one another warmly. He was a young man, born and bred in the desert, sunburned, his face sharply profiled, a picture of grace and poverty and freedom. He smiled at us, showing his magnificent white teeth, and asked us for some water. Never have I realized what a gift of heaven water is as I did here, watching the Bedouin drinking it in slow short draughts. After a time his wife approached, deeply veiled, and half a dozen children, all wanting to quench their thirst. The children, with hardly anything on but a ragged shirt, were quite enchanting. Embarrassment and curiosity were mixed in the most amusing blend in their shining black eyes. Two girls, possibly ten years old, beamed on us with the child's supreme flair for coquetry.

Twenty miles farther on we made another stop. We stood at the foot of a rock whose slanting surface was covered with innumerable curious signs. In this forsaken desert one of the great unknown geniuses of human history left behind an unusual memorial in the shape of these inscriptions carved in the rock, which Flinders Petrie discovered in 1904. The place is called Serabit el-Khadim.

These inscriptions are the first known attempts at a purely alphabetical script. They are described as proto-Sinaitic, to distinguish them from inscriptions in Sinai from a later period, and are derived from hieroglyphs. Their author was a Phoenician who worked in the turquoise mines of the pharaohs on Sinai. The rock alphabet is the basis of all the literature and recorded knowledge that has ever been written in an alphabetic script.

The language in which the inscriptions are written is a very old form of Semitic, which makes it possible to assign a precise date to them. They come from the period of Egypt's Twelfth Dynasty and are therefore four thousand years old. The Twelfth Dynasty was founded by the Pharaoh Amenemhet I and prevailed for two hundred years. The regents of this house conquered Nubia as far as the second cataract of the Nile, established turquoise mines on Sinai, and built a canal from the Nile to the Red Sea. That was in the twentieth century B.C. at the time of Abraham. When Moses passed this way the inscriptions were already more than five hundred years old.

In the afternoon, about five o'clock, it began to get dark. The day was December 7th. We turned out of a broad trough into a narrow rocky valley. Ten minutes later we stopped on the broad drive at the foot of the wall of the Monastery of St. Catherine. The wall of granite is between forty and fifty feet high. The monastery, built in the shape of a great rectangle, is completely shut in by the wall. Up to the middle of the last century there was no gate in the wall. Visitors were hoisted up in a basket. Only when his Grace the Archbishop visited the monastery was a door broken into the wall. As soon as he had entered, the door was walled in again. Today the Bedouins in the district are the monks' servants.

In every Greek Orthodox monastery there is a guest-master, a monk who looks after visitors. Here it was Father Damian, a particularly charming and friendly man. The monastery has a supply of delightfully fresh water from a mountain spring, but one has to see to one's own meals. The guest rooms are in a gallery that opens out onto the interior of the monastery. From the gallery one can see numerous courtyards and buildings connected by stair-cases and winding corridors. Centuries have contributed to the building here. Along the wall a well-preserved enclosed passage with embrasures runs around the whole monas-tery.

Everything is extraordinarily clean. Only a few of the buildings are beginning to decay. The number of monks is no longer very large. The heavy work formerly per-formed by novices and lay brothers is now done by Bed-ouins. The monastery is not poor. It is true that it has lost its properties in Rumania, but the monks still retain their estates in Turkey. In the center of the monastery, almost as though in a funnel, half sunk in the ground, stands an outwardly rather insignificant-looking church of gray granite. This is the church the Emperor Justinian had built between 561 and 565. It has been preserved intact. Only the woodwork of the roof has been restored. From the pinnacle of the wall I looked at the last red glow of sunset. The mountains plunge down steeply on both sides of the monastery. They consist of bare riven rock. Only here and there in the valley is there a thorn bush or a tamarisk. The southern slope of the mountain forms part of Horeb, the Mount of the Law. A large radiant moon was rising over the lonely scene, bathing the incredibly forsaken landscape in a flood of silvery light.

Besides ourselves, five delightful little old women were guests of the monastery. They were Greek pilgrims from Cairo who had not shrunk from the ardors of the journey. They all had the beautiful name Catherine. It was the eve of the feast day of their saint, which was to be celebrated in a Solemn Mass the following day.

The night was cold. At this height and at this time of the year there are a few degrees of frost. We rose at 5 A.M. and went down into the church. Divine service had already begun at midnight. We entered the sanctuary to the singing of the monks. The sight was a solemn but also a surprising one. In the midst of this bare mountain landscape, in this remote place surrounded on all sides by the lonely desert, the sight of the interior of the church is one of absolute beauty and great splendor.

The church is a basilica with two rows of columns. Golden and silver lamps hang from the ceiling. The ceiling is a flat wooden one with a canopy of golden stars. The iconostasis, the painted screen that separates the altar and the sanctuary from the rest of the church, dates from the sixteenth century. It is covered with pictures of the saints. Nothing in this church is later than 1800.

The cupola of the apse above the iconostasis is adorned with a mosaic from the period of the Emperor Justinian. It represents Christus Pantokrator, Christ the Sovereign Lord of the world. His face is awe-inspiringly stern and majestic. He is surrounded by four prophets. Underneath are two hovering angels that remind one of Michelangelo's angels in the Sistine Chapel. In the dry air of the desert the mosaic has retained its brilliant colors. The wall below the mosaics is lined with marble slabs—a gift to the monastery from the Emperor Justinian. They came from the Temple of Artemis in Ephesus. At the time the monastery was being built they had already been in use for more than a thousand years. Around the interior wall of the whole church runs a silver-embroidered ribbon of the width of a hand from which a number of precious old icons are suspended. The acrid smell of incense fills the church. The fathers, dignified old men with white beards, stand in the choir stalls dressed in gold-embroidered robes for the Feast of St. Catherine. A passage from the Bible is read from the pulpit. More than a hundred candles are burning. They bathe the room in a warm light. Daylight is breaking gently through the windows under the roof. The leader of the choir, Dikon Eleias, is a younger monk. His beard is still quite dark. His face, with its big brown eyes, is pale, his expression profoundly serious. He has an unbelievably euphonious voice, reminiscent of Chaliapin. Sometimes restrained, sometimes echoing powerfully through the building, sometimes rising to ecstatic heights, the voice of Dikon Eleias blends with the other monks' voices in the praise of God.

The service continues for many hours. Afterwards the reliquaries are carried in a solemn procession around the church. The reliquaries, made of gold and adorned with jewels and enamel, are distinctly ancient. A short hymn is sung in each of the four directions of the compass. Meanwhile the sun has risen high in the sky. It shines into the deep, stone-gray cloisters through which the fathers stride with measured gait. The gold of the robes and the precious stones scintillate in the rays of the sun. Looking down over the parapets, the Bedouins gaze in silence at the venerable and solemn scene.

How remote this piety is from the dissensions of this world! Since the year 565 not a day has passed on which the praises of God have not been sung in a rite that has hardly changed since the days of the Emperor Justinian, in this church built at the foot of the mountain from which three thousand years ago God gave man the Law.

The Mountain of the Law

A chapel adjoins the basilica of the Emperor Justinian in the Monastery of St. Catherine at the foot of Moses's mountain, the mountain of the Law. In this chapel is an altar. It stands on the spot referred to in Exodus, Chapter 3:

> "Now Moses kept the flock of Jethro his father-in-law, the priest of Midian: and he led the flock to the back side of the desert, and came to the mountain of God, even to Horeb. And the Angel of the Lord appeared unto him in a flame of fire out of the midst of a bush: and he looked, and, behold, the bush burned with fire, and the bush was not consumed. And Moses said, I will now turn aside, and see this great sight, why the bush is not burnt. And when the Lord saw that he turned aside to see, God called unto him out of the midst of the bush, and said, Moses, Moses. And he said, Here am I. And he said, Draw not hither: put off thy shoes from off thy feet, for the place whereon thou standest is holy ground."

In the middle of the desert, in the middle of these bare rocky mountains, which seem to have stood here since the days of creation, this is a place of incomparable dignity. It is the only place on earth that God himself has called holy. Here God called Moses to lead the children of Israel into the Promised Land, the land where Jesus of Nazareth was to be born. That was reason enough for the early

Christians to build a shrine here, however lost in the desert this place was.

Moses was brought up at the Egyptian court by a daughter of the Pharaoh. He had the rank of an Egyptian prince. Even his name was Egyptian. It is ridiculous to doubt that Moses was a historical personality. If the Jews had wanted to create a national hero they would not have given him an Egyptian name. Despite his high rank as a prince, Moses had begun to interest himself in the social conditions of the people from whom he was descended. At the time, the Jews were doing forced labor for the Pharaoh. Moses had, in anger, killed an Egyptian overseer who had whipped one of the Hebrew laborers unjustly. After this deed he fled from Egypt into the desert of Midian. There he married the daughter of the priest Jethro and lived as a Bedouin keeping his flocks. On his travels from one to another of the rare watering places in the Sinai Peninsula, he had opportunities for getting to know the country through which he was later to pass with the people of Israel.

After the service on the morning of December 8th, St. Catherine's Day, Father Damian took us into the Chapel of the Burning Bush. At the entrance to this Christian church he asked us to take off our shoes—a thing one is usually required to do only when entering a mosque. Since the time of the Emperor Justinian in the sixth century no one has entered this chapel without first taking off his shoes. Thousands of pilgrims through all the centuries have observed this reverent custom before the place which God himself declared was holy ground.

The chapel is a modest building. Its walls are covered with frescoes. Over the site of the burning bush there is a silver slab on which pictures from the Bible have been hammered. An altar has been built over it. On certain days Mass is celebrated at this altar. That the burning bush did in fact stand on this spot that is now covered by the silver slab is highly probable.

At the bottom of this valley at the foot of Horeb there are a few thorn bushes and scattered tamarisks. The mountain slopes are bare rock. A spring gushes from the mountain slope: the only one far and wide. It is obvious that Moses camped with his flocks by this spring. To see that a thorn bush was burning and yet was not being consumed, you would have to be at most within 300 to 400 yards of it. That is just the distance of the chapel from the spring.

We spent St. Catherine's Day in pleasant conversation with the fathers, discussing the affairs of the world and the concerns of the spirit. In the ancient projecting structure on the wall into which visitors used to be hoisted up with a rope Dikon Eleias sat among a lot of baskets containing small loaves baked and consecrated the day before. Down below by the wall there were about fifty Bedouin children. To the accompaniment of cheers and jokes and merry shouts, the loaves were distributed among them. Each child had brought some sort of wrapping material. These wrappings were tied into bundles and drawn up by a rope. They included an odd assortment of haversacks, some of English, some of German origin. Sometimes it was merely a scrap of material or a bit of carpet. The Dikon held up a wrapper, and the child it belonged to answered. As many loaves were wrapped up as there were members in the family. Then the bundle was tied up and thrown down. Usually it was well caught. Dikon Eleias takes the amiable view that the consecrated loaves are bound to do the Moslem children good.

Inside the walls of the monastery stands a small mosque the minaret of which peeps out modestly by the side of the church tower. The Arabs say that the prophet Mohammed once visited the monastery. There is no evidence of this visit, but the mountains of Hejaz, with the city of Medina, lie opposite the coast of the Sinai Peninsula. It is quite possible that Mohammed, for whom Moses was just as much a holy man as for Christians, once visited Sinai. Mohammed is said to have forbidden the Bedouins to molest the pious monks. When the monks politely asked what they could do to express their thanks, he asked for the erection of a small mosque on the holy site.

The Abbot invited us to see some of the treasures of the monastery. We were allowed to look at the golden reliquaries adorned with jewels. He showed us some of the most beautiful icons, glorious pieces, of which the oldest, composed of the tiniest mosaic stones, depicts Mary with the Child. It dates from the eighth century. The Abbot also showed us a golden chalice that Charles VI of France gave to the monastery, and some of the ivory crosiers of an earlier period.

Father Damian took us into the library. One of the most precious books of Christendom was discovered here: the Codex Sinaiticus.

The Codex Sinaiticus is a Bible manuscript in Greek. Of its originally 730 leaves, 390 have survived, among them the complete New Testament. The manuscript was written about 350. It probably came from Egypt. There is only one other Bible manuscript of equal antiquity: the Codex Vaticanus, an almost complete manuscript of the Greek Bible, which is now in the Vatican Library.

The Codex Sinaiticus was discovered in the Monastery of St. Catherine by Konstantin von Tischendorf, the most eminent decipherer of ancient manuscripts produced by the nineteenth century. On his first visit, in 1844, Tischendorf had found a few leaves, which he published in Leipzig in 1846, under the patronage of King Frederick Augustus of Saxony, as the Codex Friderico-Augustanus. The rest of the manuscript, which he discovered in 1859, went to

Czar Alexander of Russia. The transactions that led to the transfer of the manuscript to the Czar were very involved. The monastery received 12,000 rubles from the Czar, but the Archbishop of Sinai still preserves in his safe a letter from Tischendorf dated Cairo, September 16/28, 1859, the dates of the Roman and Greek calendars. In this letter Tischendorf promised to return the manuscript to the Sacred Fraternity of Mount Sinai after a stipulated period. In fact the manuscript was never returned, but the monks still claim that it belongs to them. With the Russian Revolution, the manuscript fell into the hands of the Bolsheviks. Their greed was greater than their belief in their unbelief. They sold the manuscript in 1933 to the British Museum. The sale caused a world-wide sensation. The sale price amounted to £100,000—the highest price ever paid for a book.

The Czar had three hundred facsimile copies made on costly parchment by the famous printers Giesecke and Devriendt of Leipzig. He gave one of these copies to the Monastery of St. Catherine, and this document is shown to visitors to the library. On the title page Tischendorf calls the manuscript "Codex Bibliorum Sinaiticus Petropolitanus." Then follows a sentence in Latin: *"Ex tenebris protraxit, in Europam transtulit—* He brought it out of the shadow and took it to Europe." The shadow was the shadow of Mount Horeb. It was the shadow of the piety that preserved the holy book for more than one and a half thousand years.

The most important fact that has emerged from the scholarly examination of the Codex Sinaiticus is that the Bible tradition has been proved extraordinarily accurate. We are in possession of the authentic text of the Gospels in the form in which they were first written down.

The following morning we set out to climb the Gebel Musa, Mount Horeb. We started at dawn, accompanied

249

by Father Damian. First, for about two hours, we followed a winding but not particularly steep path. The monastery lies at an elevation of 4,000 feet. The mountain is 7,500 feet high. The view across the mountainous landscape broadened out. Camel paths run through the valleys. Below, we saw a solitary Bedouin making his way from one place of desolation to another. The sun rose, and it became warmer. When Moses passed through this desert with the children of Israel to offer a sacrifice on Mount Horeb, the Jews carried with them the ancient legacy of their faith in the one God. Moses witnessed the most terrible defection of his people from the faith of their fathers. When he came down the mountain with the tables of the Law which were written by God, the same mountain we were about to climb, the Jews were dancing in a wild orgy around the golden calf. In his anger, the mighty man smashed the tables of the Law on the rock at our feet.

The people of Israel that he had led out of Egypt were a people of slaves. He had to travel forty years through the desert before the last of the slaves of the Pharaoh had died, and before the whole people consisted of free men, brave sons of the desert, capable of tackling the tasks that God imposed on the people of Israel. Joshua and Caleb were the only ones born in Egypt who crossed the Jordan. Aaron had to die, and even Moses was only permitted to see the Promised Land from afar: the awe-inspiringly tragic end of an extraordinary man.

The path runs for a mile along a vertical, 250-foot-high wall and then vanishes among the rocks. From this point another path, consisting of tremendous stone steps, runs another 2,500 feet up to the top of the mountain. Following the crevices in the rock, it makes a steep ascent to the summit, as depicted in the early icons.

The climb is arduous. At times the flight of steps runs across a ridge. The slopes plunge down steeply on both sides. At every pause the landscape seems more tremendous. Far and wide there is no human dwelling. Finally, we reached the summit of the mountain, a flat slab of rock measuring 70 by 100 feet. As it is impossible to see the slopes of the pyramid of which this slab of rock is the apex, one has the feeling of hovering between heaven and earth. It was here that Moses tarried in the cloud.

At one point a hollow in the rock forms a natural water tank containing clear icy cold water. This cistern, filled with the winter's snow and rain, enabled Moses to subsist here for forty days and nights.

I have seen many things on this earth, but I know of nothing so solitary, so sublime, so splendid as the view from the summit of Mount Horeb. Facing south, on the right hand lies the Gebel Katherina at a distance of ten miles. On this side lies the Gulf of Suez. Behind it there appears the dark blue shimmer of a high mountain chain that reaches as far as Abyssinia. Directly south, a few islands lie scattered about the Red Sea. To the left is the Gulf of Aqaba, and behind it in a brighter blue the Hejaz Mountains, the mountain chain that borders on Arabia, behind which lie the Arabian Desert and the Holy Cities of Mecca and Medina. White cloud ships move slowly across the sky. The sea gleams in the sunshine. No other spot could have provided a worthier setting for the event that took place three thousand years ago on this slab of rock between heaven and earth—the Lord speaking to Moses.

INDEX

253